STRONG *and* COURAGEOUS

365
DAILY DEVOTIONS FOR FATHERS

BroadStreet
P U B L I S H I N G

BroadStreet Publishing Group, LLC
Racine, Wisconsin, USA
BroadStreetPublishing.com

STRONG & COURAGEOUS: 365 DAILY DEVOTIONS FOR FATHERS

Written by Cesar Castillejos, Ken Castor, Chris Folkestad, Bryan Halferty, Steven McCready, John Mulholland, Phil Petersen, Tony Roos, Luke Trouten, Jared Van Voorst, and McYoung Yang. Compiled by Ken Castor.

ISBN-13: 978-1-4245-5475-1 (faux leather)
ISBN-13: 978-1-4245-5480-5 (e-book)

Stock or custom editions of BroadStreet Publishing titles may be purchased in bulk for educational, business, ministry, fundraising, or sales promotional use. For information, please e-mail info@broadstreetpublishing.com.

Cover design by Chris Garborg at garborgdesign.com
Typesetting by Katherine Lloyd at theDESKonline.com

Printed in China

17 18 19 20 21 5 4 3 2 1

INTRODUCTION

"This is my command—be strong and courageous!
Do not be afraid or discouraged. For the LORD your God
is with you wherever you go."
—*Joshua 1:9 NLT*

Fathers have an incredibly important role. They lead younger generations through turbulent waters, they model integrity in relationships, and they provide foundations for wise decision-making. There are times they might feel like they've got this father-business all figured out, and other times when they can feel unworthy of their generation-impacting responsibilities.

I know that my own life has been deeply impacted by my father. I still remember the day my dad stood up in church and shared that he had given his life to Jesus. I also remember watching him fighting for people who were sick, praying with families who were afraid, crying at the dinner table for a friend whose son had been injured, teaching me how to swing a golf club, quietly studying his Bible in his recliner, taking responsibility for his mistakes, supporting me in my good choices and catching me in my bad ones, letting me destroy his bare foot with my errant fastball, loving my mom, championing my brothers, and on and on I could go. Over the years, I've heard from many people the testimony I already knew: I have a good dad.

Much of what has made my father a good man is that over the years he has regularly set aside time for devotions. I learned from his example that time spent in God's presence empowers fathers to be men of character, strength, and leadership. God himself, after all, is called Father. As the Lord's Prayer begins in the old English style, God is "Our Father who art in heaven." God is also called "Abba," meaning our ever-personal Dad. God has a Son, Jesus, whom he loves. He also has children whom he has adopted as his own (like you and me). He runs with abandon toward his prodigal kids and provides for his family through the generations. In his everlasting power and conviction, God the Father has more than enough daily resources at his disposal for those ordained with the incredibly noble title of father.

This devotional book is meant to empower fathers to daily do the work they have been called to do. Each devotional offers a Bible verse, a devotional thought from some pastors near and dear to my heart, and a prayer meant to challenge, equip, and encourage dads to till the soil set before them. Every day for a year you could prayerfully read one page, be marked by its words, and strive to be the man God has called you to be for those he has entrusted to your care. Through this devotional book, may God our Father make you a strong and courageous father.

—Dr. Ken Castor

Writer, pastor, professor, and, more importantly, father of three

JANUARY

THE OFF SWITCH

"Six days you shall labor and do all your work, but the seventh day is a sabbath to the LORD your God. On it you shall not do any work."

—Exodus 20:9–10

Have you ever had a machine that was hard to turn off? Maybe there was a specific process of steps and patience needed before it could actually turn off. Maybe a switch was stuck, leaving it in the "on" position. Maybe something internally was broken, preventing anything from turning it off.

Often, this is an unfortunate picture of us. Stuck in the "on" position, we run until our circuits are fried or our batteries go dead. We tell ourselves (or our spouse) that after one more e-mail, we'll be done for the night. We convince ourselves that this phone call is important enough to step away from the family "just for a bit." We can't turn off.

God gave the Israelites a mandatory off switch. It was called the Sabbath. This off switch was a way they honored God, as they remembered that the world's problems and opportunities didn't rest on their shoulders. But it didn't only honor God; it was also good for them. They, unlike many of us, had a rhythm of rest and work, and a rest kept them from burning out. This week, consider taking some time to rest as a family. Do something that honors God and fills you and your family up.

God, the world doesn't depend on me. You are in control. I don't need to labor anxiously without rest. Help me to truly believe that this week, and to honor you through rest. Amen.

YOUR CROSS

> Then Jesus said to his disciples, "Whoever wants to be my disciple must deny themselves and take up their cross and follow me."
>
> —*Matthew 16:24*

Following Jesus is a path of great joy but also real sacrifice. Often when we hear the word *sacrifice*, we think of maybe a mission field or giving away a large amount of money. That's all well and good and is sometimes what God is calling us to do. But more often, sacrifice looks like waking up at 3 a.m. to check on a sick child, taking time from your evening to gather the family and talk about what they enjoyed about the day, or praying with a son or daughter before school. These are the little sacrifices that, when practiced through the course of years, reap the greatest rewards. What might be your "cross" today? How can you take it up and, in so doing, follow Jesus?

Father, help me to be ready to sacrifice my time and energy for those closest to me. I desire that I might love like you love. Give me strength to do this. Amen.

AFFIRMATION

> So Jacob took the food to his father. "My father?" he said. "Yes, my son," Isaac answered. "Who are you—Esau or Jacob?"
>
> —*Genesis 27:18 NLT*

Isaac had always preferred his older son, Esau, to his younger son, Jacob. After all, Esau could hunt and possessed other masculine attributes. Meanwhile, Jacob hung out at home and was also a little conniving while Esau was more simple. Isaac's heart gravitated toward his older boy. Near the end of Isaac's life, Jacob, in a crazy effort to take Esau's inheritance, dressed up like his older brother and deceived his aging father. Jacob was a bit of a sneak, but can you imagine knowing that you're second to your brother when it comes to Dad's love? That's hard to swallow.

Even though this situation is in some ways little far-fetched, experience reminds us how common it is. Many of us live with an affirmation vacancy, a place where we didn't receive like we desired. Others of us may drift toward preferring one child over another, like Isaac. The trick is to remember that when we feel the need for love, or when we feel the gravitational pull of preference, we need to remember God, who gave his one and only Son so that we might be called his kids. That's a love that can heal affirmation vacancies. That's a love that provides an example of how to let our love spill out to all in our home.

Father, teach me your ways. Help me to love like you do! I want to know your love for myself and to pass it on to my family. Amen.

OUR FATHER

"This, then, is how you should pray: 'Our Father …'"
—*Matthew 6:9*

Throughout the Bible, we find many titles for God. We learn that God is creator and powerful, that he is sovereign and knows all. But in the New Testament, when Jesus is sharing how his followers should pray, he calls him, "Our Father." Let that sink in. The infinite, sovereign creator God wants you to know him as "Dad." Not only that, but Jesus speaks about God being the type of father who scans the horizon, looking for lost sons and daughters, and then runs to them when he sees even a hint of them (Luke 19). God is a father, and the Father's love is intimate and protective and yearns to know and be known.

God, you are all-powerful, but you also desire intimacy. You want to be known as Dad. Help me to know you as a kind father today. Amen.

HALLOWED BE

"Hallowed be your name."

—Matthew 6:9

When most people hear the word *holy*, they think "moral" or "religious." That's not exactly wrong, but it misses the rich biblical meaning. *Holy* really means "set apart" or "other." A few theologians have suggested that when we see *holy*, we should think of "wholly other." God is perfect; we're not. God is all-powerful; we're not. You get the idea. In the Old Testament, priests had to perform certain purity rituals to come near God. Why? Because God is holy and they weren't. To approach God, they had to purify themselves, becoming holy.

It's interesting that Jesus says we should call God "Father" but also know he is holy. Jesus wants us to hold these two important truths together. God is beyond, and God is near. God is powerful, and God is meek. God is a warrior, and God is loving. It's as if Jesus, right at the beginning of the Lord's Prayer, was inviting us into the beautiful mystery of who God is.

When you reflect on this, you may start to stagger. It may blow you away. And if it does, you're on the right track.

Oh God, all-powerful and holy God, intimate and loving Father. Help me to be amazed by you. May I draw near to you today. Amen.

YOUR WILL BE DONE

"Your kingdom come, your will be done. On earth as it is in heaven."

—*Matthew 6:10*

In the ancient world, a kingdom was a place where the values and way of life that the king desired were put into practice. As you can imagine, this could be good or bad depending on the king. Jesus is the ultimate good King. Throughout the Gospels (Matthew, Mark, Luke, and John), he heals the sick; includes the social, spiritual, and racial outcasts into his family; and ultimately makes a public spectacle of the world's power by triumphing over it through death. The kingdom of Jesus is like no other.

As we align ourselves with this God who is both beyond and near, we must take up the cause of his kingdom. This can be hard. Within each of us is a little ruler that, left alone, would set up a kingdom that runs according to our basic desires and wants. As we learn to pray like Jesus, we must lay down our kingdoms and take up his kingdom mission. This doesn't mean that everyone becomes a pastor. It doesn't mean that we have to live at the church. It does mean that we, like Jesus, should have a heart for the outcast and vulnerable. It does mean we should familiarize ourselves with sacrifice. And it does mean that we should make Jesus our first allegiance—in all areas of life.

God, give me strength to live for your kingdom. Give me your power to love my family, my coworkers, and my neighbors. Help me to desire your kingdom! Amen.

DAILY BREAD

"Give us today our daily bread."

—*Matthew 6:11*

God is not concerned only with your spiritual needs. He is interested and desires to be recognized in and through all things; after all, he is the one who made it all. Yep, that even means the food you eat.

Previous generations had a much more intimate relationship with their food. They often raised and slaughtered the meat they ate. They depended on the rain and the sun to be "enough." While we can just pick up a loaf of bread, previous generations saw the wheat grow from the soil. So the prayer below might make more intuitive sense to a group of Jews or Christians from a few centuries ago. Still, when we pray for our "daily bread," we recognize that God is God of every square inch of creation. We remember that he made it all and cares for all of us. And we then remember that everything, even a slice of toast in the morning, is a gift of grace.

God, thank you for the easily forgotten gifts: for food and friendship, family and employment. You are generous, and I thank you for being my provider. Amen.

FORGIVE AS …

"And forgive us our debts, as we have also forgiven our debtors."

—*Matthew 6:12*

Forgiveness is one of those words that sounds beautiful but is terribly hard to put into practice. Perhaps that's the best description of it: a beautiful difficulty.

Forgiveness shows up as a beautiful difficulty when a grown woman finds the strength to forgive a mean stepfather and finds the freedom that forgiveness always brings. A beautiful difficulty takes place when a husband says, "I love you, and I forgive you," to his wife who has just admitted to a moral struggle. This beautiful difficulty shows up when a business owner hugs an employee who has just been caught cutting corners.

However, the best picture of forgiveness as a beautiful difficulty is the cross. On the cross Jesus bore the difficult weight of our sin and offered the beautiful gift of divine forgiveness. When we understand that beautiful difficulty, our calls to forgiveness become a bit less difficult.

Oh God, thank you for your forgiveness. Thank you for the cross. Help me to remember that you forgave me—all of me—and I will remember to forgive those that have hurt or offended me. Amen.

LEAD US NOT

"And lead us not into temptation, but deliver us from the evil one."

—*Matthew 6:13*

Jesus' prayer concludes with a request to not be led into temptation. Sometimes when we're struggling to overcome a temptation, we find ourselves more likely than ever to start focusing on it. The second a temptation is mentioned is the moment we can't get it out of our head. Just say the words *ice cream* to someone who's counting calories and you'll know what I mean. The solution to overcoming temptation is to focus on something better than what is tempting us.

There's a reason why Scripture speaks multiple times of fixing our eyes on Jesus. When our eyes are fixed on him, temptations become "strangely dim." Why? Because our gaze is on something far better than the diversions our culture throws at us. Indeed, our gaze is on the one whom our hearts truly crave.

God, you are worthy of my complete focus. Help me to see you in your power and strength today. May I get a glimpse of you in your love. Then I will not slip into distractions. Amen.

BE ONE

"That all of them may be one, Father, just as you are in me and I am in you."

—*John 17:21*

A team will rise and fall based on how unified it is. It doesn't matter if it's a company, a platoon, a soccer team, or a marital relationship. Relational fracture in a team environment leads to failure. The 2004 United States Olympic basketball team is one example. Although they were the best players in the world, they fell short of gold. This happened because each person wanted to be the star; they weren't unified. A team's fracture leads to a team's failure. It's that simple.

Simple, sure, but hard to put into practice. The second you have any type of team, you have broken and rebellious human beings in the same environment, and there's bound to be tension. Like porcupines cuddling in the cold, we often hurt each other as we seek connection.

But just as often as there is fracture, there is also the opposite—harmony. When two voices harmonize, a beautiful song can result. The same is true when lives merge in a team environment. This is why Jesus prays that his disciples (throughout all ages of the church) might be "one." Jesus wants harmony, not fracture.

God, today I pray for all the relationships in my life. I pray that I would be—through your work—a harmonizing voice, a team player, and a loving partner. Help me with this, God, because by myself, I slip up and make it about me. Amen.

PROOF

"May they also be in us so that the world may believe that you have sent me."

—John 17:21

The proof is in the pudding the old adage says, meaning the only thing that really matters is if something works. You get it, right? In the end, the advertising and sale price mean nothing if the product falls apart right when you open it.

Jesus continues to pray for unity, suggesting that when the church is unified, the world will believe. The proof of the church is in the unity here, we might say. That means that when it comes to unity, there is something on the line: our spiritual integrity and our testimony to a world that needs to know God's love.

God, help me to radiate your love so the world will know your love. May my home and workplace to be a picture of unity so the world will know your power and love! Amen.

OUR HELPER

"I have given them the glory that you gave me, that they may be one as we are one."

—John 17:22

Have you ever been asked to do something, maybe a particular job at work or an essay in a class, without the proper resources or training to accomplish the goal? If so, what was the result? More often than not, it's suboptimal. When it comes to Christian unity, Jesus has thankfully not left us underresourced!

In the above verse, Jesus describes Christian unity as a reachable goal. Not because we're really talented or incredibly friendly. Nope. From Jesus' perspective, Christian unity is possible because he's given us his glory, which is God's very presence in the life of his believers. The presence of God in the followers of Christ brings real and lasting Christian unity.

In a way, this is encouraging. Jesus hasn't left us to figure it out. He's given us a helper, his Holy Spirit. But, in another way, this means we have to work at it. Unity doesn't come naturally; we have to yield to others and the Holy Spirit. We have to lay down our agendas. If we really want the unity that Christ has prayed we would experience, we have to keep in step with the Spirit, saying daily, "Not my will, but yours."

God, I confess I need you. Specifically, I need your Holy Spirit in my life. I want to see you work. I want to grow as a man. For that I need your presence. Please give me your strength today. Amen.

One Body

In Christ we, though many, form one body, and each member belongs to all the others.

—*Romans 12:5*

A bicycle has many parts. The handlebars help us turn corners or keep the bike straight while cruising downhill. The gears can shift with a touch of the fingers, helping us climb hills. The pedals that connect to the gears move the chain and the rear wheel. And the brakes let us stop when the light turns red. If we took one of these parts away, the bike wouldn't work or would be dangerous to ride.

Now think of your family, your church, or even your workplace. There are those who are gifted with administration; they can organize and create systems. There are gregarious extroverts, always making new connections. Some have a kind and warm presence, the type that make you feel safe. Cautious and conservative personalities help us play it safe and not wade recklessly into new waters. Pioneers balance the cautious voices and challenge us to have faith and get out of the boat, even when it's uncomfortable. Creative types imagine beautiful God-honoring creations that inspire us to be in awe of God. Then there are the straight shooters who can look you in the eye and tell you what you need to hear. If you took away one type of person from your family, church, or workplace, the difference would be noticeable. Things would probably get off track.

God, help me to recognize and honor the diversity you have placed in my home, church, and workplace. Amen.

LEGACY

"My prayer is not for them alone. I pray also for those who will believe in me through their message."

—*John 17:20*

What do you think of when you hear the word *legacy*? Do you think about money? Or some family values passed down through generations?

Jesus prayed the ultimate "legacy" prayer as the cross got closer. In that prayer he didn't just pray for himself, though he was in the midst of crisis. He didn't even pray just for his friends and followers, though they would soon face crisis. Toward the end of Jesus' earthly life, he prayed for us. That is amazing. You. Me. The person in your small group who always shows up late. Everyone. Jesus, in one of his last moments on earth, thought about us.

What would it look like for you to think two or three generations beyond you? How might that affect your parenting? When you think about that, you start getting a vision for leaving a legacy, and you're closer having to the "mind of Christ" (1 Corinthians 2:16).

God, give me a vision for my family that is bigger than me. I pray for a vision for my family that is even bigger than my kids. I pray for a God-sized vision for my family. Help me to think about the legacy I am passing down. I desire it to be one that honors you. Please give me strength. Amen.

Set On

> Blessed are those whose strength is in you, whose hearts are set on pilgrimage.
>
> —*Psalm 84:5*

What is your heart set on? One way to tell is to think about what you spend your time thinking about. Another could be to consider where you spend your money or time. The psalmist says that the blessed have set their hearts on a journey. The word *pilgrimage* means a pursuit after something that has real meaning—something that is spiritually significant. So it's bigger than the next raise or a new house. The man who has set his heart on pilgrimage is pursuing something that is bigger than himself. The man who has set his heart on pilgrimage knows his weaknesses and moral deficiencies, and is seeking to grow in those areas. The man who has set his heart on pilgrimage is pursuing Jesus. It is that man who is truly blessed.

Father, I want my heart focus to be on you. I don't want to settle for lesser things or smaller goals. I want your plans to be my plans. So I surrender. You will be my life journey's destination. Amen.

HEARTBROKEN

"When I heard these things, I sat down and wept. For some days I mourned and fasted and prayed before the God of heaven."

—*Nehemiah 1:4*

Have you ever experienced something in your life that upset you deeply? Typically we see these experiences as negative, and they often are. But they also have the power to propel us toward action. A quick survey of history shows that the men who have affected the world most positively have been moved to action by some grave need, something that broke their heart.

Nehemiah is one example. When he heard about the destruction of his hometown, his heart broke and that led him to return to his hometown and work for its restoration. He surveyed the problem and got an understanding of what needed to be done. He gathered people to help restore the broken walls and structures. He persevered through challenges when people mocked his efforts. All of this happened because his heart broke when he heard some news.

So what gets close to breaking your heart right now? Is it a family you know that is in need? Is it neighborhood kids who need a good male influence? Is it for people to know the loving kindness of God? When you're able to answer those questions, you may, like Nehemiah, be sent into action.

Father, help me to have a heart that breaks for the things that break your heart. Help me then know what to do. Amen.

Opposition

> Tobiah the Ammonite, who was at his side, said, "What they are building—even a fox climbing up on it would break down their wall of stones!"
>
> —*Nehemiah 4:3*

What do you do in the face of opposition? It's easy to let opposition push us into a sense of defeat. Other times it's easy to lash out, launching a counterattack at the person who opposes us. Perhaps hardest of all is to persevere, pressing through the opposition.

You may remember that Nehemiah's heart had broken when he heard the news of his hometown lying in ruins. He went home and sought its restoration. But not too long into that process, he met opposition. He didn't spout back insults or sink into defeat. Instead he found strength to persevere. His secret to this is found in prayer—the first thing he did when the critics raised their voices.

When you're seeking to make a positive impact, you will encounter opposition. The opposition comes internally as you experience self-doubt and find yourself distracted. The opposition comes externally as you hear the voices of critics and questioners. Whether the opposition is internal or external, the path of perseverance begins with prayer. It's when we pray that we are reminded by God of the urgency of what we're doing and find the strength to keep at it.

God, help me to persevere. Remind me of the urgency of caring for my children. Remind me of the importance of showing your love in my neighborhood. Remind me of how the stakes are high. Amen.

CHRIST IN ME

I have been crucified with Christ and I no longer live, but Christ lives in me. The life I now live in the body, I live by faith in the Son of God, who loved me and gave himself for me.

—*Galatians 2:20*

How does it feel when you can't find your wallet? You may lose sleep or be late for work as you look under every couch cushion. If you have to drive somewhere, no doubt you feel a little jittery. Your wallet says something about who you are. In a way, it holds your identity.

But the question of identity is bigger than what's in your wallet. "Who am I?" is a question we ask in a variety of ways—and often these identity questions manifest around the topic of achievement. Many of us define ourselves by what we have done or what we weren't able to do. Deriving identity from achievement often sends us into crisis as we realize our limitations and weaknesses.

Paul gives us a different way to derive our identity. In the above passage, he says that the very core of who we are is connected with Jesus Christ. He provides our identity. And because of that, we are accepted despite our achievements (or lack of them). We are given an identity that cannot be lost because of Christ's achievement on our behalf.

Father, remind me that I am in Christ. Help me to remember that, in the end, that is what defines me. Give me the clarity of mind to remember that he is ultimately my identity. Amen.

STATUS SYMBOL

Here is neither Jew nor Gentile, neither slave nor free,
nor is there male and female, for you are all one in Christ
Jesus.

—Galatians 3:28

One of the first questions we tend to ask someone we just
meet is, "What is it that you do?" By "do," we mean what they
do for work. The answer to the question, whether we admit it
or not, determines what we think of them. If they reply, "I'm
a doctor," our respect quotient goes up and we may even feel
a bit insecure. It's easy for this harmless question to slip into
a search for status. When someone has more education or a
better job, we become insecure about our status. If someone
has a wider network, we're left wondering about our status.

Paul, writing to the Galatians, dismantles the major status symbols and positions of his day. For him, a slave is on
the same level as a free person. A Jew is on the same level as
a Gentile. A woman is on the same level as a man. No one
is above and no one is below. This is the case because before
Christ we all were in a desperate situation, and in Christ we
have been given more than we could ask or imagine. For Paul,
the ultimate status symbol is not a new car or a great job, but
the cross.

God, help me to believe that the only thing I need for
significance is you. Keep me from insecurity and pride.
Remind me of who I am in you. Amen.

FREEDOM

> It is for freedom that Christ has set us free. Stand firm,
> then, and do not let yourselves be burdened again by a
> yoke of slavery. … You, my brothers and sisters, were
> called to be free. But do not use your freedom to indulge
> the flesh; rather, serve one another humbly in love.
>
> —*Galatians 5:1, 13*

It probably wouldn't take you long to think of a movie or book where the plot is all about the pursuit of freedom. We love stories of people being freed from captivity or oppressive situations. For Americans it's woven into our cultural DNA with phrases like "home of the free" and others like it. Interestingly, the Bible is on the same page. Paul challenged the Galatians because they made their faith all about rule adherence. Paul wanted them to know that true faith means freedom from a religion strictly focused on rules and regulations.

Culturally, we love the idea of being freed from others' approval, rule-based religion, or self-criticism, and understandably so. But there is more to freedom than escaping something. In Galatians 5:1, Paul speaks about being freed from the law, but then in verse 13 he says that we have been freed for a purpose. True freedom means that we have been freed from the religious rules and regulations through Christ's work on the cross and that we are freed for the purpose of loving God and the world. Both are essential elements of true freedom.

Father, remind me that I am free from the law. Remind me that I am freed for a purpose—to love. Amen.

INVITATION

> After this I saw a vast crowd, too great to count, from every nation and tribe and people and language, standing in front of the throne and before the Lamb.
> —*Revelation 7:9*

Whether it's your child's birthday or a dinner party for family or friends from work, one of the important questions for all gatherings is, "How many people should we invite?" It may not be a popular or easy decision, but in the end, certain people are on the guest list and others aren't. This process can cause anxiety on the part of those extending the invitations and sometimes cause frustration for those not invited. Still, it's all part of the process.

When John, the author of Revelation, got a glimpse of heaven, he saw people from all continents, people groups, and economic backgrounds right next to each other. Jesus' invitation to his never-ending party isn't limited; it's open to all. Everyone is invited. While our earthly party invitations have understandable limits, what would it look like for us to live knowing that all have been invited to the heavenly banquet?

> God, help me to include, not exclude. Help me to welcome, not shun. And help me to still love those who may exclude me. For all this I need your strength. Amen.

EVANGELISM

> Pray for us, too, that God will give us many opportunities to speak about his mysterious plan concerning Christ. That is why I am here in chains.
>
> —*Colossians 4:3 NLT*

Evangelism is one word that those inside and outside the church dislike equally. It can bring anxiety as some feel obligated but not equipped—or nervous about what the person they're talking to might say. Others feel they're being pushy and worry about coming off as rude or "more holy than."

Some of this anxiety exists because we haven't always had great examples. It's easy to think of the guy on the sidewalk shouting cringe-worthy comments. In contrast to that caricature, Paul asks the Colossian church to pray "that God may open to us a door … to declare the mystery of Christ" (Colossians 4:3 ESV). Paul's method of evangelism was praying for open doors, not barging through them.

That isn't to excuse us from doing the work of evangelism. Everyone who has heard the good news of the gospel is called to pass it on. And every day there are open doors. Evangelism requires patience and watchful prayer. It involves being in relationship with those who don't know Christ. It takes being in a friendship long enough to see God crack open the door of a person's heart. It means saying something simple like, "You know, I've been wondering, how can I pray for you?"

God, give me eyes to see the open doors for your gospel! Amen.

QUALIFYING

"So now, go. I am sending you to Pharaoh to bring my people the Israelites out of Egypt." But Moses said to God, "Who am I that I should go to Pharaoh and bring the Israelites out of Egypt?"

—*Exodus 3:10–11*

Have you ever felt ill-equipped to perform a duty? Perhaps you experienced it during a tense conversation with your spouse. Maybe it was your first day at a new position. Or perhaps it was while walking out of the hospital with your first child. Whether you're experiencing it now or see it coming in the future, the question, "Am I really up to the task?" is one that haunts many men. It was the fear that plagued Moses' mind as God called him to lead the Israelites to freedom. And, in a way, Moses' concern wasn't unfounded. He wasn't completely up to the task. He apparently stuttered (Exodus 4:10), he had skipped town after killing someone in an angry outburst (Exodus 2:12), and his resume didn't fit the role. But God doesn't call the qualified; he qualifies the called.

Take some time to survey your life. Where do you have an inkling of insecurity? Is it in your role as a father? Or possibly at work? Wherever it is, know that God is there with you, and as you seek him out, he will guide your steps.

God, I confess I doubt your ability to use me. Help me to trust you. Help me to believe that you want to use me. Amen.

CHALLENGE + GROWTH

These have come so that the proven genuineness of your faith—of greater worth than gold, which perishes even though refined by fire—may result in praise, glory and honor when Jesus Christ is revealed.

—1 Peter 1:7

Lift weights and you'll find yourself sore. Decide to run a 10K race and you'll have to push through pain. Work on your marriage and you'll have to have tough conversations about those easily overlooked growth areas. Buy a house and you'll have to be disciplined and ruthless in saving for a down payment. As much as we'd like to have maturity come easy, it seems that challenge and growth are inseparable.

The people Peter was writing to (exiles scattered throughout the provinces of Pontus, Galatia, Cappadocia, Asia, and Bithynia) didn't have much money, and their neighbors and coworkers were slandering them for their faith. Even more, these exiles most likely didn't have social status and therefore had no real opportunities for advancement. All of that together created a challenging situation. But Peter says that what they did have in one another and in Christ was of greater worth than gold. Not only that, but this hidden wealth became more pure and strong in opposition. Again we find that challenge and growth are inseparable.

God, help me to welcome challenges. Give me eyes to see what you're doing in me in times of difficulty. Give me faith to believe that what I have in you is of greater worth than gold. Amen.

DESIRING GOD

> Though you have not seen him, you love him; and even though you do not see him now, you believe in him and are filled with an inexpressible and glorious joy.
>
> —*1 Peter 1:8*

No doubt you bring a picture of your wife and kids when on an extended business trip. You may even pull out your phone and scroll through a couple of pictures before the plane takes off or during a quick gas stop. Absence makes the heart grow fonder, the old adage goes.

The recipients of Peter's first letter never had the chance to meet Jesus face-to-face, but when they heard about him through the missionary efforts of the early church, something changed in them. They found themselves loving Jesus and being filled with joy as they anticipated an eternity with him.

But just as absence can make a heart grow fonder, it also can produce forgetfulness. The recipients of Peter's letter experienced a growth of desire for the Lord, not forgetfulness. Why? Because like a father does with a picture of his family, they held the reality of Jesus before them as often as possible, and this gave them great joy.

> Father, I have not seen you; help me to love you. I desire to know you; help me to desire you more. Amen.

GET AWAY

> Very early in the morning, while it was still dark, Jesus got up, left the house and went off to a solitary place, where he prayed. Simon and his companions went to look for him, and when they found him, they exclaimed: "Everyone is looking for you!"
>
> —*Mark 1:35–37*

Jesus was not worried about the crowd. Sure, he loved them. But Jesus' primary concern was connection with his Father. He knew that connection was where strength came from. Any healing and hope for the crowds rested on his intermingling with the Spirit and the Father.

But Simon (or Peter) was worried. The crowd was looking for Jesus, and if Jesus didn't show up soon, they might disappear. Then what would happen to the "movement"? Didn't Jesus understand that Simon had invested his life in this movement? If the crowd left, what would happen to his investment? He'd have to sulk back and buy his fishing gear back. Sigh.

Why did Jesus not give in to Peter's anxiety? Jesus knew that the popularity of the crowd didn't define him. He knew that his priority wasn't the court of public approval or even seeing his movement go up in the rankings. He knew that his Father's voice and the Spirit's presence are the most important, and that the identity they offer will not be taken away.

God, give me the courage to get away today. I don't have to endlessly win favor from the "crowds." What I need is to hear the voice of your favor. Amen.

THE CALLING OF WORK

The LORD God took the man and put him in the Garden
of Eden to work it and take care of it.

—Genesis 2:15

"I'm working for the weekend," we sometimes say. It's under-standable. Often our sights are set on that weekend getaway or just some relaxing time with the family. Even more, work environments can be stressful and further stir up a "5 p.m. anticipation."

Early in the book of Genesis we see God's stamp of approval on work. This may be contrary to what we've thought about the garden of Eden. Wouldn't "paradise" involve sun umbrel-las and tropical drinks? Maybe, but it also involved work. Because we were made in the image of God, and God worked by creating the world, we too have within us a compulsion to create and make—to work.

What if God placed you in your workplace just as he placed Adam in the garden? What would it look like to honor him there? What would it look like to find joy in the process of work? How could you respond to God's invitation to love both him and people right there, at work?

God, help me to find joy while I work. I want it to be more than a grind. I want my attitude at work to honor you. Help me to take pride in what I do. Amen.

HIDING

Then the man and his wife heard the sound of the LORD God as he was walking in the garden in the cool of the day, and they hid from the LORD God among the trees of the garden.

—*Genesis 3:8*

We don't stop playing hide-and-go-seek when we're young. We keep playing far into adulthood, though the stakes change and it's no longer fun. When someone we have an unresolved disagreement with walks into a store, we jet down a grocery aisle out of sight. When our boss asks how the "big project" is coming, we look down. Since we don't want our spouse or kids to know how much we drink, we keep our beer or liquor in the garage.

Why do we do this? The Bible's answer is shame. We are ashamed of ourselves, and we don't want others to see what's really going on. Often there is something close to a soundtrack repeating in our head, saying, "They won't love you if they knew."

The way of healing is to stop hiding. Only when we come out from behind the bushes do we deal shame a fatal blow. And where can we get the courage to confess? It comes from realizing that God already knows us inside and out and he still loves us. The courage comes from knowing the everlasting love of God expressed most clearly on the cross.

Father, give me the strength to step from behind the places where I'm hiding. I want to be honest. I want to be free. For this give me strength. Amen.

HEAL ME

A man with leprosy came to him and begged him on his
knees, "If you are willing, you can make me clean." Jesus
was indignant. He reached out his hand and touched the
man. "I am willing," he said. "Be clean!"

—*Mark 1:40–41*

In the ancient world, lepers were despised. No one was treated
with more disdain. They couldn't go to the temple due to the
risk of infecting others. They were shut off from family. They
had to stay at a distance from others, yelling, "Unclean!" as
they approached. It is said that rabbis wouldn't get closer than
six feet from a leper.

The leper in Mark's gospel breaks code and walks up to
the Rabbi Jesus. You can imagine the crowd gasping. And
while Scripture says that Jesus was "indignant," it's clear that
the indignation was not directed at the leper's audacity but at
the condition he suffered. And then, with the crowd watching,
Jesus touched the leper. It would have been easy to heal the man
from a distance and then invite him closer. Even more, Jesus
could have dismissed the leper for not following cultural pro-
tocol. Instead, Jesus said, "I am willing," and touched the man.

Is there something keeping you at a distance from Jesus?
Are you worried what might happen if you draw close? Are
you paralyzed by what the crowd might think? Whatever is
keeping you from him, know that he only wants to offer you
his healing touch.

God, today I believe that you are willing to heal me. You
desire to reach your hand toward me and say, "Be clean!"
Amen.

NEEDING JESUS

> Jesus said to them, "It is not the healthy who need a doctor, but the sick. I have not come to call the righteous, but sinners."
>
> —*Mark 2:17*

Can you imagine a hospital filled with people who don't need a doctor? A man in a stretcher alleging he can walk fine and doesn't need help. A young boy with a broken arm assuring a nurse that he doesn't need any help. These scenarios are pretty much unbelievable, but we don't feel the same way when imagining a church of people who think they're doing well and functionally don't need the Great Physician. That's much easier to believe. How tragic.

Early in his ministry, Jesus makes sure all who are listening understand that the whole reason he came was to heal and help—to rescue. That means two things. First, our relationship with God can't be based on our goodness but on confession of our need for Jesus. Any other way is laughable, like the sick man in the hospital pretending he's just fine. Second, followers of Jesus are called to build hospitals, not castles. Just like Jesus, we should seek out those who are in need, rather than protect ourselves from those who might have "issues." After all, every one of us needs the Great Physician; no one is beyond their need for Jesus.

Father, I confess my need for you again today. Jesus, I am just as in need of you now as I was ten years ago. Spirit of God, help me to love the sick around me like you love them. Amen.

STEP OUT IN FAITH

"But what about you?" he asked. "Who do you say I am?"
Peter answered, "You are the Messiah."

—*Mark 8:29*

When was the last time you risked something when you stepped out in faith? Maybe it was when you took a chance on a business venture or asked your beloved, "Will you marry me?" Maybe when you brought up a challenging conversation with an employer. Some find it easy to take these faith-filled steps while others are paralyzed by the pressure. Either way, often the only way forward in life is to take the step of faith.

Peter found himself in this situation when Jesus asked the disciples, "Who do you say I am?" Jesus hadn't forgotten who he was. He didn't need to be reminded of his name. Rather, he wanted them to step out in faith and boldly share who they believed he was. They had seen Jesus heal and teach, calm waters, and care for hurting people. *Could he be the Messiah?* was undoubtedly a question they had asked themselves, maybe even discussing it together, but Jesus wanted them to actually say it to him.

It was Peter who had the courage and faith to speak what he had come to believe. So now he is remembered by his faith, while we don't know anything about what the others said at that point. As the proverb goes, "Fortune favors the bold."

So, where is God calling you to step out in faith? In what is he inviting you to risk a bit?

God, you are in control. Help me believe that and to step out in faith. Amen.

FEBRUARY

COMMITMENT TO THE JOURNEY

"Come," he replied, "and you will see."

—John 1:39

No doubt you didn't know everything about your bride-to-be on the day you got engaged, and you most likely don't know everything about your wife right now. That's kind of how people work. There are layers and stories that gradually get exposed over time. We grow in our knowledge of each other over time, and over the years a spouse's or a close friend's actions and thoughts become predictable.

This same pattern exists with God. When Jesus invited his first followers to journey with him, he didn't say, "Here's a one-million-page contract and explanation offering everything you need to know about what you're stepping into." Nope. Instead, he said, "Come … and you will see." The same is true with us.

No one knows everything there is to know about God; that's part of the journey. But as we take steps after Jesus, we begin to see how predictable his kindness is and how reliable his provisions are. Today he may be inviting you to another day of trusting him, another day of coming and seeing.

God, I am committed to the journey, and I know that you are committed to me. I will come and see what you have for me today! Amen.

HUMILITY

And this was [John the Baptist's] message: "After me comes the one more powerful than I."

—Mark 1:7

Can you imagine *Time* magazine with a man on the cover and a quote at the bottom saying, "I don't have the answer. I'm not the solution"? It sounds far-fetched, doesn't it? How about an author who says, "I really don't have what you need. Wait for the one who follows me. He's the one you really need to check out"? Again, hard to imagine. Still, that's a rough parallel to one of John the Baptist's central messages: "After me comes the one more powerful than I." That was a remarkable thing to say, especially since everyone from the city and the countryside was hanging on his every word (Mark 1:5).

John the Baptist set an example for contemporary followers of Jesus. It's easy for us to get sucked up into the "look at me, notice me" approach that is often pushed in our culture. But John the Baptist resisted the pull of self-promotion because he wasn't focused on the adoring crowds or his own eloquence but on the one who would come after him. Humility happens when our focus is on "the one more powerful than I."

Father, rid me of my toxic and insecure self-focus. Help me to live focused on you. Give me your strength so I might love your world. Amen.

OPEN UP

How long, LORD, must I call for help, but you do not listen?
—*Habakkuk 1:2*

Pain happens. Whether it's the physical pain of an injury, the emotional pain of a fractured relationship, or the unexplained hurt of an accident, pain has a habit of working its way into our life. Often, trying to convince ourselves that everything will get better doesn't help (and it's even worse if a friend tells us that). The most pressing issue is the pain, and to assert optimism early proves unconvincing.

The Bible, rather than prodding us with Hallmark-esque naïveté, speaks with stark honesty. Habakkuk, for example, shares his broken heart with God, and he doesn't hold back. Throughout his exchange with God, he gradually finds himself content, even without all his hopes fulfilled. But that doesn't happen quickly, and, even more importantly, it only happens when Habakkuk is completely open and honest with God. It's only when we dare to ask God the tough questions about pain and confusion that he can begin to heal and transform us.

God, search me to see if I am hiding pain or confusion that I should be sharing with you. I do have hurt and questions. Will you be my guide in this troubling situation? Amen.

WORKERS

> Then he said to his disciples, "The harvest is plentiful but
> the workers are few. Ask the Lord of the harvest, there-
> fore, to send out workers into His harvest."
>
> —*Matthew 9:37–38*

In the face of the great need for workers, Jesus didn't mount
a marketing campaign, craft an elevator pitch, or hire a con-
sultant. Instead, he said that we should "ask the Lord of the
harvest." This goes against our instinct. In the face of great
need, it makes sense to send out e-mails and make phone calls,
saying, "Please?"

Jesus says that we should pray for workers as a first step
because God is "the Lord of the harvest." That means he's in
control. Jesus is inviting his followers to acknowledge that
prayer is the first and most important step, even as the world is
filled with overwhelming needs. This of course doesn't mean
that the actions of evangelism, service, and social justice aren't
important; they're vital. It just means that the priority is to ask
"the Lord of the harvest" to provide for the need.

> Father, I acknowledge that you are the Lord of the harvest.
> Send workers to address the needs around the world and
> in my city. Amen.

Reset My Soul

In the beginning God created the heavens and the earth.
—*Genesis 1:1*

We experience our pain and problems differently when we understand who is in control and trust the process he pulls us through. We have an important role to play in our lives, but the hero in our story is not us.

The words of Genesis 1:1 echo throughout Scripture as a reminder of who has been in control since "the beginning." Mark 1:1, John 1:1, and 1 John 1:1 all remind us of the need to reset our soul and put our trust in the one who set creation in motion.

Issues in our lives can pull us away from God's presence. Over time, the weight of the world gets shifted onto our shoulders. When we cannot see past our present problems, we need to reset and remember that in the beginning—before the issues at hand, before the obstacles of the day, and before the difficult decisions ahead—God created the heavens and the earth.

God is in control. Not us.

God, reset my soul and grant me strength to put my trust in you. You have been the author of creation since the beginning. May I find rest in that reality. Amen.

TRAINED EARS

> So Eli told Samuel, "Go and lie down, and if he calls you, say, 'Speak, LORD, for your servant is listening.'" So, Samuel went and lay down in his place.
>
> —*1 Samuel 3:9*

When listening to music, a musician with a trained ear hears more than the average person. The everyday listener will simply hear a song, but a musician will hear the musical texture, the rhythm, and the key. A trained ear will be able to pick up more and understand the fullness of music.

Eli recognized that God was speaking to Samuel, but Samuel did not have a trained ear yet. Instead of explaining what the Lord was doing, Eli taught Samuel how to listen and how to respond. Taking Eli's advice, Samuel went back to bed and was able to hear the voice of the Lord.

As we disciple our children, it may be easier to tell them what to believe. It may be simpler to tell them what God requires, rather than train them how to listen for the voice of the Lord. But we do a disservice to our children and stunt their spiritual growth if we don't train their ears to hear God's voice. We need to trust that God desires to teach our children and help them develop the ears to hear the fullness of his music.

God, give me peace as I disciple those under my care. Give me ears to hear your voice and the patience to trust your process. Amen.

STRENGTH

The Lord is my shepherd; I have all that I need.

—*Psalm 23:1 NLT*

We see billboards along the highway, advertisements in the paper, and banners on our screens all attempting to pull us into our next purchase. The world has a way of convincing us that something is missing from our lives. Many subscribe to a pattern of thinking that says, *If I just get this, then I'll have all I need.*

Having new things is not the issue. Purchasing new toys is not the problem. The heart of the matter is wrapped up in believing that our fulfillment comes from what we have, not who we follow. The issue is that we shop for satisfaction, when our shepherd is all we need.

Our strength is found in the simplicity of our needs. All we need is the Lord. Anything else is extra. We don't need to scramble for more. We don't have to buy the next best thing.

Our shepherd is sufficient. In him, we have all we need.

God, simplify my desires. When my heart desires more things, help me desire more of you. When my mind believes that I am lacking, remind me that you are all I need. Amen.

GUIDANCE

Your word is a lamp to my feet and a light to my path.
—Psalm 119:105 ESV

As we walk through life, we find ways to increase the distance we can go. We run far and fast as we achieve our way to the next best opportunity. The question, "What's next?" directs our path. The question, "Now what?" dictates our speed. We desire more and let life's opportunities guide our steps.

If we invite God into the conversation, we ask for a two-year forecast or a five-year plan. We want him to reveal a clear and accurate picture of the life ahead of us, so we can decide whether we want to take that path. But when we go to God for guidance, we need to understand that speed and distance are not his priority.

We want headlights, but God's Word is a lamp. A lamp can only light up the next few steps of a journey. If we look ahead too far, if we move our feet to fast, we may forget who we're walking with. When God guides our steps and we go at the pace he reveals, we will be going the right direction, toward him. And we will be going the right way, with him.

God, as you light the next steps of my journey, give me the courage to walk in your ways. Guide me closer to you as I lean in to the plans you have for my life. Amen.

TRUST IN THE LORD

> Trust in the LORD with all your heart, and do not lean on your own understanding. In all your ways acknowledge him, and he will make straight your paths.
>
> —*Proverbs 3:5–6 ESV*

We experience life differently when we trust in the Lord with half our heart and lean hard on our own understanding. The biggest difference is our level of anxiety. When we get swept up in the conflict and confusion of the day, our paths get crisscrossed and we lose our way. We acknowledge the Lord in some of our ways and work hard to pull ourselves out of the mess.

Peace and confidence are byproducts of trusting the Lord. Yet we believe that we'll get there through our own efforts. Life gets the best of us when we continue down the path of self-reliance. But God's grace steps in when we take ourselves out of the equation. When we place our trust in the Lord and acknowledge him in all our ways, peace and confidence will find their way into our hearts and minds.

Lord, give me opportunities to breathe deep today. May I breathe in your presence and exhale my control. I stand before you with open hands and an open heart. Take what is yours and leave peace in my soul. Amen.

USE MY WORDS

The tongue can bring death or life; those who love to talk will reap the consequences.

—*Proverbs 18:21 NLT*

What we say matters. When we say it matters. How we say it matters. Sticks and stones can certainly break bones, but words can crush a spirit. We underestimate the power of our words, and can undermine our motives if we do not consider the art of conversation. When we pay mind to what we say, we can heal the hurting, restore the weary, and create community. But a loose lip can lead to division and destruction.

After you squeeze toothpaste out of its tube, trying to put it back in is a mess. So, too, are our words. We can try to move forward, but our words are out there. We can try to clean up the mess, but we can't take back what was said. When we understand that our words have the power to bring life or death, we are responsible for using them well.

The words children use reflect the words they hear. If we use our words wisely, we can help those around us to understand the power of their words. When we speak words of affirmation to others, we set a good example of how to use words well.

God, help me be quick to listen and slow to speak. Help me use my words wisely to affirm and build others up. Speak life into me and guide my conversations today. Amen.

SURRENDER

You can make many plans, but the LORD's purpose will prevail.

—*Proverbs 19:21 NLT*

Planning helps us prepare for the unknown. It provides a sense of stability as we journey through life. It has been said, "If you fail to plan, you plan to fail." But sometimes we need to put our plans in perspective.

How many things in our lives have turned out the way we planned? What should that teach us?

Our plans may fail, but that doesn't mean we're lost. Our plans may be fulfilled, but that doesn't mean we're found. We find ourselves not in the fulfillment of our plans, but in the fulfillment of the Lord's purpose.

The most difficult part of planning is surrendering our plans to him and his purpose. It is a good thing to plan, but when we bind ourselves to our plans, we run the risk of losing hope. When we get married to our plans, we set ourselves up for disappointment. But when we plan with open hands and pursue our plans with the freedom to fail, we can embrace the Lord's purpose with joy, even if we're taken off the path we created for ourselves.

God, as I journey through life in pursuit of you, remind me that your purpose will prevail. Loosen my grip on the plans I have for my life. Open my hands and my heart to joyfully receive the purpose you have for me. Amen.

BE MY LIGHT

> Do not gloat over me, my enemies! For though I fall, I will rise again. Though I sit in darkness, the LORD will be my light.
>
> —*Micah 7:8 NLT*

Our strength is not measured by how many times we fail. It is not calculated by the number of mistakes we make or the amount of losses we accumulate. The true measure of our strength is found in our source. If we subscribe to the system of self-reliance, the ceiling of our strength is our greatest effort. But if we put our hope in the Lord and find our strength in him, we can rise from our failures and be fearless when darkness descends.

We can fail with confidence when the Lord is the source of our strength. We can sit in the darkness, knowing that the light of the Lord shines brightest in dark times. We do not have to rush out of life's struggles when we know God's strength sustains us in the shadows.

The day will come when we realize that our own efforts are not enough. But the sooner we come to that realization, the sooner we can rest in the power of God and be led by the light of the Lord.

> God, be my strength. Lord, be my light. Keep my eyes on you when failure finds its way to me. May your light lead me when the shadows of life surround me. Amen.

NO LONGER ANXIOUS

"Therefore I tell you, do not be anxious about your life, what you will eat or what you will drink, nor about your body, what you will put on. Is not life more than food, and the body more than clothing? Look at the birds of the air: they neither sow nor reap nor gather into barns, and yet your heavenly Father feeds them. Are you not of more value than they?"

—Matthew 6:25–26 ESV

Many minor things in life consume our care. We find things to worry about and often perceive little things as big problems. But if we take the time to understand the real issue at hand and whose hand we hold as we journey, we will experience a peace that settles our souls.

The issue at hand might be significant in our eyes but already taken care of in God's eyes. Part of the problem is that we confuse our wants with our needs. We get locked into our own desires, and anxiety arises when we are left in want. But Jesus reminds us that our heavenly Father values us more than the birds of the air. He reminds us that our needs have been provided for. If we can rest in that reality, our anxiety will fade away and peace will be present.

God, may your provision bring me peace so I can pay mind to the significant struggles that surround me. Give me perspective and increase my trust in you. Amen.

LOVE

> Love is patient, love is kind. It does not envy, it does not boast, it is not proud. It does not dishonor others, it is not self-seeking, it is not easily angered, it keeps no record of wrongs. Love does not delight in evil but rejoices with the truth. It always protects, always trusts, always hopes, always perseveres.
>
> —*1 Corinthians 13:4–7*

Happy Valentine's Day! These verses are often shared at weddings, which is great, but the apostle Paul never mentioned a wedding. That's not to say that these verses can't be applied to marriage; they certainly can be. But the application is so much richer and deeper than just that.

Some people recommend taking out the word *love* in the verses and inserting our own name. If we do, we'll soon realize that we're really *not* those things 100 percent—but Jesus is. So the idea is to continue to rely on Jesus, not ourselves. We might do okay for a while, but before long we'll drop the ball. We want to be patient and slow to anger with our kids, but it's really hard sometimes. Don't shame yourself into thinking that if you fail at love, you have somehow upset God. It just shows us how much more we need God—in marriage, in parenting, and in our jobs.

> God, show me your love today. Grow me in my imperfect love and develop me more into the likeness of Christ. Amen.

COMPASSION

> When he saw the crowds, he had compassion for them, because they were harassed and helpless, like sheep without a shepherd.
>
> —*Matthew 9:36 ESV*

Compassion for another grows when we understand their story. It unites the mind and the heart. We may see the circumstances surrounding a situation, but when we understand the context, our heart gets involved and compassion springs forth. *Compassion* means to "suffer with." When we have compassion for someone, their problems become our problems. Their pain becomes our pain.

Jesus saw the crowds, and he also knew their situation. Compassion was his natural reaction. When he saw the harassed and helpless people, he had compassion at first sight. Their circumstances did not change in that moment, but their story did. Jesus entered their struggle in that moment, making their problem his own.

We are called to be people of compassion, not judgment. If we take time to understand the stories of those we serve, compassion will be close by. If we teach our children to have compassion at first sight, we can help them see beyond themselves. If we seek to extend grace to those in need, compassion will become a natural part of our lives.

God, lead me into a life of compassion. Give me eyes to see the needs of those around me. Disrupt my comfort and give me the courage to respond with compassion. Amen.

LIFE WITH CHRIST

Take My yoke upon you and learn from Me, for I am gentle and humble in heart, and you will find rest for your souls.

—*Matthew 11:29 NASB*

The busyness of life often brings us to our knees. We work hard, play hard, crash hard, and then pray hard. When we run out of gas, we run to our source. We pray for rest, and hope to be refueled so we can get back out there. Jesus meets us in our exhaustion, in our brokenness, in our struggles. But he also calls us to a new way of working and reveals a new road to resting.

A yoke is a wooden frame that holds two oxen together so they can work side by side. As the stronger ox moves, the weaker ox is pulled along. When both oxen are strong, the work load is lighter for both. This is the picture of work that Jesus paints for us.

Life alone is exhausting. But when we are yoked with Jesus, he is not a pit stop. He's a presence. When we are working by his side, we can rest while we labor, knowing his strength is sufficient.

Life with Christ by our side takes us further faster. When we are yoked with Christ, his humbleness rubs off on us, and rest for our souls is always one step away.

God, teach me to walk in your ways. May I experience rest as you draw me into your presence. Amen.

COURAGE

> But Jesus immediately said to them: "Take courage! It is I.
> Don't be afraid." "Lord, if it's you," Peter replied, "tell me
> to come to you on the water." "Come," he said. Then Peter
> got down out of the boat, walked on the water and came
> toward Jesus.
>
> —*Matthew 14:27–29*

When we are committed to comfort, it's difficult to experience all that God has in store for us. Whether because of the fear of failure or the fear of the unknown, we choose to stay in the boat when we let our fears dictate our direction. Courage is not the absence of fear but the presence of peace when fear is at hand. When our object of hope is greater than our object of fear, we can be courageous.

In the midst of their fear, Jesus said to his disciples, "Take courage! It is I. Don't be afraid." In other words, "Be courageous because I am here. And I am greater than your biggest fear." We can experience peace when we put Jesus on the proper pedestal. When our courage comes from Christ, we will be able to do the unimaginable. We will be able to step out of the boat into the unknown with confidence, and accept his simple invitation to "come."

> God, give me peace when fear surrounds me. Help me to be courageous and follow you into the unknown. Build my trust so I can experience all that you have in store for me. Amen.

CREATIVITY

"For it will be like a man going on a journey, who called his servants and entrusted to them his property. To one he gave five talents, to another two, to another one, to each according to his ability. Then he went away."

—*Matthew 25:14–15 ESV*

One of the first things we do when we get something new is look for instructions. We open the package and find the directions. Instructions are helpful, and it is wise to follow the directions. But what do we do when life gives us something without any instructions? How do we fare when we get an opportunity to use our creativity?

In Jesus' time, it would take a servant nearly twenty years to earn one talent. So the servant who received five talents of his master's property had a heavy responsibility to handle. The servants were given a lot to work with, but the master left them without any instructions. Each servant had an opportunity to exercise his creativity and make his master proud.

By the grace of God, we have received gifts and talents to be used for his glory. God guides us, but he leaves us without any specific instructions. Instead, he gives us opportunities to use our creativity and come up with ways to make him proud of his investment in us.

God, awaken my creativity. Inspire my imagination. And help me to be a good and faithful steward of the gifts and talents you have bestowed upon me. Amen.

PREPARATION

And a voice came from heaven: "You are my Son, whom I love; with you I am well pleased." At once the Spirit sent him out into the wilderness.

—*Mark 1:11–12*

There are seasons in life that are confusing and puzzling. The circumstances that surround us can make us question God's motives and even doubt God's love for us. When we find ourselves in seasons of wilderness, it's important to have the right posture. We need to have a posture of receiving, a commitment to growing, and a focus on the future.

As Jesus was being baptized, God affirmed him, saying, "You are my Son, whom I love; with you I am well pleased." The puzzling part of the story is that immediately following Jesus' affirmation, the Spirit led him into the wilderness. When he was with the wild animals, Jesus didn't question what God said in the waters. Equipped with God's love, he battled in the wilderness for forty days.

Sometimes our sin leads us into the wilderness, but other times God leads us there. Seasons of wilderness reveal and shape our foundation. We don't have to question his love when we find ourselves in the struggle. We need to remain in his love, trust in the process, and let the season of wilderness prepare us to do powerful things.

God, keep my eyes on you when I find myself in the wilderness. Shape me in the shadows, and prepare me for the path ahead. Amen.

COMMITMENT

And when they could not get near him because of the crowd, they removed the roof above him, and when they had made an opening, they let down the bed on which the paralytic lay. And when Jesus saw their faith, he said to the paralytic, "Son, your sins are forgiven."

—*Mark 2:4–5 ESV*

When obstacles arise or roadblocks impede our path, our commitment to the task at hand is tested. How we handle the hurdles of life reveals what is important to us. If our commitment to the task is stronger than the object in the way, we will use our creativity to complete the task. But if our commitment is frail and our dedication is faint, we will find comfort in quitting.

A crowd could not stop the paralytic's friends from getting him to the feet of Jesus. A roof could not make them quit. Their faith in Christ and their commitment to their friend were far greater than the obstacles that were in the way. Jesus noticed their faith and honored their commitment. By God's power, the paralyzed man walked. By God's grace, the man's sins were forgiven.

A commitment to getting others to the feet of Christ is a commitment worth fighting for. Believing in the power of Jesus will take us past any obstacle and over any hurdle we find in the way.

God, increase my commitment to you. Help me see the opportunities beyond the obstacles. And grant me the fortitude to stay the course when quitting sounds comfortable. Amen.

Presence in Storms

That day when evening came, he said to his disciples, "Let us go over to the other side." Leaving the crowd behind, they took him along, just as he was, in the boat. There were also other boats with him. A furious squall came up, and the waves broke over the boat, so that it was nearly swamped.

—*Mark 4:35–37*

In life, we can hope for bright days full of sunshine, but dreary nights and stormy skies are part of the journey. The twists and turns we experience can leave us feeling swamped with struggle. But we find our hope in God's presence during the storms of life.

Jesus took his disciples on an evening journey on the lake. There were other boats on the same waters, but when the winds picked up, Christ was in the boat with his disciples. When the waters rose, Christ was there. When the waves began to sink the vessel, Christ was there.

Living a life with Christ means having Jesus with us in the storm. When the sickness comes, he is in our boat. When loss overwhelms us, he is with us. When confusion capsizes us, he is our comforter. During the storm, it is better to be in a boat with Jesus than out on the waters without him. God, may I find my comfort in you and experience peace through your presence. When the storms of life overwhelm me, be the hope that carries me to the other side. Amen.

JUST BELIEVE

While Jesus was still speaking, some people came from the house of Jairus, the synagogue leader. "Your daughter is dead," they said. "Why bother the teacher anymore?" Overhearing what they said, Jesus told him, "Don't be afraid; just believe."

—Mark 5:35–36

When life doesn't go as planned, we often fear the unknown and put our faith in a new plan. We listen to our fears and head toward hopelessness. Our internal doubts are reinforced by a spirit of negativity. We give power to the critics as their words extinguish our hope. But Jesus overhears our distracting internal dialogue and desires to give us a new voice to listen to—a voice that says, *Do not be afraid. Just believe.*

As a commander in an army directs the soldiers, Jesus spoke those words to Jairus as a command—an imperative, not a suggestion. Jesus didn't declare it to the crowd; he spoke past his doubters directly to Jairus. As with Jairus, Jesus desires to pull us out of our hopelessness and beyond our fear. He wants us to put our faith in him, not a new plan. His words may not always be louder than the words of his critics, but they are more powerful and come from a higher authority.

God, give me ears to hear your voice when doubt sets in. Restore my faith in you when my plans fail. Move me beyond my fears to a place of belief, hope, and promise. Amen.

LIKE A LITTLE CHILD

"Truly I tell you, anyone who will not receive the kingdom of God like a little child will never enter it."
—*Mark 10:15*

When we take a new job, we need to go through two things: an application process and a training period to make sure we can carry out the required tasks. So if we believe the kingdom of God is bigger than any job we apply for, we would expect that entrance also requires a strenuous process. But Jesus defies our expectations and explains that receiving the kingdom requires humbleness and humility, not an application and training.

The process to enter the kingdom isn't strenuous, but it isn't easy either. To become "like a little child" means becoming dependent. It means stripping away all that makes us strong and self-reliant, and that goes against "growing up" and becoming independent. But it makes complete sense if we want to be grafted into the kingdom and become dependent on the King.

When we are self-reliant, we buy into the lie that we are all we need. But when we commit to humbleness and humility, we realize how much we need God in our lives. If we receive the kingdom like a little child, humbly and dependently, we will be able to accomplish more than we ever could on our own.

God, humble my spirit and make me more reliant on you. Help me become like a little child so I can receive the kingdom with awe and wonder. Amen.

SERVANT LEADERSHIP

"For even the Son of Man did not come to be served, but to serve, and to give his life as a ransom for many."

—*Mark 10:45*

It is the call of our culture to climb the ladder of power and authority. Many people find their life purpose in that pursuit. We prize promotions and are defined by the titles we hold. We use others to get what we want and invest in relationships only if it benefits us to do so. Yet Jesus had a different pathway to power and influence. Christ's path was paved with service and sacrifice. Jesus not only served but was also a servant. His actions came out of his character, out of who he was.

Positions of power and authority are honorable positions to hold. However, the attitude of entitlement that comes with those positions is something we need to let go of. When we take the path of Christ, seeking to serve and sacrifice for the sake of others, we will create a culture that reflects the kingdom.

God, give me the eyes to see the ways I can be a servant today. Give me the courage to step into those opportunities. Help me develop the habit of helping others, so service and sacrifice become a natural rhythm of my life. Amen.

GRACE

" 'I am no longer worthy to be called your son. Treat me as one of your hired servants.' And he arose and came to his father. But while he was still a long way off, his father saw him and felt compassion, and ran and embraced him and kissed him."

—Luke 15:19–20 ESV

When we make choices that bring us away from the Lord, we convince ourselves that we need to earn our way back. Our poor decisions bring us to a distant land, and we begin to lose our identity as a child of God. If we do not understand the depth of God's grace, we try to direct God in dealing with our disobedience.

In the parable of the prodigal son, the son had a plan and a proposal. The plan was to go home, and the proposal was to become a hired servant of his father. He did not understand the grace of his father and bought into the lie that he had to earn his way back into the fold. But the father had a different plan and a different proposal. His plan was to lovingly welcome his son home, and his proposal was a family celebration.

The parable is about the grace of the father, not the efforts of the son. We cannot give to our children what we do not have for ourselves. Once we receive God's grace in our own lives, we can extend it to those we love.

God of love, be by my side. God of grace, be my guide. Amen.

SACRIFICE

And he said to them, "Truly, I say to you, there is no one who has left house or wife or brothers or parents or children, for the sake of the kingdom of God, who will not receive many times more in this time, and in the age to come eternal life."

—*Luke 18:29–30 ESV*

The weight of sacrifice is not a light load to carry. Sacrifice is a loss that evokes pain, but it also ushers in something new. Jesus doesn't call us to sacrifice for the sake of loss, but for the sake of the kingdom. When we put Christ and the kingdom at the top of our priority list, we'll be able to look beyond the object of sacrifice to what is gained through our loss. The promise is that the benefits will outweigh our sacrifice, not only in this time but also in the age to come.

When we choose to live a sacrificial life, we'll experience life to the full. We'll experience a life with Christ as our supply. And with him as our supply, we have enough life to pour into our homes and into our families.

Lord Jesus, help me to focus on you and your kingdom. Give me the strength to surrender all I am and all I have to you. Pour into my life so I can begin to see the joy beyond the sacrifice. Amen.

ROUTINES

Jesus said to her, "Everyone who drinks of this water will be thirsty again, but whoever drinks of the water that I will give him will never be thirsty again. The water that I will give him will become in him a spring of water welling up to eternal life."

—*John 4:13–14 ESV*

Our daily routines can condition us into comfortable living. We settle for repeated rhythms and expect our lives to change. Day after day, month after month, year after year, we find life in the things that satisfy only our immediate needs and desires. Our hearts long for so much more, but we settle for so much less.

Too often we live for the temporary, but Christ invites us into the life our souls are longing for. If we allow Jesus to disrupt our daily patterns of living, we can develop the eyes to see the alternative life that Christ offers. A life that satisfies beyond our temporary needs and desires. A life that generates more life. A life that brings light to our work and our play. A life that spills over into our families and our friends.

God, help me encounter you beyond my daily routines. Disrupt my comfort so I will be open to receiving the life that you graciously offer. Mold my heart so I will desire the eternal things you place before me. Amen.

RECOGNIZING CHRIST'S PRESENCE

The woman said, "I know that Messiah" (called Christ) "is coming. When he comes, he will explain everything to us." Then Jesus declared, "I, the one speaking to you—I am he."

—John 4:25–26

Understanding is not a prerequisite of having faith. It is possible to cling to a promise when we find ourselves in the midst of confusion and doubt. Sometimes we are distracted by our circumstances. Sometimes we are blinded by our own expectations. Sometimes Jesus is standing right in front of us, but we're so consumed by our pursuit of him that we fail to recognize his presence.

The Samaritan woman had an unplanned encounter with a Jewish prophet by Jacob's well. The conversation brought her past to light, uncovered her questions, and revealed her faith in the promise of the coming "Messiah." She didn't know all the details, but she knew one thing for sure: "The Christ is coming to explain everything." When she declared her faith in that promise, Jesus revealed his true identity to her.

Life will bring us through valleys of doubt and clouds of confusion. But when we have faith and cling to the promise of the coming Messiah, we may come to find that Christ was with us the entire time.

God, when confusion and doubt overwhelm me, help me put my hope in you. When I am blinded by my circumstances, give me faith to know that you are near. Amen.

MARCH

PARTICIPATING

When Jesus looked up and saw a great crowd coming toward him, he said to Philip, "Where shall we buy bread for these people to eat?" He asked this only to test him, for he already had in mind what he was going to do.

—*John 6:5–6*

Good leaders see needs before the needs present themselves. They anticipate and prepare for problems before they happen. Good leaders provide solutions, but great leaders invite others into the solution. Even if a leader can resolve the issue alone, there is value in having others participate in the action. Servant leaders don't have a "watch me" attitude. They increase effort and effectiveness by asking others, "What should we do?"

Before the feeding of the five thousand, Jesus invited his disciples into the miracle by asking Philip for his opinion. Jesus was fully capable of performing the miracle as a show for all to see, but he chose to use his disciples to be his hands and feet that day. As fathers and leaders, may we see the value in inviting others to be part of the miracles God desires to perform through us.

Lord God, thank you for inviting us into the story. Thank you for choosing me to participate in your work here on earth. May I invite others into the work you have called me to do as I serve you and your kingdom. Amen.

EMBRACING ABUNDANCE

The thief comes only to steal and kill and destroy; I came
that they may have life, and have it abundantly.

—John 10:10 NASB

There are seasons of life when we struggle just to get by.
There are also seasons when we are lulled into the trance of
daily existence. Something deep within us knows that we were
created for more than working jobs and paying bills. Something in our soul hungers for more than survival. But when
the busyness of life hunts us down, we resort to managing life
and controlling circumstances.

The roadway out of that routine is following Christ and
accepting his offer of abundant life. If we receive the life that
Jesus offers, we'll be able to bring life to those around us.
To have something in abundance means to have more than
enough. Experiencing abundant life is so much more than
survival.

Living abundantly doesn't only shape how we live; it shapes
who we live for. When we have more life than we need, we'll
create ways to give our lives away. We'll joyfully pour our lives
into our families, our neighbors, or the strangers we meet—
and still have more to give.

God, help me to not settle for survival. Give me a heart
that desires the abundant life you offer. Stir within me
a spirit of generosity so I can joyfully bring life to those
around me. Amen.

A NEW COMMANDMENT

"I give you a new commandment, that you love one another. Just as I have loved you, you also should love one another. By this everyone will know that you are my disciples, if you have love for one another."

—*John 13:34–35 NRSV*

If love becomes our default posture, we're heading in the right direction. If we choose love, we'll be following the new commandment Jesus gives us. But when we try to love one another with our own strength, we fall short of what Christ calls us to. Our greatest efforts of loving one another can only take us so far.

The love that Jesus loves us with comes from the Father. Christ explains the foundation of his love, saying, "As the Father has loved me, so I have loved you" (John 15:9 NRSV). He then passes the love baton to us with the commandment to love one another. This love for others becomes a signpost of our commitment to Christ.

The weight of loving one another is a lighter load to carry when we're filled with the Father's love for us. His love will fill in the gaps when our best efforts fail. When we tap into the unending supply of the Father's love, we will be able to love one another well.

Heavenly Father, your love for us stretches beyond the heavens. Your supply is more than enough. Fill my heart and soul with your love so I can love others more generously. Amen.

TO ALL PEOPLE

To the weak I became weak, that I might win the weak. I have become all things to all people, that by all means I might save some. I do it all for the sake of the gospel, that I may share with them in its blessings.

—1 Corinthians 9:22–23 ESV

Whether through a common interest or a shared hobby, a powerful connection can happen when we realize what unites us. Strong, lasting relationships are built when we celebrate the uniqueness of others and embrace the things we have in common. As our relationships develop, the needs of others become our needs, their struggles become our struggles, and their joys become our joys. Humility happens when we choose to leave our self-serving agendas to create the best opportunities for those around us.

When we grasp the blessings of the gospel, we will do what is necessary and become who we need to become so those around us can experience Christ in a life-changing way. The kingdom comes when we meet people where they are—physically, emotionally, and spiritually. When people see our willingness to enter their world for the sake of the gospel and its blessings, doors are opened, walls come down, and people take a step closer to Christ and his kingdom.

God, increase my joy when I consider the blessings of the gospel. Give me courage to reach out to others for the sake of the gospel. May my character reflect yours as I seek to enter the lives of those around me. Amen.

Growth

> But we all, with unveiled face, beholding as in a mirror the glory of the Lord, are being transformed into the same image from glory to glory, just as from the Lord, the Spirit.
>
> —2 Corinthians 3:18 NASB

Unlike our bodies, our spirits don't stop growing. And over time, as our bodies begin to deteriorate, our spirits are still being transformed into the God's image. We don't arrive at a place in our faith journey where we are fully formed. With open hands and God's grace, we need to allow the Holy Spirit to guide our growth.

We are never too old, too weak, or too broken to reflect God's glory. If we get to a place where we're settling for suitable, we need to reclaim the childhood desire for growth. We need to pull ourselves out of the glory days and look forward to the next level of glory that the Lord wants to bring us to. We give our children a glimpse of God's glory when we age but grow stronger—when our bodies break down but our spirits build up. As we reflect the glory of the Lord, may our hearts be open and our spirits ready.

Lord, continue to pour into my life so I can reflect your glory. Keep me humble. Make me willing. I am thankful that you are not done with me yet. Amen.

THE GIFT OF GRACE

God saved you by his grace when you believed. And you
can't take credit for this; it is a gift from God.
—*Ephesians 2:8 NLT*

God's grace is a gift that has been paid for by Christ on the
cross. The work we do in the name of Jesus, the service we
render for the sake of the kingdom, should express our gratitude for that gift. We diminish the meaning of the cross when
we attempt to earn God's grace through our works. If we have
a spirit of entitlement, we cannot truly receive God's grace,
because we believe it is owed to us. And if we believe we
earned the gift, we expect others to do the same.

The biggest obstacle between the gift of grace and those
who need to receive it from us, is the belief that we were the
ones who paid for it. When we awaken to the reality that grace
is a gift from God and that we did nothing to earn it, we can
give it away with freedom and generosity. If we joyfully receive
the gift, we will joyfully give it away to those around us. And
when we extend grace to our children amid their mistakes,
they will walk away with a clearer understanding of the love
that Christ has for them.

Lord, thank you for grace. Open my heart and my hands
so I can freely receive and give the gift you have lavished
upon me. Amen.

PURPOSE

> For we are God's masterpiece. He has created us anew in Christ Jesus, so we can do the good things he planned for us long ago.
>
> —*Ephesians 2:10 NLT*

Our lives are not a made up of random events pieced together by the hands of time. We were created with intention and purpose by the hands of God. The Greek word *poiema*, which is translated "masterpiece," describes a work that only God can do. As an artist creating with intention, God has crafted us. He has made us as a beautiful depiction of the work he is doing in the world.

No two people are alike. Each of us is uniquely gifted to do the good works God has prepared for us to do. Crafting our history, weaving in our giftedness, and fastening our future, God continues to mold us for his purpose. He wants to use us to bring life to those around us and to encourage those under our care. When we embrace our uniqueness and live with purpose, we can confidently step into God's calling for our lives.

God, open my eyes to see what makes me unique. Help me discover my unique role in your kingdom. As I seek the good works you want me to step into, continue molding me to make me more like you. Amen.

HOW TRUE POWER ACTS

Who, being in very nature God, did not consider equality with God something to be used to his own advantage; rather, he made himself nothing by taking the very nature of a servant, being made in human likeness. And being found in appearance as a man, he humbled himself by becoming obedient to death—even death on a cross!

—*Philippians 2:6–8*

If we want to be achievers in our culture, we need to commit to moving up the ladder of success. But no matter how high we climb, no matter what title we hold, we will never find ourselves "being in very nature God."

It is an honor to have a high position of power, but the challenge is found in how we use the position. If we have an attitude of entitlement, we will seek ways to have people meet our needs. If we have a spirit of humbleness, we will use our position of power to create ways to serve others.

Jesus relentlessly pursued the path of humility. This path led him beyond serving others and brought him to the cross. Committing to a life of humility will lead us to service and sacrifice. When we choose to pursue that path, we will find ourselves in good company.

God, give me the strength to pursue a path of humility. Help me see my life through a lens of humbleness, so I do not miss an opportunity to serve others. Amen.

FOCUS

Finally, brothers and sisters, whatever is true, whatever is noble, whatever is right, whatever is pure, whatever is lovely, whatever is admirable—if anything is excellent or praiseworthy—think about such things.

—*Philippians 4:8*

It's often easier to focus on what's wrong with the world than it is to see the beauty around us. Our minds gravitate toward what needs fixing, what went wrong, or what could have been better.

What we think about shapes what we see. The posture of our mind shapes how experience life. If we're constantly thinking about what could go wrong, we'll see the shortfalls and identify the issues. If we have the posture of a critic, we'll pinpoint the problems.

But if we shift our focus, we can see and experience the beauty that has been hidden in plain sight. When we focus our minds on what is true, noble, right, pure, lovely, admirable, excellent, and praiseworthy, we will find something to celebrate. Thinking about those things helps improve our vision. We'll see the goodness in others more clearly and experience more joy in our lives.

God, shift my focus and sharpen my mind. Help me to think about all that is true, noble, right, pure, lovely, admirable, excellent, and praiseworthy so I can experience more joy in my life. Amen.

VISION

> These all died in faith, not having received the things
> promised, but having seen them and greeted them from
> afar, and having acknowledged that they were strangers
> and exiles on the earth.
>
> —*Hebrews 11:13 ESV*

When we live pursuing a vision, we sweep others into the movement. But we need to understand that the vision is of secondary importance to the pursuit. Hebrews explains that the people of faith did not receive the things promised. They did not see their vision fulfilled. Did that make them failures? Did that void their noble living? Did that make their lives a waste? Of course not.

If the vision itself is of primary importance, an unfulfilled vision voids all that precedes. In other words, if your dreams are dashed, your pursuit was a waste of time and effort. But if the dream is secondary to the pursuit, a strange thing happens. When you lose, you still win. If you don't get the championship ring, your dignity remains. If you don't get the job, your life is still intact. If your dream doesn't materialize, you can still inspire others to pursue theirs.

Living in pursuit of a vision will shape how we live. If the pursuit of our vision is of primary importance, we can still inspire others to pursue their dreams even if we only greet ours from afar.

God, give me eyes to see that you surround me as I live in pursuit. May my pursuit inspire others to dream big and go after their vision. Amen.

SHEPHERDING

> Care for the flock that God has entrusted to you. Watch over it willingly, not grudgingly—not for what you will get out of it, but because you are eager to serve God.
> —*1 Peter 5:2 NLT*

As fathers, we have been put by God into a position that requires a high level of responsibility. He has made us shepherds of our families. But there is freedom in understanding that our flock is ultimately his. He is the chief shepherd who entrusted a flock to us, and it is our role to nurture and care for that flock.

As we disciple our flock, our motives matter; we can't be selfish. Our attitude matters; we must be willing. Our focus matters and shapes how we care for our flock. When our priority is our flock, the weight of responsibility can overwhelm us. But if we shift our focus to God, the giver of the flock, we can trust that he will fill in where we fall short. When we trust the chief shepherd, who has called us into this role, we can eagerly serve him by caring for those entrusted to us.

God, thank you for the flock you have entrusted to me. As I disciple my flock, remove any selfish motives that are present. As I seek to serve you, instill a spirit of eagerness within me so I can serve with freedom and joy. Amen.

MESSENGERS OF THE GOSPEL

How beautiful on the mountains are the feet of the messenger who brings good news, the good news of peace and salvation, the news that the God of Israel reigns!

—*Isaiah 52:7 NLT*

We often think of missionaries as those who live in some far-off land. We look up to these people for their dedication and service, and we respect them for the sacrifices they make in order to bring the gospel to those in need.

When we walk across the street and share our faith with our neighbors, we are accomplishing the same goal as those missionaries working around the globe. Our calling to share the gospel with those around us is no less noble or important than the call of those serving in other areas.

How can you help your family be messengers of the gospel in your neighborhood this week?

God, help my family to be messengers of the gospel. May we take every opportunity to share our faith with our neighbors and those within our community. Amen.

CEASE STRIVING

"Cease striving and know that I am God; I will be exalted among the nations, I will be exalted in the earth."
—*Psalm 46:10 NASB*

We often see this verse translated "Be still, and know I am God." It hangs on banners in sanctuaries. It is quoted by well-meaning Sunday school teachers while trying to calm the squirrely boys and girls. This translation above, however, using "cease striving," speaks to the Father's heart.

As fathers, we are constantly told how much more there is to do to be a good father. Work harder, love better—the pressure lies on our shoulders. But "cease striving and know that I am God" speaks to us. God is still God, and there is nothing that our striving can or will change about that. Have confidence that God is seated on his throne, and know that sometimes we need to take a step back from our strivings to realize that.

God, help me to better understand your place on the throne—both of this world and of my heart. My strivings and work won't change that. Let me have confidence to stop striving after things that don't matter. Amen.

DISCIPLESHIP

> I have no greater joy than this, to hear of my children walking in the truth.
>
> —*3 John 1:4 NASB*

Few things bring dads more joy and happiness than when we see our kids excelling. That's why many of us do what we can to make sure our kids are able to participate in sports camps, take music lessons, and attend good schools. We want to see our kids have every opportunity to excel in what they do. That's just what dads do.

As believers, we want to see our kids also growing in their relationship with God. It seems obvious, but it's too important not to point out that our kids' growth in their relationship with God is far more important than any other skill or achievement they could attain.

We can't make our kids follow Jesus any more than we can make them hit a ninety-mile-per-hour fastball, but we can do things to make sure our kids are exposed to the truth of God's Word. That might look like sharing our faith stories with our family, or helping our kids connect to the children's and youth ministries at a local church. However we choose to go about it, there's great joy to be found in leading our children to truth.

> God, thank you for my children. Help me to lead them to an understanding of who you are. Help them to grow in their relationship with you. Amen.

FOCUS ON JESUS

Fixing our eyes on Jesus, the author and perfecter of faith, who for the joy set before Him endured the cross, despising the shame, and has sat down at the right hand of the throne of God.

—*Hebrews 12:2 NASB*

Keeping our eyes on Jesus sounds a lot easier than it really is. Our jobs, our family, our friends, our hobbies, our social contacts, and so much more are all fighting for our attention. There's no shortage of books and blogs that tell us what to believe and how we should be living our lives.

Life often feels more like a car ride through a heavy rainstorm. The road becomes uncertain when we can't see more than a few feet ahead of us. We want to keep moving forward, but we can't see the familiar markers that tell us we're headed in the right direction. The only way it gets easier is if we're following the guiding tail lights of someone ahead of us.

Jesus Christ has gone before us to make a way for us. If we can focus our eyes on him, he will lead us through the distracting storms of life and help bring clarity to our path. We fix our eyes on him when we spend time in his Word and prayer. Are your eyes fixed on him, or are you more focused on the worries you can't see?

God, you've made a way for me through your Son, Jesus Christ. Help me to not be distracted by other voices calling for my attention, but to fix my eyes on you, the author and perfecter of my faith. Amen.

HE REJOICES OVER US

> The LORD your God is with you, the Mighty Warrior who saves. He will take great delight in you; in his love he will no longer rebuke you, but will rejoice over you with singing.
>
> —*Zephaniah 3:17*

Do you remember the first time you tucked your son or daughter into bed? You got their blankets set up just right, tucked them in, said a prayer, and probably sang a lullaby or two. We've all been there. Whether we are good singers or not, we usually end up singing to our children. We watch as their faces light up and they sing along with us. It's a special experience.

The verses above, and our experiences as fathers, give us a new perspective of our heavenly Father. When we read that he takes delight in us, forgives us, and sings over us with joy, we get it. We might not feel like we deserve it, but our own experience as fathers singing over our children helps us understand how God loves us.

The next time you tuck your kids in, take time to sing with them. Then remind them of the love that you have for them, as well as the love that their heavenly Father has for both of you.

God, thank you for the experience of being a dad. Thank you that you've given me a glimpse of your love for me. Help me to know your love and to share it with my children. Amen.

MODELING

Brothers, join in imitating me, and keep your eyes on those who walk according to the example you have in us.
—*Philippians 3:17 ESV*

Do you have someone in your life who is worth following? Are there other men in your church who you look up to? How about men who love Jesus and live their lives for him? Paul says it simply: Follow their example.

Are you setting an example worth following for your children? Would you be proud to have your children imitate your life? They are watching and learning. There are plenty of examples not worth following in our world. You have an opportunity, even an obligation, to set an example worthy of being followed.

God, thank you for the men you've placed in my life who have modeled a Christlike lifestyle for me. Help me to be that same example to my children, and to others who are watching me. Amen.

LOVE YOUR WIFE WELL

Husbands, love your wives, just as Christ also loved the
church and gave Himself up for her, so that He might
sanctify her, having cleansed her by the washing of water
with the word, that He might present to Himself the
church in all her glory, having no spot or wrinkle or any
such thing; but that she would be holy and blameless. So
husbands ought also to love their own wives as their own
bodies. He who loves his own wife loves himself.

—*Ephesians 5:25–28 NASB*

The standard by which we are to love our wives has clearly
been set high, according to these verses. We are to love them
as "Christ … loved the church" and as we "love … [our] own
bodies." We are to love them sacrificially and selflessly.

In order to love our wives well, we must be willing to make
sacrifices for them. We must believe that their needs are just as
important as our own needs. When we do this, not only do we
love them well, but we also model the love that we have been
shown by Christ.

God, help me to love my wife as I have been loved by you.
Help me to put her needs ahead of my needs. Help me to
have the strength to make sacrifices for the good of my
wife. Help me to love her well. Amen.

THANKFULNESS

I will give thanks to the LORD with my whole heart; I will tell of all your wonderful deeds. I will be glad and exult in you; I will sing praise to your name, O Most High.

—Psalm 9:1–2 NRSV

What are you thankful for today? Is that an easy question to answer, or does it take time to think of something? Often, it's difficult for guys to articulate the things we're thankful for. It's not that we aren't thankful; we just don't always know how to verbalize it.

Take some time today to write down everything you're thankful for, no matter how small or big. Take time to talk with God and thank him for the things on your list. Then, tell someone else about your thankfulness for God's provisions. You'll be surprised at all you have to be thankful for—and how verbalizing it helps you truly understand and feel your thankfulness.

God, help me to be a man with a thankful heart. Remind me of all I have to be thankful for, and help me be quick to share my thankfulness with others. Amen.

SELF-CONTROL

So I do not run aimlessly; I do not box as one beating the air. But I discipline my body and keep it under control, lest after preaching to others I myself should be disqualified.

—*1 Corinthians 9:26–27 ESV*

Running aimlessly. When you read those words, what picture forms in your mind? Do you see a marathon runner *aimlessly* running a race? Imagine this man dragging his feet, getting distracted by the crowd, and randomly stopping along the way to check his phone.

Now picture a focused runner in the same race. His eyes are fixed straight ahead of him. He can hear the crowd cheering him on, but he keeps a steady footfall moving forward. He checks his watch, but only to make sure he's at the pace he's trained for.

Are you living your life focused or aimless? Are you running with a plan in place, or are you making things up as you go? How can you discipline yourself to stay focused at the task at hand?

God, help me to run the race with focus and perseverance. Remind me of what I am running for. May my actions be worthy of the reward. Amen.

JUSTICE

> Speak up for those who cannot speak for themselves;
> ensure justice for those being crushed.
>
> —*Proverbs 31:8 NLT*

It's easy for us to show our support for those who are well-liked and respected. Showing our support for those who aren't as popular is much more difficult. Even so, it's our responsibility to speak up for those who cannot speak for themselves. This is an especially important lesson for us as parents.

The verse above describes ideas that the Old Testament king Lemuel learned from his mother. As king, Lemuel was put in a position of power and influence, so the words that his mother shared with him guided him as he guided others.

How are we teaching our children to treat others? Are we teaching them to treat all people equally and to speak up for those who cannot speak for themselves? The lessons that we teach today will guide how our children live their lives in the future.

God, help me to set an example of how to treat others. Help me to be a voice for those who cannot speak for themselves. Help me to set a legacy of justice for my children. Amen.

LISTENING

Know this, my beloved brethren. Let every man be quick to hear, slow to speak, slow to anger, for the anger of man does not work the righteousness of God.

—James 1:19–20 ESV

Quick to hear, slow to speak, and slow to become angry. It's not natural, is it? Our instinct as men is to take control and fix things. We are quick to offer advice and criticism and quick to jump to conclusions. But this often leads to fighting, bitterness, and grudges.

James' words remind us of the importance of listening first and foremost. When we do this, we show that we care for the others involved in the conversation or situation. When we listen first, we remind ourselves that we're not the only ones who this affects. When we listen first, we aren't the experts. We aren't the ones trying to swoop in and fix everything with a quick answer.

God, help me to listen—to those in my family, those at work, and those I'll interact with today. Help me to hear their story and respect them in my conversation. Amen.

PRAYER

> Therefore confess your sins to each other and pray for each other so that you may be healed. The prayer of a righteous person is powerful and effective.
>
> —*James 5:16*

We could easily skip past the first part of this verse and jump straight to "the prayer of a righteous person is powerful and effective." That's the good stuff! We want to know that when we pray, it is going to be effective.

We can't skip ahead though. The first part of this verse gives context to the second. James is reminding us of the importance of confessing our sins to one another. As men, we aren't good at that. We confess our sins to God in private prayers, but it's much more difficult for us to confess our sins to one another.

Confessing our mistakes and sin is not a form of weakness, but instead an example of righteousness. Are there people in your life to whom you need to confess? If so, make a plan today to do it.

God, thank you for the forgiveness that we have through your Son, Jesus Christ. Thank you that you promise that when we confess our sins to you, you are faithful to forgive. Help us to also confess our sins to those we have affected with our actions. Amen.

FREEDOM IN CHRIST

> For I do not understand my own actions. For I do not do what I want, but I do the very thing I hate. … Wretched man that I am! Who will deliver me from this body of death? Thanks be to God through Jesus Christ our Lord.
>
> —*Romans 7:15, 24–25 ESV*

How many times have you found yourself saying these same words? You know what's best for you but just can't seem to follow through with it.

Romans 7 records Paul's frustration with his inability to do the right thing. It's worth noting, though, the question that Paul asks: "Who will deliver me?" He doesn't ask *what* he needs to do or *how* he can try harder. Instead, he asks *who* can deliver him. Paul realized that there wasn't anything he could do on his own, but that he needed a Savior.

You're not good enough or strong enough to overcome your sin on your own. None of us are. But Jesus has already won the battle for you. Accept what he has done for you, and walk in victory through him.

God, you know my desire to do the right thing even though I continue to fall short of your standard. Help me to not try to be my own hero, but to fully accept what Jesus has done for me on the cross. Thank you that you have not only forgiven me but also freed me from the bondage of sin. Amen.

CONFIDENCE IN GOD

> Great is our Lord, and mighty in power; His understanding is infinite.
>
> —*Psalm 147:5 NKJV*

Have you ever wished you had someone to talk to who understood what you were going through? Sure, others are willing to listen, but they just don't understand. Have you ever wished that there was someone who could help bring clarity to your uncertainty?

This verse reminds us that God's understanding is infinite. The previous verse even says that he not only knows the number of stars in the sky but he calls them all by name. There is no feeling, situation, emotion, or problem that is beyond his comprehension.

There's a whole list of qualities that we can ascribe to God, but have you thought of him as understanding? Approach him with confidence; you will not catch him off guard.

God, thank you that you are an understanding God. I take assurance in knowing that whatever I'm facing is not beyond your understanding. Help me to trust you with my uncertainty today. Amen.

PASSION FOR THE GOSPEL

> For I am not ashamed of the gospel, because it is God's power for salvation to everyone who believes, first to the Jew, and also to the Greek.
>
> —*Romans 1:16 HCSB*

We all have things we're passionate about—our favorite sports team, our preferred truck manufacturer, our love for bacon. These are things we love, and we are not ashamed of it.

But do we feel the same way about the gospel? Is it as easy for us to share with others the thankfulness we have for what God has accomplished in our lives through Jesus, as it is to talk about the stats from last night's game?

The gospel is God's power for salvation for all who believe! How can we proudly share our story of what the gospel has done for us with others today? How can we incorporate the importance of boldly living out and sharing the gospel into our family DNA?

> God, please help me to see the need of the gospel in the lives of those I spend time with this week. Then help me to have the confidence I need to share the saving message of the gospel with them. Amen.

MENTORSHIP

We loved you so much that we shared with you not only God's Good News but our own lives, too.

—*1 Thessalonians 2:8 NLT*

Who are the people who've invested the most into you spiritually? It could be a father, a pastor, a Sunday school teacher, or a mentor. Chances are good that you've spent a fair amount of time with these people. They know you well, and you know them.

The verse above paints a beautiful picture of a mentor or parent. Sharing God's good news is important, but so is sharing life. When you share your life with someone else, it builds trust. When you invite other people into your life, they get to observe you living out what you're sharing.

Who are you sharing your life with? How are you sharing God's good news with them? By doing both, you're showing them that you truly love them.

God, help me to be a man who lives what I preach. Help me to not only tell others about you, but to invite them into my life so they can see me prioritizing your good news. Amen.

PARENT LEADERSHIP

As for me and my family, we will serve the LORD.
—*Joshua 24:15 NCV*

There are a lot of things that we don't have control over, and as dads, that's scary. We want to be able to ensure our kids have a safe, secure, and wholesome environment to live in. But as we look around the world, it seems that much of it has turned its back on God.

We don't have control over the whole world, our country, or even our own community, but we do have control over what happens within our home. Today, will you choose to declare that your family will serve the Lord? Will you commit to leading the way by serving the Lord? Will you teach your children about who God is and how they can serve him?

God, I declare to you today that my desire is for my family to be one that serves you. Help my family and me to not lose focus on you, and to continue to put you first in everything that we do and say. Amen.

FATHERHOOD

"Pray, then, in this way: 'Our Father who is in heaven, Hallowed be Your name.'"

—Matthew 6:9 NASB

When teaching his disciples to pray, Jesus started by addressing God as "Father." This authoritative definition that Jesus ascribes to God is the main image describing our relationship with God throughout the New Testament. It paints a beautiful picture of the nature of our relationship with God, as well as our role as fathers.

Fatherhood is one of the highest callings we receive, because it most clearly models our relationship with God. It also has a direct impact on our children's understanding of God. Our role as fathers is not insignificant and should not be taken lightly.

What have we learned about our relationships with God through our experiences of being a father? What examples of fatherhood are we leaving for our children? These are questions that should both motivate us and draw us to our knees.

Father, thank you for the privilege of being a father to my children. Help me to model my relationship with you to my children as I interact with them. May my time with my children help in correctly forming their understanding of you. Amen.

BUILDING A FOUNDATION

> Start children off on the way they should go, and even
> when they are old they will not turn from it.
> —*Proverbs 22:6*

Being a dad is hard work. We want the best for our kids, and so we do our best to teach them and train them. We make sure they're attending good schools, get them plugged into local church ministries, and set guidelines and expectations for them. And sometimes, we receive pushback from them because of it.

It is important to remember, though, that we're not the ones who mold and change their hearts. That is the work of their heavenly Father. Our job is to start them off on the way they should go—that is, to point them toward Jesus in all circumstances. Our window for influence in our children's lives is limited; we must use it to point them to Christ.

The proverb above encourages us that our role matters now and in the future. Our time with our children, as limited as it may be, is building a foundation that will not fail them. Our work is hard, and sometimes thankless, but it is worth it.

God, give me the strength to parent well. Help me to stand firm on what I know is important. Help me to set my children off in the way they should go, knowing that you are leading them, guiding them, and calling them to yourself.

MOTIVATION

We always thank God for all of you and continually mention you in our prayers. We remember before our God and Father your work produced by faith, your labor prompted by love, and your endurance inspired by hope in our Lord Jesus Christ.

—1 Thessalonians 1:2–3

Here we see Paul thanking God for the believers in Thessalonica. It's particularly interesting to see what Paul is thankful for: work produced by faith, labor prompted by love, and endurance inspired by hope in our Lord Jesus Christ. Their relationship with Christ influenced their daily life, and Paul noticed it.

When we allow our relationship with Christ to impact our whole life, our motivation changes. We live our life led by our faith in Christ. We begin to serve others out of a love that we have received from Christ. And we have the motivation to continue the work, even when it's difficult, because of the hope of eternity that we have in Christ.

When we try to live our life apart from Christ, our work is just a job, an obligation that we need to fulfill. We tend to lose heart without hope. Is your life filled with faith, hope, and love, or is it marked by duty and obligation?

God, help me to be a man whose work is produced by my faith in you, and whose labor is prompted by my love for you and from you. May my endurance to continue be prompted by the hope for eternity that I have in Christ Jesus. Amen.

APRIL

ACCESS TO GOD

> Now we can come fearlessly right into God's presence, assured of his glad welcome when we come with Christ and trust in him.
>
> —*Ephesians 3:12 TLB*

It's all about who you know, right? We all want to be that guy who has the connection to courtside seats at the big game, or the one who has the ear of the boss at work. The connections we make often come with benefits.

How quickly we forget that we have direct access to God, the creator of the universe! We forget that we can speak with him, seek him for advice, and even ask him for help. And not only can we approach him, but he gladly welcomes us into his presence. We know that this is true only because of what Jesus Christ has accomplished for us on the cross.

Are you apprehensive about speaking to God? Do you feel like your issues or problems are too small to bother him with? Do you forget that we can speak to God and that he listens? Because of your relationship with Jesus, you can boldly approach him. Spend some time today just talking with God. He's looking forward to spending time with you!

> God, thank you that I can come to you and speak to you. Thank you that I don't need an appointment or even a reason. Thank you that you listen to me and that you answer my prayers. Amen.

EFFECTIVE MINISTRY

For this very reason, make every effort to supplement your faith with goodness, goodness with knowledge, knowledge with self-control, self-control with endurance, endurance with godliness, godliness with brotherly affection, and brotherly affection with love. For if these qualities are yours and are increasing, they will keep you from being useless or unfruitful in the knowledge of our Lord Jesus Christ.

—*2 Peter 1:5–8 HCSB*

We all want to be effective. We want to be the best fathers, husbands, leaders, friends, teachers, and men that we can be. Very few people go through life just wanting to be average.

In the verses above, Peter lists eight characteristics of an effective person. While it may be easy to see them as tasks to be completed, this isn't a list that will ever completed in full. If we're to be effective, we need to "make every effort" (this will take work and time) to continue to grow in these areas.

Do you have more of these qualities in your life today than you did last week or last year? This is a list to be revisited. Whether this is your first year following Jesus or you've been following him for decades, it's important to continuously work on increasing your faith, goodness, knowledge, self-control, endurance, godliness, brotherly affection, and love.

God, help me to never feel like I have accomplished all that there is for me in you. May I continue to be intentional about growing in these qualities. Help me grow in my effectiveness as these qualities become more evident in my life. Amen.

Faithfulness

Above all, fear the Lord and worship Him faithfully with all your heart; consider the great things He has done for you.

—*1 Samuel 12:24 HCSB*

What are some great things that God has done for you? Have you ever stopped to ponder his goodness in your life? What great things has God done for your family? Being thankful seems so simple, but we often forget the importance of remembering God's goodness and faithfulness in our lives.

Find some time today to start a list of the great things that you've observed God doing in your life. Ask your wife and kids to brainstorm with you, and then go over your list together. To consider something is to carefully think about it. Don't just rush through your list to accomplish the task. Instead, carefully consider God's greatness in your life.

We are called to be men who "fear the Lord and worship him faithfully" with all our hearts. This becomes much easier to accomplish when we're regularly thinking about all the great things God is doing in our lives. As you lead your family, allow your thankfulness to God lead you to be a man who fears and worships the Lord with all your heart.

God, your great works in my life and my family are endless. Help me to never stop considering all the ways you're active and working in our lives. May I live a life that is marked by my worship of you. Amen.

PERSONAL DEVOTION

> So give yourselves to God. Stand against the devil and he will run away from you. Come close to God and He will come close to you. Wash your hands, you sinners. Clean up your hearts, you who want to follow the sinful ways of the world and God at the same time.
>
> —*James 4:7–8 NLV*

There's only room for one leader in your life. We can't serve God and the evil one. It just doesn't work. James is pointing out our tendency to want to follow God but still give the devil authority in our lives. He says that we have to choose who we will follow.

Through Jesus, God has given us the ability to stand against the devil's temptations in our lives. We are no longer controlled by the power of sin. We have the ability to stand against sin and say no. James says that when we do this, the devil will run from us.

When we decide to stand against the devil's schemes and instead draw near to God, not only will he draw near to us, but the devil and his temptations will also become less and less powerful in our lives.

> God, help me to follow after you alone. Remind me of the victory that you have already accomplished over sin in my life through Jesus, and give me the strength to stand against the devil in my life. Thank you for your promise to draw near to me as I draw near to you. Amen.

LOVING GOD

> Loving God means keeping his commandments, and his commandments are not burdensome.
>
> —*1 John 5:3 NLT*

This sounds like a conversation we could have had with one of our children: "If you love me, you will prove it by doing what I have asked you to do. I am not asking you to do anything that I know you can't do." We know that the best way for our children to show their love for us is for them to do what we've asked of them.

It's no different for us. The best way we can show our love and appreciation for our heavenly Father is to follow the commandments he has given us. We display our love for him not just through the words we say to him but also by the way we live our lives.

Actions truly do speak louder than words. How are you showing your love for your heavenly Father today?

God, I love you! Help me to live a life that displays my love for you through my obedience to you. Thank you that following your commands is possible for me because of the power of the Holy Spirit living within me. Amen.

SERVICE

As each has received a gift, use it to serve one another, as good stewards of God's varied grace.

—*1 Peter 4:10 ESV*

God has uniquely gifted each of his children. He has created each member of your family with talents and abilities that are unique. As you look at your family, can you identify how each person has been gifted? How can you help your wife and children understand their giftings?

Once you have identified your giftings, it's time to discover how you can use your gifts, as individuals and as a family, to serve others. God has not gifted each of us uniquely for our own benefit. Use your gifts to serve and help others. As you do, you'll discover that your family is far stronger together than each person is alone.

God, thank you that I am created uniquely. Help me to use my gifts to serve others. Help me to be a good steward of what you have given me, and grant that, by my doing so, others might experience your love and grace. Amen.

EASTER

About three in the afternoon Jesus cried out in a loud voice, *"Eli, Eli, lema sabachthani?"* (which means "My God, my God, why have you forsaken me?").

—*Matthew 27:46*

Dads, this Easter reach down into your soul and let praise flow from your heart in singing praise to the King.

Men have an issue with singing in church. Rumors of feminine influences and wishy-washy love songs about Jesus. The truth is we have been misinformed about what worship is. The New Testament teaches that worship is first a choice to engage. It's supposed to be an offering; in other words, it should cost. Then it's connected to the power of God on a mission. Mission and worship are inseparable.

Perhaps the most powerful place to see this demonstrated was on Calvary's cross. Jesus—hanging on that old wooden tree, having chosen to engage—brought a costly offering, his very life. He meaningfully took part in the very mission of God.

This bloodied and beaten Savior, crucified and dying, lifted his voice and sang in worship. He worshiped his father with Psalm 22. Men, if you ever doubt the masculinity of worship, the man Jesus, hanging by nails to a cross—finds within his heart a desire to sing praise to God.

This Easter, let's not make excuses. Let's make a joyful noise.

Lord, I repent of my worship attitude. Forgive me for making it about me. Help me engage and worship you. Amen.

LIVING UP TO OUR WORTH

> As a prisoner for the Lord, then, I urge you to live a life worthy of the calling you have received. Be completely humble and gentle; be patient, bearing with one another in love. Make every effort to keep the unity of the Spirit through the bond of peace.
>
> *—Ephesians 4:1–3*

Do you set rules and guidelines for your children to follow so you'll love them more? Do you place expectations on them so they can earn your love? No. You love them and want to see them succeed. You have set standards for them because you know what they're capable of and you want to see them achieve their full potential.

When Paul says to "live a life worthy of the calling that you have received," he's not saying that these are things we need to do to earn God's love or prove ourselves to him. Instead, he is making it clear that we have received the high calling of being a child of God and that we should be living our lives in a way worthy of such a calling.

When you think about your life, do the words *humble, gentle, patient, bearing with one another in love,* and *unity* describe you? These are the qualities present in a life that is living up to the high calling it has received. Allow these words to motivate you to a higher standard of living—not so you can earn God's favor, but so you can live up to what God already sees in you.

God, thank you for the value you see in me. Thank you that you've called me to be your son. Help me to live in a way that reflects the life you have called me to. Amen.

ATTITUDE

> Rejoice in the Lord always; again I will say, rejoice. Let your reasonableness be known to everyone. The Lord is at hand.
>
> —*Philippians 4:4–5 ESV*

It's easy to rejoice when things are going well. When you receive that job promotion that you've been waiting for, or when your kids do well on the test that you fought over last night.

But how can we rejoice when it doesn't seem natural? How do we rejoice when we lose our job, the furnace goes out and we don't have money to replace it, our kids are constantly fighting with one another, or we receive news from the doctor that cancer is affecting us or someone we love?

Paul understood that rejoicing in the Lord wasn't always easy or natural. After all, he wrote these words while sitting in a prison cell. Thankfully, he does cast some light on how it is possible: "The Lord is at hand." Paul reminds us of the Lord's promise that he is with us always. We can rejoice in knowing that God is aware of our circumstances and that he is with us, just as he was with Paul in that prison cell.

As you lead your family, do so with an attitude that rejoices in the Lord in all circumstances. As you do, you are modeling your trust in the Lord's provisions to your family.

God, thank you for the promise of your presence in my life. Remind me of your presence when things are difficult. Help me rejoice in you always. Amen.

GODLINESS

> But you, man of God, flee from all this, and pursue righteousness, godliness, faith, love, endurance and gentleness. Fight the good fight of the faith. Take hold of the eternal life to which you were called when you made your good confession in the presence of many witnesses.
>
> *—1 Timothy 6:11–12*

When dealing with your kids, have you ever said, "That's not how we do it in this family"? You want them to know that the standard your family holds to is different from the standard they see around them. You want them to know that because they are a part of *your* family, they are held to a higher standard.

That's the kind of conversation Paul is having with Timothy. He is reminding him about his identity as a child of God. Timothy is called to a greater standard of living. Paul calls him to action with words like *flee, pursue, fight,* and *take hold.* He is reminding him that being a child of God requires action, that he can't just expect these things to happen to him.

The same is true for you. You are a child of God, and you've been called to a high standard of living that's only realized with a commitment to action. Flee from the evil that is around you, and pursue what is good. Be willing to fight for your faith. As you do this, keep in mind the end destination— eternal life with Christ.

God, thank you for the reminder that I am your child. Thank you that you have not only called us to a higher standard, but that you are also empowering us to victory as we pursue and fight for our faith. Amen.

STRENGTH IN WEAKNESS

But he said to me, "My grace is sufficient for you, for my power is made perfect in weakness." Therefore I will boast all the more gladly of my weaknesses, so that the power of Christ may rest upon me.

—2 Corinthians 12:9 ESV

We aren't all that willing to admit our weaknesses, are we? We don't like to confess that we get lost while driving, much less that we are struggling. We are men—the leaders of our family—and people are counting on us. We can do this on our own. We have to. Right?

Wrong.

It's time we rid ourselves of that mentality and embrace the fact that we aren't the superhero we sometimes believe we need to be. It's time we realize that we lead best when we allow God's grace and power to be evident in our lives. We are strongest when we lead and live with a dependence on God's work in our lives. As he has said, "My grace is sufficient for you, for my power is made perfect in weakness." Let's make room for God's power by admitting that we can't do it all on our own.

God, forgive me for wanting to do things my way and on my own. Forgive me for not seeking help when I need it, from others or from you. Help me to admit my weaknesses to you today. I invite you to come and work in my life. Amen.

THANKFULNESS

Oh give thanks to the LORD; call upon his name; make known his deeds among the peoples!

—*Psalm 105:1 ESV*

One of the first things we teach our children to say is, "Thank you." We want them to know the importance of having a thankful heart. So we teach them to send thank-you notes for gifts, say thank you to our hosts, and to say a prayer of thanks before a meal.

In God, we have so much to be thankful for. This verse instructs us to not just say thank you to God for all that he has done for us, but also to tell others of our thankfulness. We are to "make known his deeds among the peoples."

Today, what can you share with others about what God has done for you? How can you share your thankfulness to God with your family and friends?

God, thank you for your many blessings in my life and in the lives of my family. Help me to be quick to share and tell others of all that you've done. Amen.

GOD IS GREATER

For the foolishness of God is wiser than human wisdom,
and the weakness of God is stronger than human strength.
—*1 Corinthians 1:25*

It seems strange to read about God's foolishness and weakness. But what Paul is trying to help us understand is that in all things and in every way, God is greater.

We live in a do-it-yourself world where many of us want to figure things out on our own. We think that if we ask for help, we're admitting that we are weak. This verse reminds us that even at our greatest and strongest, we still don't compare to God.

Isn't it encouraging to know that God is not only wise and strong, but that he is also on our side? We can confidently come to him, knowing that he is more than sufficient to help us in every situation we will ever find ourselves in. And likewise, when our kids come to us for help, we can do our best to guide them by pointing them to God.

God, help me to rest in your strength and your wisdom. Help me to trust you to help me and not try to accomplish everything in my own strength. Thank you for the wisdom and strength that you gladly share with your children. Amen.

LEADERSHIP

"Here is a simple rule of thumb for behavior: Ask yourself what you want people to do for you; then grab the initiative and do it for them!"

—*Luke 6:31 MSG*

Sometimes it's the simple things in life that make the most sense. The idea behind the verse above is taught in preschools all over the world. But it is no less true in our homes, businesses, and lives. Do to others what you want done to you.

Are you modeling the behavior you want to see in your kids and those you have authority over? It's easy to want to lead out of power and authority, but the best way for us to lead is through treating others the way we wish to be treated.

People will often listen to our words, but they're more likely to follow our example. Your kids are watching you. They will follow the behaviors, attitudes, and actions that they see modeled for them. Are your words of instruction also being lived out in your own life?

God, thank you for this simple reminder today. Help me to live my life in a way that is worthy of being replicated by my children. Help me to lead by example in the way that I treat and interact with my family. Amen.

CONTENTMENT

> Keep your life free from love of money, and be content with what you have, for he has said, "I will never leave you nor forsake you."
>
> —*Hebrews 13:5 ESV*

As fathers, we want to be the ones who provide for our family. We want to give them not only what they need but also what they want. We want to be able to bless them with things that are fun.

So how we can find contentment even without the things that money can buy? How can we help our family to understand contentment in what we have? The answer begins with understanding who God is.

God is our creator, our provider, our sustainer, and our defender, and he is deeply in love with us. When we have a right understanding of who God is and what he does for us, our priorities and values begin to change. Knowing that God has promised to never leave or forsake us should bring comfort. We can do our best to provide for our family, but we should also know that God has promised to care for us. *He* will provide.

> God, help me to rest in the promise of your never-ending presence in my life. May I value your presence more than the love of money or possessions in my life. Amen.

GRACE AND FORGIVENESS

> Make allowance for each other's faults, and forgive anyone who offends you. Remember, the Lord forgave you, so you must forgive others.
>
> —*Colossians 3:13 NLT*

Forgiveness and grace are powerful things. Along with love, they could probably fix almost any problem in any part of the world. That sounds like a bold statement, doesn't it? Consider a situation in your life or with your family. If you went to someone in your family and asked for forgiveness or granted forgiveness, what would happen? How would it change the feel in your household?

When the apostle Paul uses the word *allowance*, it sounds like a directive to expect faults and mistakes. He realizes the nature of the church and relationships and how messy they can be—even our relationships with our kids. We never *intend* for them to get messy, but we get tired, we become frustrated when bank account isn't where we want it to be, we lose our jobs, and we are affected by everyday life. We expect people to make allowances for us, so we should do the same through the power of the grace of God.

> God, help me to remember that you grant me grace. You forgive my faults. Now give me the ability to do the same for the people in my life. Amen.

DELIGHT IN GOD

Take delight in the LORD, and he will give you your heart's desires. Commit everything you do to the LORD. Trust him, and he will help you.

—Psalm 37:4–5 NLT

Something unique happens when we delight in God. It's one thing to delight in a certain kind of food or a hobby or even a job. But it's altogether different when we delight in God, because he starts to plant within us new desires—desires for more of him, for more love, peace, grace, and the list goes on. As a dad, if you delight in God, then he will start to shape your desires to be in alignment with his. You'll begin to be committed to him with every aspect of your life, including your kids. True commitment to God will inform how you see yourself and your family. It doesn't necessarily make parenting easier, but it certainly gives you wisdom, grace, and perspective for whatever comes your way.

If our vehicle seems out of sorts, we take it to a mechanic. If our own life and faith seems out of sorts, we need to recalibrate ourselves in relation to God and recommit ourselves to him.

God, in this moment I commit myself, as well as my family and my desires, to you. Help me to be in alignment with your will for my life. Amen.

GOD'S WILL

This is what the LORD says: "You will be in Babylon for seventy years. But then I will come and do for you all the good things I have promised, and I will bring you home again. For I know the plans I have for you," says the LORD. "They are plans for good and not for disaster, to give you a future and a hope."

—*Jeremiah 29:10–11 NLT*

Often, verse 11 of Jeremiah 29 gives people a sense of excitement about their future because they can see that God has plans for good. But how often do we forget what verse 10 says? They will be in captivity for "seventy years." God lets his people know that the future is bright, yes; but his will doesn't necessarily change circumstances overnight.

As dads, sometimes we just want to know what the plan is and then we are settled. But we must also realize that the plan may include a process. We want our kids to understand things right away, but we must recognize that God is patient with us because we too are in process. Sometimes God even allows the process to take a longer than we might like. Trust this day that God has great plans and a will for you and your kids, and also know that it's a process. Even though it doesn't seem like much is happening, that doesn't mean God isn't working.

God, help me to trust your will for my life and for my kids' lives as well. Give me the ability to be okay with process. Amen.

REMOVE THE CLUTTER

"Blessed are the poor in spirit, for theirs is the kingdom of heaven."

—*Matthew 5:3*

When Jesus is speaking to an audience that is already poor, it seems odd to be encouraging even more poverty. The words "poor in spirit," however, speak to more than just an economic status—although that is a part of it. Ultimately, what matters is that when one's life is void of clutter, there is a greater awareness of God. When everything is stripped away, a new level of trust in God is experienced—physically, spiritually, mentally, financially, and emotionally.

Jesus encourages his followers to be drawn into a deeper level of trust. As dads, sometimes we can fill our lives—or our kids' lives—with so much clutter or activities that we're unable to sift through what really matters at a much deeper level. Consider what you might need to strip away from your life. How can you model a life of simplicity for your kids so they understand what it means to be poor in spirit?

God, draw me into a deeper relationship with you, and help me to remove the clutter so I can trust even more in you. Amen.

GENEROSITY

> "But when you give to the needy, do not let your left hand know what your right hand is doing, so that your giving may be in secret. And your Father who sees in secret will reward you."
>
> —*Matthew 6:3–4*

As dads, it can be so easy to be generous to our kids. Sometimes we feel compelled to give them the things or opportunities we never had when we were young. So when our kids ask us for something, it can be hard to say no. But do they also see us modeling generosity in other ways? What if our *no* to them is because it's a *yes* to something else or someone else?

Jesus talked about the rich, the poor, and money a lot. Giving always seemed to be a top priority for him—he even *gave* his life. Some might say that our wallet is the final thing to be converted to Jesus.

It seems sort of ironic to ask, but do your kids "see" you giving in secret? Do they see you looking out for the poor, the marginalized, and the vulnerable? Consider having a conversation with your kids about this today. Ask them what they think about generosity.

God, help my heart to be in alignment with the heart of Jesus. Cultivate a heart for the poor within me that would lead to generosity. Amen.

MONEY

"Don't store up treasures here on earth, where moths eat them and rust destroys them, and where thieves break in and steal. Store your treasures in heaven, where moths and rust cannot destroy, and thieves do not break in and steal. Wherever your treasure is, there the desires of your heart will also be."

—*Matthew 6:19–21 NLT*

Do you remember ever hearing children comparing their dads to other dads? They might say, "Well, *my* dad has this kind of car," or "Oh yeah, well, *my* dad has *this* kind of car." One-upping is an art form that continues to this day.

It's so easy to fall into the trap of wanting all the "right" stuff, the "right" toys, and the "right" amount of money. Jesus warns against this kind of idolatry, because he recognizes the toll it takes on our heart and soul. It shows who we really are and what we really desire. Talk to your kids about how they view money and possessions, and ask them what really matters to them.

God, help me to not make money and possessions idols in my life. I confess that I often put too much stock in "things." Help me to put my trust in you even more today. Amen.

PROVIDENCE

"So do not worry, saying, 'What shall we eat?' or 'What shall we drink?' or 'What shall we wear?' For the pagans run after all these things, and your heavenly Father knows that you need them. But seek first his kingdom and his righteousness, and all these things will be given to you as well."

—*Matthew 6:31–33*

Providing for a family can be one of the most rewarding—and yet most worrisome—roles a dad can have. The moment our first child is born, we start to think about providing on a whole new level. It can also give us even more perspective on the verses above. If we think this much about providing for our families, how much more does God think about providing for us!

But the reality is that providing can be a daunting task. What if we lose our job? What if an unforeseen bill comes in the mail? Whatever the case, it seems the way of Jesus is to not worry. That is truly easier said than done, but it's not impossible.

Be present in each moment, and plan to the best of your ability, but know ultimately that God will provide. It may not be what as you imagined it, but as you cultivate a life of faith, you grow into the habits of a life free from worry.

God, give us this day our daily bread. Help me to trust that you will provide for my family. Amen.

PERSISTENT PRAYER

"Keep on asking, and you will receive what you ask for. Keep on seeking, and you will find. Keep on knocking, and the door will be opened to you. For everyone who asks, receives. Everyone who seeks, finds. And to everyone who knocks, the door will be opened."

—*Matthew 7:7–8 NLT*

Jesus tells us that our heart's motivation in prayer, as we seek the Holy Spirit, is persistence. Keep on! We are promised that as we seek God, we will find him—every time. Prayer might seem like a challenging thing at times, but as you keep on praying, you will grow—guaranteed.

For today's devotion, consider how you can pray for your kids. What do they need? How do you see them growing? What do you like about them? What gifts are they developing? Ask God to help them grow in that gift. Or maybe a time of prayer looks like five minutes of silence. Seeking God can be done in silence and solitude as well.

God, help me to grow in prayer. Teach me how to pray for my kids. Remind me what I love about them. Amen.

THE KINGDOM OF GOD

> Here is another illustration Jesus used: "The Kingdom of Heaven is like a mustard seed planted in a field. It is the smallest of all seeds, but it becomes the largest of garden plants; it grows into a tree, and birds come and make nests in its branches."
>
> —*Matthew 13:31-32 NLT*

Jesus often talked about the kingdom of God or the kingdom of heaven. It's much greater and richer than an afterlife destination; it's a way of life. It's the reason Jesus asks us to pray that his kingdom would come on earth as it is in heaven.

When you think of living in the way of Jesus—the kingdom of heaven—what comes to mind? Jesus is often comparing it to something small and seemingly insignificant, but over time (perhaps a long period of time) it grows and has purpose.

In the illustration above, Jesus talks about the kingdom of heaven being a home or a refuge. In a lot of ways, parenting can be modeled after this illustration. It starts out simple, but over time our relationship with our kids grows and changes. The question is, does it grow into something with purpose? As a dad, are you a safe refuge for your kids?

> God, develop me into the dad you want me to be. Help me to pattern my life after the way of Jesus, and may your kingdom come. Amen.

APRIL 25

POSSESSIONS

> Jesus told him, "If you want to be perfect, go and sell all your possessions and give the money to the poor, and you will have treasure in heaven. Then come, follow me."
>
> —*Matthew 19:21 NLT*

In Western culture, consumerism is the air we breathe. We have holidays that celebrate getting more—more stuff. We love stuff, and it's hard to think of life outside those terms. If we take our kids to a store, they are bombarded with the same idea—to get more.

Yet Jesus appeals to a different kind of living. He attributes a desire for perfection to getting rid of stuff. He calls his followers to a life of simplicity and getting rid of things that can dominate our life. He recognizes that we sometimes even organize our lives and our calendars around our stuff. We purchase extra storage units to become a house for our stuff, and all the while our heart is more and more cluttered and has no room to be mindful of God, much less those who have virtually nothing. As a dad, following Jesus looks like a life of simplicity and generosity. Think about how you can model this kind of living for your kids.

God, help me to declutter my life so I am wholly devoted to you. Amen.

LEADING THROUGH SERVING

"It shall not be so among you; but whoever would be great among you must be your servant."

—*Matthew 20:26 RSV*

When Jesus appealed to his disciples about leadership, status, and positions of power, he gave them an upside-down way of thinking. He said the best leaders are the ones that not only know how to serve but actually participate in serving.

When our kids are young, sometimes it seems like we're constantly serving them because they can't do things themselves. But over time, if we aren't intentional about giving them responsibility, our kids will expect us to keep serving them. It's a challenging balance to not only be a servant within our families but also encourage our kids to adopt an attitude of service as well.

One of the best ways to model this kind of leadership is to get out with your family and find a way to serve within your community, whether it is volunteering at a soup kitchen, a homeless shelter, or perhaps your local church. The best leaders are the ones who are willing to get their hands dirty and serve.

God, help me to model a life of joyful servitude so my kids will grow into humble servant leaders as well. Amen.

INVESTMENT

> "His master replied, 'Well done, good and faithful servant! You have been faithful with a few things; I will put you in charge of many things. Come and share your master's happiness!'"
>
> —*Matthew 25:21*

In Matthew 25, Jesus tells an interesting parable about a master who gives three different servants various amounts of money. Two of them invest their amount and it grows, while the third servant buries it. This parable can have multiple meanings, but one of the most popular applications is the idea of investment. It's not just concerning our finances, although that is an important aspect; it's also important to consider our gifts and talents as well.

Are you using the gifts God has given you to invest in and make a difference in the world? How do you invest in the lives of your kids? Today, think of one way that you can make an investment in your kids' lives. The reward of your investment is invaluable.

God, thank you for investing in me by sending Jesus so I can be in relationship with you. Help me to understand more of what my gifts are, so that I can invest them into my kids, my family, and ultimately the world. Amen.

A LIFE OF SACRIFICE

"Greater love has no one than this: to lay down one's life for one's friends."

—*John 15:13*

As men, we've heard so many times that being "tough" or "strong" looks like standing our ground, not letting our emotions get the best of us, and having a stiff upper lip. These ideas were constructed by different cultures over time, but they are not the way of Jesus.

Being a man—even more, a man of God—involves love, sacrifice, and friendship. We could say the truest man was revealed in the person and character of Jesus. He was a man who deeply loved people. The disciples weren't just his followers or students; they were together for nearly three years. We must assume they became close friends, and then one day he made the ultimate sacrifice. He lost his friends, and they lost him. But the sacrifice was far greater than anyone would realize.

What does sacrifice look like for you as a dad to your kids? How can you show true love today? Maybe it looks like setting aside your desires so you can get on the floor and play—or even have a tea party when it seems like the least "manly" thing to do. Maybe it's something much bigger and more complex. How can you show love in *that* situation?

God, thank you for making the ultimate sacrifice for me. Help me to live a life of sacrifice. Amen.

THE HOLY SPIRIT

"When the Spirit of truth comes, he will guide you into all truth. He will not speak on his own but will tell you what he has heard. He will tell you about the future."

—*John 16:13 NLT*

In a previous devotion, we discussed partnership in parenting. But there's another partner that we can also rely on—the Holy Spirit. It's important and sometimes challenging to cultivate a relationship with our earthly partners; we could say the same for our relationship with the Holy Spirit. As you deepen your relationship with God, ask that you'll also be continuously filled with the Holy Spirit. It'll serve as sort of a road map for your faith life as well as your parenting life. (Even though men stereotypically don't like to use maps, right?)

Another name for the Holy Spirit is "Counselor." Take some time right now to consider God as a counselor—one who listens, and one who comforts. What do you need to get off your chest? What are you struggling with as you try to be a dad? In what areas do you need direction, guidance, or comfort?

God, continue to fill me with your Holy Spirit. Lead me into truth—the truth of who you are, the truth of who I am, and the truth of who my kids are. Amen.

Faith / Doubt

> Then he said to Thomas, "Put your finger here, and look at my hands. Put your hand into the wound in my side. Don't be faithless any longer. Believe!" "My Lord and my God!" Thomas exclaimed.
>
> —*John 20:27–28 NLT*

Depending on your background, you may have heard that having doubts about God is somehow a bad thing. One thing to recognize in the story of Thomas, is that Jesus never rebukes him for his doubt or turns him away. Jesus simply invites Thomas to touch him and then encourages him.

Faith and doubt are almost always pitted against one another, but it may be better to see them as companions that complement one another. If you're having doubts about God or your ability to be a father, invite faith into the mental conversation as well. Consider that your doubt may actually be strengthening your faith.

It's okay to wrestle a little. We see it over and over in Scripture. Then, also create a safe environment for your kids to wrestle with things in their lives, whether it be their faith, questions about God, or just questions about life in general. Draw them in deeper, and don't turn them away. Ask them questions like, "Why do you think that?" Encourage them by saying, "That's a really good question. Tell me more about that."

God, I believe, but help my unbelief. Thank you for not shaming me when I have doubts. Amen.

MAY

COMPARISON

When Peter saw him, he said to Jesus, "Lord, what about this man?" Jesus said to him, "If it is my will that he remain until I come, what is that to you? You follow me!"

—*John 21:21–22 ESV*

Sometimes it's easy to look at others and compare our situation to theirs. With other dads we might compare salaries, home sizes, car styles, and the list goes on. We may wonder if we are providing everything that our kids need or at least as much as the other dads. We might say, "At least I'm better than *that* person," or "If only I were as good of a dad as *that* person." It's a constant game of comparison, and we start young.

When Jesus was talking to Peter about *Peter's* life, Peter wanted to compare his future with that of another disciple. Jesus basically says, "It's not your concern, Peter. Be concerned about Peter—about yourself! *You* follow me." It seems the best cure for comparison is simply turning to Jesus and following him.

Think about what comparisons you might be making in your own life, particularly as a dad. How can turn your attention back to Jesus?

God, help me to follow you and focus on you. May I turn away from the temptation to compare myself with others. Amen.

COMMUNITY

And they devoted themselves to the apostles' teaching and
the fellowship, to the breaking of bread and the prayers.

—Acts 2:42 ESV

It seems that the early followers of Jesus found it imperative to form a community after his death, resurrection, and
ascension. They focused on just a few things that they devoted
themselves to regularly. We eventually started calling this
community "church," except that church has taken on many
different forms over the last two thousand years or so.

Ultimately, community is essential for followers of Jesus.
Are you and your family plugged into a community? It doesn't
matter the size or the building; what matters is togetherness
and breaking bread and devoting yourselves to learning about
God in the Scriptures. If you are currently attending a church,
is it causing your family to grow in your faith?

God, help me to continue to be part of a community that
is enriching for my family and me. Even when it gets hard,
help me to strive toward unity. Amen.

SHAME

Therefore, there is now no condemnation for those who are in Christ Jesus, because through Christ Jesus the law of the Spirit who gives life has set you free from the law of sin and death.

—Romans 8:1–2

As dads, sometimes when we think about our parenting at any stage of our kids' development, it can bring great pride, great shame, or perhaps something in between. And sometimes when our kids fail at something or make a mistake, we might think that *we* failed or *we* made a mistake.

First and foremost, the apostle Paul tries to make it clear to us that as we find our worth and identity in Christ, we are encouraged to not put any additional and unnecessary shame on ourselves for the brokenness we experience in the world. Once we find our identity in Christ, we recognize that we need grace upon grace.

Our kids are the same way. We should expect them to make mistakes. They, too, are going to experience brokenness. That doesn't mean that it's a direct reflection of our parenting. Do your best to provide a grace-filled environment for your kids. When they make mistakes, help them to not feel shame but instead receive grace from you. And then talk about the mistake. What can they learn from it?

God, grant me grace for every situation I encounter with my kids today. Amen.

TRUST

And we know that God causes everything to work together for the good of those who love God and are called according to his purpose for them.

—Romans 8:28 NLT

We usually reference the above verses when something bad happens, so we can have hope amid our potentially negative circumstances. Just a few verses before this, the apostle Paul appeals to our weaknesses. This all certainly applies to difficult things that we may have already experienced, but a handful of the verses in this chapter deal with the future tense as well. It's almost as if he is telling us to prepare our hearts for whatever comes our way and to ultimately know that when (not if) life gets hard, God is still working.

Even when your kids don't listen, God is still working. Even when you feel like you can't provide your kids with what they need, God is still working. Even when you can't seem to get along with your kids, God is still working. If you love God, you can trust him knowing that he is still working. God, help me to trust you even when things get hard, and please keep working on me, in me, and around me. Amen.

TRANSFORMATION

> Do not conform to the pattern of this world, but be transformed by the renewing of your mind. Then you will be able to test and approve what God's will is—his good, pleasing and perfect will.
>
> —*Romans 12:2*

It's easy to get distracted by what we see and hear in culture about how to raise our kids, how to make money, how to lose weight, how to gain weight, what to buy, what not to buy, and the list goes on. None of these things are inherently bad to consider, but in the verse above, the apostle Paul is concerned about the ways of culture dominating every thought we have and controlling us.

Transformation requires a move of God not only in your heart but also in your mind. Renewal is needed within your thought life so you can suppress the cultural distractions and instead focus on God. What kind of mind shift needs to happen for you to see God more clearly today? How can you begin (or continue) to think about your kids in a God-honoring way?

> God, help me to give not just my heart and soul to you, but my mind as well. Continue to renew my thoughts. Amen.

A STRONG FOUNDATION

"Therefore everyone who hears these words of mine and puts them into practice is like a wise man who built his house on the rock. The rain came down, the streams rose, and the winds blew and beat against that house; yet it did not fall, because it had its foundation on the rock."

—*Matthew 7:24–25*

The storms of life can come from any and every direction. It is during these storms that our foundation is tested. The stronger the storm, the greater the test.

Jesus painted a picture of a storm that hit from all angles. The rain came down, the streams rose, and the winds blew and beat against the house. But the foundation was solid and the house withstood the storm. The foundation was not built during the storm; it was built before the winds picked up. It was not made by the storm; it was made for the storm.

Jesus explains that the foundation of our faith is built through action. It is not built on hearing God's Word, but being obedient to it. It is built by taking the words of Christ and putting them into practice. Before you go through difficult days, you need to do the hard work of obedience and build a strong foundation that can weather the storm.

Lord, help me rely on you before the difficult days. Guide me as I build a strong foundation of faith in you. When the rains come, help me stand with courage and confidence. Amen.

FRUIT OF THE SPIRIT

> But the Holy Spirit produces this kind of fruit in our lives: love, joy, peace, patience, kindness, goodness, faithfulness, gentleness, and self-control. There is no law against these things!
>
> *—Galatians 5:22–23 NLT*

Often, when trying to rely on our own strength and will power to be men of God, we fall short. Jesus embodied the kind of person we all hope to become. God recognizes this need we have, and so he sent his Spirit to not only guide us and lead us into truth, but to also develop character within us. A good fruit tree is planted in good soil, watered, trimmed if necessary, and given the right amount of sunlight.

Much like a fruit tree, we require a good foundation and proper care. We require the Holy Spirit as followers of Jesus. If we find ourselves to be people (and dads) who follow Jesus but aren't exhibiting any of the qualities above, perhaps we need to ask God to continue to fill us with the Holy Spirit. If you've never done that before, take a moment and pray for it now.

God, fill me with your Holy Spirit today so I can become more and more like Jesus Christ. Amen.

PROCESS

And I am sure of this, that he who began a good work in you will bring it to completion at the day of Jesus Christ.

—*Philippians 1:6 ESV*

Sometimes our kids want instant gratification. Things need to happen *right now*. In our age of greater technology, everything is available at the click of a button, and when this becomes the norm, we project this mentality onto every aspect of our lives without even thinking about it.

That includes our relationship with God and our relationship with our kids. It's hard to find stories in the Bible where a person has an encounter with God and immediately becomes a complete person. Even the apostle Paul. When he said yes to God, he was still blinded temporarily. He went through a process to become the man God intended him to be. Even after lots of ministry, Paul still confessed his issues and areas of growth.

We should expect that our lives are a process. They are not microwaved. So don't feel rushed or like you're behind. Are you where you ultimately want to be with God or with your kids? Maybe not, but are you in a different place today than you were yesterday or a year ago? Most likely.

God, help me to be patient with the process and know that you're transforming me to be more like Jesus. Amen.

ATTITUDE

You must have the same attitude that Christ Jesus had.
—Philippians 2:5 NLT

Science and experience have shown us that at a very early age, our kids start imitating us—our mannerisms, our speech patterns, even our facial expressions. It can be fun to watch and sometimes a little scary too. And as they grow and we spend even more time with them, they watch how we handle all kinds of situations. We might not even have to say anything, because they're watching our attitude, behavior, and demeanor.

What does your attitude reflect in general? Do you see the same patterns in your kids? The apostle Paul encourages us to have the same attitude of Jesus, and he later goes on to describe that attitude. Ultimately, he sums it up in one word: humility.

God, give me the grace to align my heart and my attitude with yours. Help me to be more like Jesus with my attitude today. Humble me and let my kids see an attitude of humility as well. Amen.

PARTNERSHIP

The LORD God said, "It is not good for the man to be alone. I will make a helper suitable for him."

—*Genesis 2:18*

As followers of Jesus, we were never meant to do life alone. As dads, it's important for us to have a partner, whether it be a spouse, a mother, a sibling, or just a friend, to help us out. God's creative intention was for partnership and community. He even models what relationship looks like through an expression of the Father, Son, and Holy Spirit. Learn to first be in a partnership with God as you continue to trust him with your life. If you have a partner in your wife, then on this Mother's Day, take the opportunity to express your gratitude for her partnership along with you—but also continue to be in conversation about how you can support and encourage one another going forward.

You were never meant to do this alone, and if your children learn from you the importance of partnership, community, and trust, then they, too, will realize that they are not alone.

God, help me to realize that I was never meant to do life alone or to parent alone. May I trust in you and learn to be in even greater partnership with my "helper." Amen.

BRINGING PEACE

> Let the peace of Christ rule in your hearts, since as members of one body you were called to peace. And be thankful.
>
> —*Colossians 3:15*

The people of Colossae were only familiar with a certain kind of peace when the apostle Paul wrote these words. They knew of a peace that was only accomplished through conquering war by Caesar and the Roman Empire. But Paul says let the peace of Christ be the ruler in your heart. This is a provocative statement, because most certainly the peace of Christ looked very different from the peace that was accomplished by Caesar. It looked like mercy, humility, love, and sacrifice, not dominating or conquering force.

Sometimes, as dads, we think we'll make peace in our homes by asserting more authority and more power. But it's quite the opposite for followers of Jesus. The only way we bring peace is *through* peace. When it seems like there is chaos with your kids, a natural reaction might be to puff up more, raise your voice more, and be more expressive with your actions. But try establishing a demeanor of peace before engaging in the situation. It will feel counterintuitive at first and may take time to get used to, but ultimately you'll be modeling a way of peace for your kids.

God, grant me peace amid the chaos. Amen.

DOUBT

Then the eleven disciples went to Galilee, to the mountain where Jesus had told them to go. When they saw him, they worshiped him; but some doubted.

—*Matthew 28:16–17*

This is, without a *doubt*, one of the greatest passages in the New Testament. I like to imagine the disciples arriving at the top of this mountain covered in dust, pushing each other, making fun of one another, and giving the slowest members of the group a hard time.

When they get to the top, Jesus is there. He is standing with them—present, powerful, and purposeful. Matthew tells us that when they saw him, some worshiped, but amazingly, some doubted. The word *doubt* here means to "stand in two places." In other words, they were there physically, but spiritually and emotionally they were somewhere else.

Gathered in front of Jesus was the full spectrum of discipleship. From passionate worshipers to those who were troubled, doubting, and confused. What's absolutely staggering is that Jesus doesn't make their current reality a prerequisite for his Great Commission. In the very next verse he gives this group the instruction to go and change the world. Clearly there's enough room on Team Jesus for those who are struggling.

Lord, I'm just like these disciples on any given day. I can move from faith to doubt and back to faith again. Thank you that you know that and you call me to your mission regardless. Amen.

ANGER

Human anger does not produce the righteousness God desires.

—James 1:20 NLT

Can you remember a time when your mom or dad got angry with you? What did that feel like? Were they able to be angry while still being loving?

Getting angry with our kids can be pretty common. Anger is not necessarily the issue; how we control our anger or manage it is what's imperative. James is not telling us, "Don't be angry." He's encouraging us to consider our anger and how it affects us as individuals and the people we love.

Think about a moment when you got angry with your kids recently. Were you able to express your anger in love? You can tell your kids that a particular situation made you upset; they need to know that. They also need to know *why* that situation made you upset. Then, take time to talk about how anger can affect them. Ask them how it feels to be angry. Brainstorm together with your kids what you can do when you get angry.

God, help me in my anger. Develop in me patience and self-control so I can still show love to my kids when I'm angry. Amen.

ACTION

But don't just listen to God's word. You must do what it says. Otherwise, you are only fooling yourselves.
—*James 1:22 NLT*

As you grow in your relationship with God, some of the natural desires that develop are prayer, reading Scripture, and joining together with a Christian community. When James spoke about doing "what it says," he was referring to a kind of action that results in justice—hope for the hopeless. Just a few verses later, he speaks of caring for the widows and orphans—the poor. Evidently, these two people groups were largely neglected, and often the prophets before Christ called out the people of God on their neglect. James seems to say that following Jesus looks like standing with the marginalized, the poor, and the broken, because faith without works is dead.

How can you model this kind of lifestyle with your kids? Maybe start out small by considering how you interact with a cashier or a restaurant server. How do you interact with people of different ethnic backgrounds or even the poor? Your kids will imitate your actions, so consider acting out justice.

God, give me your heart for broken people. Help me to consider ways that I can stand with them and care for them, because ultimately you cared for me. Amen.

LOVE DEEPLY

> Above all, love each other deeply, because love covers over a multitude of sins.
>
> —*1 Peter 4:8*

Sometimes hearing the words "Above all, love" over and over may sound like a broken record. It really is that simple, but it's also important to recognize the complexity of the final half of the verse: "covers over a multitude of sins." Peter is not trying to say the "sins" never took place or that we should somehow deny them. This is more of a proactive statement that if we love one another deeply and live in a rhythm of love, we may be less prone to participating in the brokenness of sin. Sin is still real and still present, but love is far more powerful. It's also a reactive statement in that love can heal sin. It doesn't take away from the fact that the sin occurred, but love has the power to heal and restore.

How might this look for your kids or for you? You're all going to make mistakes, there's no denying that. But if you continuously move toward love, you all will experience healing and restoration.

God, show me love today, and help me to show others love as well. Amen.

HOSPITALITY

Cheerfully share your home with those who need a meal
or a place to stay.

—*1 Peter 4:9 NLT*

In ancient Eastern culture, hospitality was paramount. To say
that it would be an honor to have someone over for dinner
would be an understatement. In Western culture, however, we
seem to be always on the go. We don't usually stop to have a
meal for hours at a time with guests, instead frequenting the
drive-through on our way to the next event. Hospitality may
be a dying art, but let's revive it.

It's important for our kids see how we interact with guests
who come to our homes—no matter how nice our homes are,
no matter how great the meal is, and no matter how long they
stay. Your kids are watching you when you plan for company.
For followers of Jesus, there is something sacred about sharing a meal together in a home with another family. When you
break bread and talk about life and faith and whatever else
comes up, it's a holy moment. Make room for more of those
moments.

Interestingly, in the book of Revelation, Jesus makes mention of knocking at a door and coming in to share a meal.
Perhaps there's something to that.

God, help me to be open and proactive in inviting people
into my home. Amen.

HUMILITY / TRUST

> Therefore humble yourselves under the mighty hand of
> God, that He may exalt you at the proper time, casting all
> your anxiety on Him, because He cares for you.
> —*1 Peter 5:6–7 NASB*

In American culture, it seems like everyone wants to be the
best and get to the top. In fact, we encourage it. It's in our DNA
to succeed, and it's the air we breathe. And getting to the top is
often in conflict with humility and trust; those character traits
are seen as weak or passive.

As followers of Jesus, however, humbling one's self is the
start of true character and integrity. As dads, we can struggle
with this. Often, we want to display to our kids that we have it
all together, because if we show any weakness, then they might
not trust us or feel secure with us. But we follow a God who,
in Jesus, submitted himself to death on a cross because of his
humility. Let's trust that our humility will lead to greater trust
in God, and in the meantime rid ourselves of the insecurity of
being honest about our fears and anxieties. We don't have to
impress God—good thing!

God, I admit that I cannot do this on my own. I need you.
I am not invincible. Fill me with trust. Amen.

WORLDLINESS

Do not love this world nor the things it offers you, for
when you love the world, you do not have the love of the
Father in you.

—1 John 2:15 NLT

There is so much about our world that is enticing—and it
should be. We were created in the image of God, so we're creative beings. Humankind has come up with some truly unique
creations. However, there are also certain worldly creations
that distract us from God. In a lot of ways, they reflect the
opposite of the character that God wants to produce within us.
There's no need for a list of these; you know the things in your
life that lead you away from God.

Instead, think about the love of God. What would it
look like for you to be so filled with the love of God that you
wouldn't have enough room in your heart for the things of
this world? The goal isn't to escape anything; that just produces fear and separation. The goal is to be confronted with
the challenges of the world and not be phased by them (or
at least controlled by them). Have a conversation about these
things with your kids so they'll know how to engage them
when they're no longer at home.

God, prepare my heart to be secure in you. Help me to
resist the temptations of the world that lead me away from
you. Amen.

PAIN AND JOY

> "He will wipe every tear from their eyes, and there will be no more death or sorrow or crying or pain. All these things are gone forever."
>
> —*Revelation 21:4 NLT*

As followers of Jesus, it's important for us to live with hope no matter our circumstances. The hope we have in Jesus leads to something like what John wrote about in Revelation. He saw an image of no more sadness, just pure joy. The question is, how do we start living in that reality right now? And how do we encourage our kids to understand that as well?

At a fairly young age, most kids get the concept of joy and pain. Try having a conversation with your kids and have them imagine what it could look like to have a world where there's no more pain, suffering, or sadness. Have them describe what true joy looks like to them. It could be something serious or something silly. The idea is to get them in the habit of thinking futuristically—imagining a future with nothing but joy and then beginning to live in that future right now. This is what hope in Jesus can look like. Get creative!

God, develop a greater hope within me to see your kingdom come and your will be done on earth now as it is in heaven. Help me to imagine a world without pain. Amen.

NEWNESS

And the one sitting on the throne said, "Look, I am making everything new!" And then he said to me, "Write this down, for what I tell you is trustworthy and true."
—*Revelation 21:5 NLT*

Our kids like new things. New shoes, new toys, new phones, new cars—it doesn't matter what it is as long as it's brand-new. And we like to be able to get them new things.

There's a different kind of newness that comes with being a follower of Jesus. Each day seems like a new opportunity to grow in our faith, to encounter someone in need of the love of God, or to simply breathe another breath of air. God promises to make us new in this life, and even in the end, there is a vision that God will make *all* things new. It's almost as if Jesus takes every broken thing and restores it, repurposes it, or revitalizes it.

Where do you need newness in your life? What new thing can you do to show your love for your kids today? Consider the newness of each day; it's another opportunity to show your kids how special they really are.

God, remind me that my kids are a blessing to me. No matter what challenges I face as a dad, help me to never forget that they are a gift. Amen.

SMALL BEGINNINGS

"Do not despise these small beginnings, for the LORD rejoices to see the work begin, to see the plumb line in Zerubbabel's hand."

—*Zechariah 4:10 NLT*

Grand visions are just that. Grand. Big. But each of them begins with the smallest of steps. The rebuilding of the Lord's temple after the people returned from Babylon was no different. Before the ornate interior was the roof. Before the roof, the walls. Before the walls was the floor. Before the floor was the foundation. And that foundation? It began with a single brick set into the ground. According to Zechariah, it was Zerubbabel who laid that very first brick of the foundation and it would be Zerubbabel who would set the final stone. A single brick is a small thing. A small beginning. A very crucial beginning. Parenting is a lot like that.

As fathers, we often have grand goals for our kids and families but we don't know where or how to begin. Start small with a kind word or gentle nudge. Then, keep building.

God, you do not despise the small things. Compared to the grandness of the Lord's temple, a single brick seems so tiny, so meaningless, and so purposeless. Often, we feel like that small brick. But you find joy in those bricks, those small beginnings, because without them, there is no completion. Help us to be willing to take that small step as we begin. Amen.

FAVORITES

Now Israel [Jacob] loved Joseph more than all of his
children.

—Genesis 37:3 NKJV

Playing favorites was nothing new to the family of Jacob. His
own mother, Rebekah, preferred him over his brother, Esau,
and together they had tricked Isaac into giving Jacob the
birthright meant for Esau. And when Jacob played favorites
with Joseph, he unknowingly set his son on a collision course
with pride and arrogance, which caused many problems with
his older brothers.

Each one of our children has different gifts and talents,
and these were given by God. As fathers, we may be tempted
to look upon some of those gifts with greater favor than others, but when we do this, we can transfer this favor to our kids,
creating bad feelings among siblings and resentment toward
parents.

As fathers, let's pay close attention to the way we show love
to our children, according to who God made them to be.

Father, you do not play favorites. You reveal your grace to
all through the sacrifice of your Son, Jesus Christ. And,
while you give different gifts and measures of grace, your
love for each of us is total, complete, and perfect. Help me
to love my children in this same way. Amen.

LISTEN

Hear O Israel: the LORD our God, the LORD is one.
—*Deuteronomy 6:4*

The verse above is the beginning of the daily Jewish prayer, commonly called the *Shema*, which is Hebrew for "listen." It sets the tone for the rest of the prayer because it orients the pray-er to whom he is praying to.

It is God's people, Israel, who must listen as God is described—his name, nature, and character.

It is the Lord who is God. He was the deliverer of the people from slavery in Egypt.

It is the Lord who is one. Not one of many, but one God. Sole deliverer.

It is we who must listen, because we are surrounded by gods that "are not gods" (Jeremiah 16:20). Fathers call their children to hear about "the LORD our God," the one and only Lord and Deliverer, so they will not be confused. Fathers who do this will be speaking honestly, clearly, and consistently about the "who" of God.

We can only do this proclaiming when we know him personally.

Father, I'm here to hear about you. The only God. The one true God. My God. You are clear and direct with me; please give me that same clarity when I tell my kids about you. Amen.

Total Love

Love the LORD your God with all your heart and with all
your soul and with all your strength.

—*Deuteronomy 6:5*

Once we have acknowledged the "who" of God (our God, one
God), a response is required. An action. The right response is
to love God with all of who we are, because love is a verb. This
love is full and complete—all of our heart, all of our soul, and
all of our strength.

Fathers have the daily opportunity to not only love the
Lord totally but to also show this same love to our kids, not
as just an act toward them but also as a demonstration of love
toward God. They experience this "heart love" when they see
our emotion, our "soul love" when they see our sincerity, and
our "strength love" when they see us exert energy for them.

Our kids learn about total devotion to God from us, so let's
love them well!

God, please show me the areas in my life where my active
love for you falls short of your command. Is my heart in
it? Do I feel emotional love for you? Does my love for you
indicate effort? Am I striving to love you with all of me?
Thank you for being devoted to me. Amen.

COMMIT

> And you must commit yourselves wholeheartedly to these commands that I am giving you today.
>
> *—Deuteronomy 6:6 NLT*

We live in an overcommitted age, and so much of what we do requires total commitment. Our electronic devices make us available 24/7. The activities that our kids participate in take more time, money, and effort than ever before. As soon as one activity ends, another begins—and usually on a different night than the previous ones, requiring us to adjust our schedules yet again.

God also has a requirement—not to an activity or availability, but to his commands. We need to commit to them, to follow and obey them. As dads, the way we obey God's commands reveals much about our commitment to him. Being committed means more than just knowing the commands; we also need to follow them and understand that they keep us focused on him and that they protect us.

When you show your total commitment to God's commands to your kids, you show them where your heart is.

God, open my heart to your commands. Allow me not just to learn them and teach them but to be committed to them and to see them as a gift to me that keeps me in line with your will and protects me from hardship and evil. Amen.

MAY 26

REPEAT

Repeat them again and again to your children. Talk about
them when you are at home and when you are on the
road, when you are going to bed and when you are getting up.

—*Deuteronomy 6:7 NLT*

We learn best by repetition. We learn best by repetition. We
learn best by repetition. (No, that is not a typo!) We study
words to learn to spell. Playing a musical instrument is simple muscle memory. We drive the same route every day so we
know how to time it right to hit nothing but green lights. And
many of us have spent hours shooting free throws.

The commands of God are no different. We read the Scriptures not just for a way to live, but to know and understand the
way of Jesus. We learn them and then talk about them, always.
We become so familiar with God's Word that it overflows out
of us, and we talk about it with our kids every chance we get.
We make the most of every moment with our kids because
passing on the faith is our primary task.

When we drive. When we lie down. When we rise. Always.

Father, help me to fall so in love with your Word that it
overflows and absolutely infects every conversation with
my kids. I want to study and learn your commands again
and again so they are always on my mind. Amen.

PUT ON

> Tie them to your hands and wear them on your foreheads as reminders.
>
> —*Deuteronomy 6:8 NLT*

Male humans love to "do." We feel most comfortable when we are taking action, whether at play, at home, or at work. We fear being seen by others as lazy. At times, we "do" so much that we're simply busy as opposed to actually accomplishing something of value.

But when we tie God's commands to our hands, we're acting upon them. We go beyond understanding and put them into practice. We actually serve others; we do something. Wearing these commands on our head happens when we're transparent about whom we serve and why we do what we do. We talk about Jesus and are unafraid to share the motivation for our actions. These things are not "busy work," but incredibly important and valuable.

When we wear God's commands, our kids get to see us live out what we say we believe. When we act upon those beliefs, they learn that what we believe is more than something we simply intellectually assent to. Rather, it is who we are.

> Lord, as I listen to, love, commit to, and repeat your commands, let me act upon them. Daily I meet people in need of you—not just your words, but you. As James says, my deeds reveal my faith. Let them be bold! Amen.

WRITE

Write them on the doorposts of your house and on your gates.

—*Deuteronomy 6:9 NLT*

Take a moment and look at the clothes you're wearing. Chances are there's a brand label clearly visible for all to see. We're walking advertisements, and we provide this service free of charge. In fact, we pay the brand. Perhaps we simply like the style or the fit, but more likely the brand means something to us.

When we write God's commands on our doorposts and gates, we are advertising him. And he has paid us to do this. First Corinthians 6:20 tells us that we have been bought for a price—his Son, Jesus Christ. By accepting this, we put him on display; he is our brand, and we belong to him—not in the form of a catchy saying, but in the form of our actions of love, mercy, and grace.

This begins at home as we show these things to our wives and children. Put Christ on display!

God, as I dress today, help me to look at each label on my clothing and ask myself what those labels and logos say about the brand. Then give me the presence of mind to ask how my thoughts, words, and deeds reveal you to all those I'll meet today. Amen.

BE STRONG

"Be strong and courageous, for you must go with this people into the land that the LORD swore to their ancestors to give them."

—*Deuteronomy 31:7*

The heart of God is one of strength and courage. While we know this for many reasons, it is most obvious through his Son, Jesus. God didn't simply give his people a set of rules and regulations to follow; he entered into their world, going with his people into the activities of their lives. He struggled, faced temptation, and knew hunger and thirst. He was tired. He worked. He laughed. He confronted sin and selfish attitudes. And he is still with us today.

In the same way, a dad enters the world of his kids. He plays with them. Works and labors with them. Instructs them from a close proximity. This requires strength and courage because it seems easier just to give orders and make rules.

Just as followers of Christ are comforted by the closeness of God, kids find comfort when Dad is near.

Lord, I want to be strong and courageous! I want to follow the example of Jesus, entering into the lives of my children. I want to know their experiences, their hurts, and their successes. I want to know them deeply. I want them to know that I am with them. Amen.

WONDERFULLY MADE

I praise you because I am fearfully and wonderfully made;
Your works are wonderful, I know that full well.
—*Psalm 139:14*

It's easy for us to think about and apply this verse to ourselves as individuals, and it's easy for us to think about and apply these verses to our kids. Until …

Milk is spilled. Mud is tracked in. The trash does not make it to the curb in time. Your son wants a drink of water before bed. Your daughter asks, "Why?" And … now another drink of water.

You just want five minutes of peace and quiet. Even in these moments, God's truth rings out: humans are fearfully and wonderfully made.

Father, you made each of my children in your very image. In that image you set purpose and intentionality. No details were left to chance. Each and every aspect of my children was made to bring you glory and reveal something about yourself. I love the joyous moments, and it's so easy to see you in them. But life is also filled with challenges and unexpected—and sometimes disappointing—actions. You are there too. Let me see you then. Amen.

GENTLENESS

A soft answer turns away wrath, but a harsh word stirs up anger.

—*Proverbs 15:1*

Gentleness is a fruit of the Spirit, an evidence that God is at work in us as the Holy Spirit takes residency in our heart. Because of this, the way we speak to our children can reveal the degree to which the Holy Spirit influences and impacts our lives.

Our kids ask us so many questions while seemingly telling us every thought that crosses their minds, especially when they're young. This can try our patience, and we need to remember that they want to include us in everything that they do. The way we respond to them will often be directly proportional to the level of inclusion they will offer to us as they get older. Perhaps you've experienced this. Do your older children share with you? Evaluate how you've responded to them in the past.

Gentleness requires that we be present in the moment, remembering that our words are powerful and that gentle ones are best.

Lord, I remember many harsh words said to me in response to something I'd said or done. Frequently, that led to escalation and greater misunderstanding, then harder feelings and more harsh words. Help me to reflect on those moments, and give me the desire to respond in ways that honor you. Amen.

JUNE

ACT JUSTLY

> He has shown you, O man, what is good; and what does the LORD require of you but to do justly, to love mercy, and to walk humbly with your God?
>
> —*Micah 6:8 NKJV*

God has shown us what is good. Not merely through his law, although his law is good. Not only by dealing with those who reject those laws. Not only by keeping his Word. God shows us what is good through his Son, Jesus. Jesus was the physical representation of justice. He brought healing. He cast out demons. He brought hope. He righted wrongs. And, finally, he paid the penalty for our sin in an ultimate act of justice.

We act justly when we behave as he did. We can bring healing, cast out demons, bring hope, and right the wrongs around us, first in our homes and then in our churches, communities, and the world. To act justly is to remember that we love others because Jesus first loved us.

God's justice is not only final; it is also ultimately complete. And it is utterly hopeful and hope filled. As we act justly with our kids, may it also be hope filled.

Lord, you've shown me what is good, in your Word and in your actions. History is filled with freedom and salvation. It's also filled with bondage and seemingly hopeless situations. Teach me to act justly in a world that so desperately needs it. Amen.

MERCY

He has shown you, O man, what is good; and what does the LORD require of you but to do justly, to love mercy, and to walk humbly with your God?

—*Micah 6:8 NKJV*

"Mercy!"

Perhaps you cried that out as an older brother or uncle twisted your arm behind your back or applied just the right amount of pressure in the wrong spot. "Mercy" is what we say when we give up, when we need deliverance from someone or something.

Mercy is also what we need from a just God because of our disobedience to him. And mercy is what God offers to us. He gives this to us because without it, we are a poor and pitiable people. We are hopeless, lost.

Just as we loved it when that uncle would release us from his grip, we love it when we receive mercy from God, when we know we're caught in a twisted mess of life. But to "love mercy" here is not to love mercy received but mercy given. This is good. This is required—to love the giving of mercy to those who do not deserve it, just as we recognize the undeserved mercy from God.

This week, consider mercy when what is deserved is punishment. This, after all, is God's heart.

God, I love receiving your mercy because I know just how much I need it. Help me to give that same mercy to those in need. Amen.

WALKING HUMBLY
WITH GOD

He has shown you, O man, what is good; and what does
the LORD require of you but to do justly, to love mercy,
and to walk humbly with your God?

—Micah 6:8 NKJV

Before you read today's devotion, go take a walk with your
kids. Seriously.

Now that you're back … how was that? Were they pulling
you all over? Going off the road into people's yards? Going off
the sidewalk into the street?

Walking with people requires humility. Someone is going
to want to walk faster or slower than the other. Someone will
want to go look at something that the other may not want to
see. Someone may want to walk farther. Or, they may want to
just stop in the middle of the road and be done with it. In any
of these situations, humility will be required of someone.

Walking with God is no different. His ways are not our
ways. And he is the leader, the pacesetter. Where he goes, we
follow. Our humility is in following him, step by step, walking
with him. He leads with love.

Walk humbly with God and bring your kids along, leading
them with love.

God, I want to walk with you. I trust that you know where
we are, where we are going, and when we will get there.
Lead me with love. Amen.

SELF-SACRIFICE

"The Kingdom of Heaven is like a treasure that a man discovered hidden in a field. In his excitement, he hid it again and sold everything he owned to get enough money to buy the field."

—Matthew 13:44 NLT

We sacrifice the most for the things we most desire. We will commit to a thirty-year loan to own a home and to up to a six-year loan for an automobile. We work forty, fifty, even sixty hours a week (or more) to get a promotion at work. When it comes to our kids, we will work hard to get them onto the best youth sports teams and into the best schools. And with each of these things comes a cost.

There is, however, something greater than any of the above. God's kingdom. Jesus tells us that God's kingdom is so valuable that it would be like finding a treasure hidden in a field, then selling everything we own to buy that field to get the treasure.

What might it look like for us to pass God's kingdom on to our kids? What might we have to give up for that to be the most important thing?

God, I have experienced the glory of your kingdom, and I want nothing more than for my family to know about it. Please help me honestly evaluate my sacrifice for you. Amen.

THE MOST IMPORTANT LESSON

"For this is how God loved the world: He gave his one and only son, so that everyone who believes in him will not perish but have eternal life."

—*John 3:16 NLT*

This text is likely the most recognizable text in the Bible, if not in the English language. You will see it in the end zone at most football games and just behind the catcher or on the baseline at a baseball game. It will be just behind the backboard at a basketball game and along the racetrack at an automobile race. It will be held high in a town parade by churches and individuals alike. Why?

Because in it we find the most important lesson that there is: God loved us so much that he sent his Son, Jesus, to perish in our place. This is the gospel message in one simple sentence.

Of all the things that we teach and tell our families, it is this message that is the most important. A great way to do that is to read the verse, replacing "the world" and "everyone" with first our names and then the names of those around us. Do this often, and we will all know the greatest lesson.

Father, you loved us so much that sent your Son to pay for our sins. He took our place, perishing for us so we may have eternal life. You did this for each of us personally. Teach me to be grateful for it and to pass it on. Amen.

Giving Good Gifts

"You fathers—if your children ask for a fish, do you give them a snake instead? Or if they as for an egg, do you give them a scorpion? Of course not! So if you sinful people know how to give good gifts to your children, how much more will your Father in Heaven give the Holy Spirit to those who ask?"

—*Luke 11:11–13 NLT*

There is nothing like the face of a child on Christmas morning, especially in that "first see" moment as they come downstairs or turn the corner into the room where the Christmas tree is. The look of pure joy.

Fathers love to give gifts to their children, and we will do whatever we can to give them exactly what they ask for. No bait-and-switch or generic gift will do. Giving them what they want is not just indulging a selfish desire on their part; it also indicates that we have clearly heard them and want to see them happy, joyful, and fulfilled.

The Father in heaven also knows what is in our best interests: the Holy Spirit. This is the most important gift. As you give gifts to your children, remember that these are symbolic of the gifts that the Father has given to us.

God, you know exactly what I need. When I ask for the Holy Spirit, that is what I receive. You do this because you are a good Father who loves to shower his children with what is best for them. Thank you for showing me what good gifts are. Amen.

DON'T SHRINK

"I never shrank back from telling you what you needed to hear, either publicly or in your homes."

—*Acts 20:20 NLT*

As Paul was preparing to leave the elders from Ephesus, he essentially gave them his resignation notice. He told them that he loved them and that from day one it was his desire that they know Jesus and his good news. He spoke of his hard work among them, and how this often required confronting them with truth.

Confronting others is one of the most difficult things that we do. When the person we will confront is a family member, it is even more difficult. But confrontation is a part of being a father. It is necessary.

When it came to telling people what they needed to hear, Paul did not shrink back, and as fathers, we must not be afraid to be honest with our children and speak truth into their lives. What they need to hear beyond any other message is the truth of the gospel and the good news of Jesus Christ. We have to confront them on their sin and point them to Jesus as the one who took care of it. We must not shrink back.

I am thankful for the people in my life who did not shrink back from telling me a truth that I needed to hear. They demonstrated courage in doing so. Please give me that same courage to not shrink back from telling my children what they need to hear. Amen.

Honoring Parents

Children, obey your parents because you belong to the Lord, for this is the right thing to do. "Honor your father and mother." This is the first commandment with a promise: If you honor your father and mother, "things will go well for you, and you will have a long life on the earth."

—*Ephesians 6:1–3 NLT*

As children, we were under the authority of our parents and had to obey them. But in that obedience, we may or may not have honored them; this was determined by our attitude. As adults, while we are no longer bound to obey our parents, we are to honor them.

Think of what this demonstrates to our kids:

- We honor our parents when we ask for advice; this demonstrates that we view our parents as wise.
- We honor our parents when we speak kindly of them; this demonstrates respect.
- We honor our parents when we spend time with them; this demonstrates value.
- We honor our parents when we defer to an activity they would prefer; this demonstrates humility.

In each of these, we are teaching our kids how we honor our parents—and they are learning how to honor us.

Lord, my parents have taught me so much about life. While imperfect, they sought to love me and care for me. Help me to honor their efforts by respecting and valuing them in ways that my own children see, so they will be blessed. Amen.

HOPE

"That's how it works with my words. They don't return to
me without doing everything I send them to do."

—Isaiah 55:11 CEV

We teach and train our kids in the faith, and we take them to
church, Sunday school, youth group, and Bible camp. We send
them on mission trips, and we pray for and with them. Even
so, they sometimes make decisions that lead them away from
Jesus. We are crushed, heartbroken, and overwhelmed with
sadness and sorrow. Does this sound familiar? And yet …

Isaiah 55:11 is so filled with hope. This Scripture teaches us
that the faithfulness of God's Word is ever fruitful. His words
are not pie-in-the-sky naiveté but truth. Promises. Believable.
Inspired. Inspiring. Trustworthy. Full and complete. And they
do everything that God sends them to do.

Father, I so much want my kids to know who you are. I
want them to know and experience your power and majesty. I want them to know your peace and promises. I want
them to come to you with their burdens and lay them at
your feet and find rest. I want them to know that the joy
of your salvation is greater than anything that might bring
them temporary happiness here on earth. I want them to
know you deeply and intimately. I want them to escape
the sorrows of their sin and instead know freedom. I want
each of these things and more, because you want them for
my kids. I praise and thank you for your words of hope.
Amen.

Courage (Father's Day)

Be watchful, stand firm in the faith, act like men, be
strong. Let all that you do be done in love.

—1 Corinthians 16:13–14 ESV

There is a crisis of fatherhood today. The US Census Bureau
says 24 million children (one in three) live in homes without
their own dad. But children with dads involved in their life are
more successful in school, more confident, more sociable, and
less likely to have a list of adolescent problems. Clearly, dads
play a large role in the success of children.

This verse includes four descriptions of a godly man. He
is alert, stands firm in the faith, is strong in his courage, and
loving. A challenging list! This describes a dad who is engaged
and aware of what's going on in his children's lives. This is a
dad who is careful to pass along his faith by his words and also
in the way he models it to his family. This is a dad with a purpose who doesn't give up when tests and conflicts arise. All of
this is embodied in a bold love that makes him willing to put
his wife and children first and treat them with respect. It takes
courage to be a godly man.

God, being a dad is an amazing privilege. With your help,
I'm up for the challenge again this year. My family needs
me to follow you. Help me to be a dad that makes a difference. Amen.

ENCOURAGE

> Fathers, do not provoke your children, lest they become discouraged.
>
> *—Colossians 3:21 NKJV*

One of the biggest challenges in being a father is dealing with the poor behavior our children sometimes demonstrate through their thoughts, words, and deeds. What did Paul mean by "provoke"?

Earlier in this chapter, Paul told the Colossians to "put off" the things that lead to spiritual death: anger, wrath, malice, blasphemy, and lying. Each of these behaviors are provoking in nature. When we respond in these ways to our children, we are bound to discourage them.

Once we have taken off the things that lead to discouragement and death, we are to replace them. We do this when we "put on" the following: tender mercies, kindness, humility, meekness, longsuffering, bearing with one another, forgiveness of one another, and love. We are to be ruled by the peace of God, let Christ's words live within us, sing spiritual songs to one another, and do everything in the name of Jesus.

When we do not provoke our children, we encourage them to come to us and be in relationship with us. They will grow to trust us, and in turn they will demonstrate this new "outfit" to those around them. Be an encourager!

Father, help me evaluate the way I speak with my children. I want to be encouraging to them. Give me opportunities today to be humble, forgiving, peaceful, and kind. Amen.

EAT MEAT

You are like babies who need milk and cannot eat solid food. For someone who lives on milk is still an infant and doesn't know how to do what is right. Solid food is for those who are mature, who through training who have the skill to recognize the difference between right and wrong.

—*Hebrews 5:12–14 NLT*

There's nothing like a properly cooked piece of meat. After we have eaten it, we feel full and satisfied.

As our children grow and get older, we watch their eating habits change and we adjust. What made them full at one year old barely makes a dent in their hunger when they are seven. And when they are seventeen? Forget it. Keeping up with that appetite is nearly impossible!

The same is true with spiritual nourishment. When our kids are young, we give them spiritual milk; we introduce them to people like Adam and Eve, Noah, Moses, Samson, King David, Jesus, Mary, and perhaps the disciples, as well as basic Bible stories. But as they get older, we start digging into "meatier" concepts like sin, salvation, and the Trinity. We want them to know the difference between right and wrong, true and false. Dads help their kids grow in their faith by giving them the right spiritual food.

God, help me see how "hungry" my kids are, and help them see that what they need is more of you. Let them be unsatisfied with a little bit of spiritual food, and allow them to feast on the meat of your Word and be completely filled. Amen.

THE CLOSEST FISH

Then he said to them, "Follow me, and I will make you
fishers of men."

—*Matthew 4:19 NKJV*

A lot of work goes into catching fish. We need to have all the right equipment: a rod and a reel, fishing line, bait and tackle, and a fishing license. If you don't want to fish from a dock or the shore, you'll need a boat. Then after accumulating all this gear, you'll be faced with the toughest decisions of all: where to fish and when to go. Often, we make these decisions by talking with family and friends or by going online. Because who wants to go fishing and catch nothing?

When Jesus spoke to his earliest disciples, he invited them to go "fishing" with him. But rather than go away to a far of place, Jesus and the disciples "fished for men" throughout the region of Galilee. Why? Because those "fish" were close by. At the end of his ministry, Jesus told his followers to go out and make disciples, beginning nearby in Jerusalem and then spreading to the ends of the earth.

We, too, have fish near us. They are our children. We have all the equipment necessary, and because they are our kids, we know who to fish for and how to catch them. We are intimately connected to them, knowing their eating habits, when they rest, and when they are active. Go fishing for them. Today.

God, I can be a fisher of men in my very household. Help me to see that you have given me all I need to catch them for you. Amen.

JUNE 14

DISCIPLINE WITH LOVE

"For the LORD disciplines those he loves, and he punishes each one he accepts as his child."

—*Hebrews 12:6 NLT*

"This is going to hurt me more that it will hurt you."

As a child you may have heard the phrase, and as a parent you've likely thought it, if not said it, yourself. Fathers know the truth of this statement because, while discipline is part of being a father, it is not a joyous one.

Our task is to ensure that what we do in those moments is not vengeful punishment but loving discipline. Loving discipline has one goal in mind: restoration. It seeks to bring people together, to right wrongs, to show that justice is possible, and to point to a time when all there will be is peace.

Our example for this is God's love for us. He disciplines us through the consequences of our actions and choices, and through the Scriptures and conviction from the Holy Spirit. He allows consequences because his desire is for us to be restored to him. This discipline reveals that we are not only loved by him, but that we belong to him. And this belonging came at great cost—the sacrifice of his Son for us. It truly did hurt him more than it hurt us.

As we discipline our children, let us do so with the intent of restoration and return, and let it be done in love.

Father, I am thankful for your discipline. It is designed to restore me to you and to make me more like your Son. As I discipline my own children, help me guard my heart and act out of love. Amen.

Divine Discipline

As you endure this divine discipline, remember that God is treating you as his own children. Who ever heard of a child not disciplined by its father?
—*Hebrews 12:7 NLT*

"Who ever heard of a child not disciplined by its father?"

The question asked in this verse is rhetorical, regardless of the answer. On one hand, our response is, "Of course I've not heard of this. Discipline of children is part of the parental responsibility." On the other, we say, "Yep, I knew kids like that growing up. They ran wild and caused all sorts of problems. And we have some kids on our street whose parents never confront their behavior."

When God disciplines us, he is showing to everyone that we are his. The fact that we endure it is the evidence that we are in the hands of a loving father. By default, a father must discipline his child. If not disciplined, the child seemingly belongs to no one.

God, you set the example for discipline. You allow me to endure it first because I need it, and second because it shows that you are indeed a loving father. If you let me run wild, it would say much about your character as well as mine. Help me to treat my children as mine, and as you treat me. Faithfully, honestly, and with great discipline. Amen.

STAY ALERT

Be sober, be vigilant; because your adversary the devil walks about like a roaring lion, seeking whom he may devour.

—*1 Peter 5:8 NKJV*

The word *sober* in this verse has nothing to do with alcohol or drunkenness; here it means to have a clear mind, to be alert. To be vigilant means to be looking both outward and inward for something, to be ready. But ready for what?

The adversary. Our enemy, the devil. Sometimes we believe that this adversary is out sneaking around, hiding in the bushes or creeping in on us. But the imagery used here by the author of Hebrews is that of a roaring lion. We know he is coming. In fact, he is announcing himself. We hear him. The soberness and vigilance is not about looking for him to arrive, but about being prepared for his arrival.

Fathers work with their kids so they not only know the roar of this lion, but also know what to do when he arrives. We do this best when we are prepared and when we are sober and vigilant.

Lord, my adversary is coming. I know he is because I can hear him. He is roaring and he wants to devour me. He wants to devour my kids and my family. Help me to be sober and clear minded. Help me to be vigilant and ready. And help me to teach my kids how to stand strong against him when he arrives. Amen.

JUST ONE GENERATION

When all that generation had been gathered to their fathers, another generation arose after them who did not know the LORD nor the work which He had done for Israel.
—*Judges 2:10 NKJV*

A lot can happen in one generation. Nations can rise and nations can fall. Resources can be increased or lost forever. Just in one generation.

Throughout Deuteronomy, we see God giving many instructions to Moses; they spoke about worship, the building of the tabernacle, and many other things. And in many instances, these instructions ended with God saying something like, "And when your children ask about why you do this, tell them that I delivered you out of slavery." The reason given was simple: to keep the people from forgetting what God had done. But in just one generation, the knowledge of the past was gone. The people still had the rituals to follow, but they didn't know why.

As fathers, it's our role to talk about the amazing things God does. We give glory and praise him for his deeds and work. We talk about the "why" because we need constant reminders of who God is.

Let's teach our kids to remember.

Father, it's so easy to forget. To forget what you have done, and to forget to pass our faith on to our kids beyond Sunday. We forget who you are, and we forget how you have delivered us from our sin. Help us to remember daily your love and sacrifice for us, and to share with our children the hope and promise of delivery for them. Amen.

WASHING FEET

> So he got up from the table, took off his robe, wrapped
> a towel around his waist, and poured water into a basin.
> Then he began to wash the disciples' feet, drying them
> with the towel he had around him.
>
> —*John 13:4–5 NLT*

Jesus was a servant and demonstrated this with his disciples the night before he died. After they entered the room where he would eat his final meal, he picked that moment to do the lowliest task a servant could do: wash feet. Jesus did this not out of false humility or to receive praise. In fact, one of his disciples, Peter, chastised him for it.

Fathers wear a lot of hats in the home. We provide food, shelter, and clothing for our families. We chauffer our kids to and from school, sports practice, the doctor's office, and work. One of the easiest ways to share the gospel with them and to teach them the character of God is to serve them in the way Jesus served others.

Each day, we have opportunities to wash the feet of our families through selfless—and sometimes humiliating—acts of service. We can clean up *their* mess. We can show mercy and grace when judgment is warranted. We can consider them greater than ourselves and spend time with them in ways that honor them and not us. Serve like Jesus.

> Master, I am the servant, you are my Lord. I am here to
> serve you so that others see you. Help me remember that
> when I serve my family in honesty and humility, that I
> magnify you alone. Amen.

DISCERNMENT

"You must distinguish between the unclean and the clean."
—*Leviticus 11:47*

Beginning in Genesis 3, we find humanity struggling to discern the difference between evil and good, and it is in this struggle that we find people making choices that separate them from God and other people. Cain failed to bring God a righteous offering. David didn't look away from Bathsheba. And while his son Solomon asked for (and received) wisdom from God, he was led astray. In the New Testament, we find Peter refusing to eat with Gentile believers.

We are no different. In Romans 12, we're told to be transformed by the renewing of our minds. These new minds teach us the difference between right and wrong, and then the Holy Spirit gives us the ability to choose right over the wrong. Finally, we pass this on to our children. We do this when we tell our children about God, life in Christ, and power from the Spirit, and when we help them make right choices. We talk with them about choices because at some point they will be confronted by them on their own.

As we pray for knowledge and wisdom, may we also ask for the desire to do the right thing.

God, your Word is clear about right and wrong. Through it, show and teach us what obedience looks like, and give me to courage to do the good. Amen.

PHYSICAL TOUCH

> So the LORD said to Moses, "Take Joshua son of Nun, a man in whom is the spirit, and lay your hand on him. … Give him some of your authority so the whole Israelite community will obey him."
>
> —*Numbers 27:18, 20*

Physical contact affirms what is being verbally communicated. We tell our kids, "I love you" and often follow it with a hug, kiss, or pat on the back. When we discipline our kids, we may place our hand on their shoulder to indicate our seriousness. Touch can provide a feeling of safety and security.

In Numbers, Moses is told by God to bring Joshua before the people and to lay his hand on Joshua, showing approval as power shifts from the aging Moses to the younger Joshua. In 1 Timothy 4, Paul tells a younger Timothy that Timothy received his gifts when the elders laid hands on him, and to live up to those gifts.

Your kids seek your approval of their actions, words, and thoughts. As you tell your thoughts, encourage them as often as possible and correct them when they need it. May we remember the power of loving, kind, appropriate, and frequent touch.

> You are a God of touch. When you created man, you literally touched the dust of the earth to do so. You breathed life into our nostrils. When your Son, Jesus, was on earth, he healed many by physically touching them. And your Spirit literally dwells within us; we are your temple. Help me to value touch. Amen.

LONG-TERM PLANS

> Salmon begot Boaz, and Boaz begot Obed; Obed begot Jesse, and Jesse begot David.
>
> —*Ruth 4:21–22 NKJV*

What began as the story of a woman in search of someone to care for her daughter-in-law ended twenty-eight generations later with Jesus Christ. Boaz had no way of knowing this when he took Ruth as his wife. God, however, knew exactly what he was doing because he is interested in long-term plans.

Long-term plans are why, when he set up rules and regulations about worship, he told the parents to tell their children "why" when they asked questions about those rules and regulations. Long-term plans are why God considered the character of those whom he chose—and chooses—to lead his people. Long-term plans are why the same Gamliel who spoke up in defense of the apostles in Acts 5:33 was also the mentor of Saul, "who was also called Paul" (Act 13:9). Long-term plans are the only reason why we even know the names of Ruth and Boaz.

We have no idea what God will do with us, our children, our grandchildren, and beyond. But we participate in those plans when we are obedient today, because we set each following generation on a trajectory of future obedience. Remember the long-term plans of God.

> God, you are all-powerful, in every place, and all-knowing. You alone know what the future holds and the role that I and my offspring will play. Help me to choose obedience to you today. Amen.

HAPPY

How happy I was to meet some of your children and find them living according to the truth, just as the Father commanded.

—*2 John 4 NLT*

Can you imagine what it must have been like to read these words in a letter from John? While anyone is pleased to hear nice things about their children, how much more valuable and encouraging are these words when they're about the things that really matter!

When we faithfully live in obedience to God, share the gospel with our kids, read God's Word with them, pray and serve with them, and demonstrate repentance and call our children to it, we are leading them down the narrow path of personal connectivity and relationship with Jesus Christ.

Our kids will ultimately make choices of what to do with the wisdom and knowledge of Christ. And the grace of God and our faithfulness to him create the environment necessary for our kids to make choices that honor God.

Father, you give us commands to follow, not just about our own obedience and rule-keeping but about the way we are to pass on the faith to our kids. Create in me the desire to obey you in all things, so that my own children may be followers of you and live by the truth you tell. Amen.

WELL DONE

"His master replied, 'Well done, good and faithful servant! You have been faithful with a few things; I will put you in charge of many things. Come and share your master's happiness!'"

—*Matthew 25:23*

There is only so much one can accomplish in a given day. There are actually twenty-three hours, fifty-six minutes, and four seconds in the average day. And in that time, a number of things need to be done:

- We will sleep.
- We will eat.
- We will go to work.
- We will praise God.
- We will spend time with family.
- We will drive our kids to events.

How can we do each of these things with the intent and purpose of glorifying God and being faithful to him? God has put us "in charge" of just a few things.

The way to join in the happiness of God is to be faithful in the few things he has given us, and take full advantage of every moment of each day. Then we will hear, "Well done."

God, there is both so little and so much time every day. Time passes by so quickly that at the end of the day, I sometimes wonder where it all went. Each day is a gift, and every moment an opportunity for faithfulness. Help me to serve you each day. Amen.

STAND STRONG

> Keep yourselves in God's love as you wait for the mercy of our Lord Jesus Christ to bring you eternal life. Be merciful to those who doubt; save others by snatching them from the fire; to others show mercy mixed with fear—hating even the clothing stained by corrupt flesh.
>
> —Jude 21–23

Waiting for things is not only an important part of life; doing so with patience is a trait of a believer in God. We are in the space between the resurrection and return of Christ, and as we wait, we parent our children and lead our families.

Kids are different, even kids from the same household. We can parent them similarly, and each one will have a different temperament and personality. Perhaps you have a child who is anxious and filled with doubts; be merciful, gracious, and kind—always. Maybe one of your children is in grave danger; act decisively and quickly, for time is of the essence. Does your child need to be convicted of sin? Share with that child the total character of God and talk about love and justice.

God is merciful to us and has placed children in our care that we might love them well. Know them and what they need.

Father, there are times when I doubt and am in need of mercy. Make me aware of your mercy that I may be merciful. Other times, the situation is pressing and I need an immediate evac! Help me see this in others. I know I have sins to be convicted of, so do that for me. Help me repent of my sin and point others to repent of theirs. Amen.

WHAT YOU WEAR

Since God chose you to be the holy people he loves, you must clothe yourselves with tenderhearted mercy, kindness, humility, gentleness, and patience.
—*Colossians 3:12 NLT*

What kind of clothes should a father wear? A suit and tie for an important meeting? A uniform for work? Maybe a ratty T-shirt and jeans for oil changes and mowing? Or how about some casual Saturday clothes with his favorite team logo for the college football game?

The mixture of polyester and cotton isn't nearly as important as what a man wears in his heart and actions. For fathers, this is especially true because, whether we like it or not, a dad is a strategic representative of God the Father. What a dad says and does has significant ramifications.

So when a dad "puts on" mercy in the midst of trouble, or when he chooses patience over raising his voice in frustration or when he consistently encourages those around him, his family will take notice. "If that's what God the Father is like," they'll say, "then I can trust God."

God, help me to be clothed in your qualities and characteristics today. Let me be a proper representative for you to my family. Amen.

A DEVOTED MAN OF PRAYER

> Devote yourselves to prayer with an alert mind and a thankful heart.
>
> —*Colossians 4:2 NLT*

Stop everything you're doing, even if just for a few minutes, and pray. Put aside your anxieties, put to rest your weighted burdens, and have a conversation with God. Take a moment to pray for your own relationship with God. What has he done in your life that makes you thankful? Where do you need to realign yourself with his Spirit? What requests, what needs, could you put in his hands? Take a moment to ask God what his plans are for you. Devote yourself to prayer.

Now take a moment to pray for your family. What has God done in your family that makes you thankful? Where does your family need to realign its priorities with the Holy Spirit? What requests and what needs do you have for your family that you could entrust to the Lord's hands? Take a moment to ask God what he sees when he looks upon your family. Devote yourself to prayer.

> God, remind me to be constantly talking with you. Don't let me neglect coming to you in prayer. May I become a devoted man of prayer for the sake of my family. Amen.

EVERY OPPORTUNITY

> Live wisely among those who are not believers, and make the most of every opportunity. Let your conversation be gracious and attractive so that you will have the right response for everyone.
>
> —*Colossians 4:5–6 NLT*

Who are the people around you who need God? Take a deep breath, close your eyes, and consider those who are close to you that, for one reason or another, are not following God. Is there someone in your family? Perhaps one of your friends? A coworker? A neighbor?

Having the right response for someone is not really about knowing how to win an argument. It's much more about living in such a way through the circumstances of life that others take notice. You want others to see a wellspring of strength and a daily resource in you. You want them to think, *There's something different about him. He has a peace that I need.*

When that moment comes, you'll want to be ready to share about the source of your strength and courage. It is in the everyday moments that your life has its greatest impact. How others see you in the routines, accidents, stresses, and relationships will reveal to them who you truly are and what you truly have. How you live in your everyday life could make the difference between someone finding God or continuing to live apart from him.

God, let me live consistently in your patterns every day, so I may be ready to share at any moment how great you are. Amen.

REPRESENTATIVE

> So we are Christ's ambassadors; God is making his appeal through us. We speak for Christ when we plead, "Come back to God!"
>
> —*2 Corinthians 5:20 NLT*

To "represent" someone means to "re-present" them. In other words, if you represent someone, it's as if you're making them present again. Make sense? No? Maybe? Okay, let's try to illustrate it this way:

Let's say there was a king who came to a land and did many good things for people. Let's say this king supplied daily bread, extended mercy to those in trouble, and gave himself on behalf of those in his kingdom. Then, let's say the king asked you to become his representative to those people. In effect, he was calling you to be his ambassador. He was entrusting you with his authority and words. When you would speak, the words you spoke would represent the king's words. When you would act, the patterns of your life would enact the king's grace or justice. As the king's representative, it would be as if the king was right there, living through you.

And so it is with us as we live our lives for Christ, as his representatives.

> God, let me speak as you would speak, act as you would act, and represent you to everyone I come in contact with today. Amen.

BEING CONTENT

Not that I was ever in need, for I have learned how to be content with whatever I have.

—Philippians 4:11 NLT

It could never be said that Paul had it easy. Maybe you can relate to what he went through. His life was riddled with ups and downs. He faced hardships and successes, agony and abuse, rejection as well as acceptance, and shame but also joy. Paul had made huge mistakes and caused tremendous pain that scarred his past, but his life changed dramatically when he met Jesus. He began to help others and learned to share himself vulnerably. Instead of bullying his way to victory, he would sometimes go hungry. Instead of being celebrated, he would sometimes suffer loss.

Yet, because of Jesus, Paul found contentment. He learned that no matter his circumstances, he was grounded in who he was because of who Jesus was in his life. He found confidence in what he was called to do because of what Jesus was calling him to do.

As a father, where do you find contentment? What enables you to stand courageously? What helps you feel secure in who you are and what you're called to do?

Hopefully, you will find your inner strength in the life and power of Jesus Christ today.

God, help me find my sense of worth, my sense of peace, and my sense of identity in you. Let me trust you fully for the contentment I so desperately seek in my life. Amen.

TRUSTING GOD TO SUPPLY

> And this same God who takes care of me will supply all
> your needs from his glorious riches, which have been
> given to us in Christ Jesus.
> —*Philippians 4:19 NLT*

Consider all the things that have been set before you. What
do you have? What do you lack? What raises you to your feet
in joy? What brings you to your knees in sadness? Whose
steps are crossing your path? What words are ready to come
out of your mouth? What passions are ready to well up in your
heart? What sights are you absorbing with your eyes? That's
quite a list. Whether you have much or whether you have little, your life is full.

Considering all that is set before you, what do you need?

God the Father has unlimited resources. Do you have
responsibilities set before you? What does God have at his
disposal that could help you fulfill your calling? Do you have
people in your life who need your love? How could God supply your needs in such a way that you could unconditionally
love them? Do you lack strength or courage within yourself
today? How might the Lord of all creation want to bless you
heart, mind, soul, and strength?

> God, let me seek you first and there find my needs sup-
> plied in you. Amen.

JULY

PRIORITIES

Now all glory to God our Father forever and ever! Amen.
—*Philippians 4:20 NLT*

The temptation we fathers struggle to overcome is the need for approval, affirmation, or adoration from those around us. We want respect from our children, love from our wives, recognition from coworkers, and good standing within our community. We strive for these conditional social rewards. Something missing within us longs for acceptance, and so we shift our attention to the accolades this world so teasingly offers.

Perhaps we didn't get the approval we needed from our own fathers. Or perhaps we know we are inwardly more fragile than the lofty expectations we have placed upon ourselves. Or perhaps we are tempted to place the spotlight on ourselves. For whatever reason, if we're not proactive, our priorities can become misguided. We can be tricked into thinking, *If only others would lift me up.*

It has been said that the chief end of man is to bring glory to God. The honest question that every father needs to face is this one: In all sincerity, who do I want to see glorified in my life today?

God, whenever I am swayed to seek my own stance upon your pedestal, remind me of who you are and what my priorities should be. Amen.

BLESSING

May the grace of the Lord Jesus Christ be with your spirit.
—*Philippians 4:23 NLT*

At the end of his letter to his friends in the city of Philippi, Paul gave a blessing: "May the grace of the Lord Jesus Christ be with your spirit."

Does anyone in your family or within your network of friends need to receive a blessing like this from you? As a dad, you're in a privileged and unique situation to speak life into those who need your love. You have the incredible opportunity, through your words, to curse or to encourage those closest to you.

God wants you to extend his blessing upon others. So, today, receive the grace he has for you through Jesus and then be intentional about sharing that grace with those you love. Jesus loves you, has given his life for you, and offers you unrelenting relationship. Now do the same for others in his grace-full power.

God, may you give me more than enough grace, so I may overflow upon my family. In the name of Jesus. Amen.

CHANGING LIVES

> This same Good News that came to you is going out all over the world. It is bearing fruit everywhere by changing lives, just as it changed your lives from the day you first heard and understood the truth about God's wonderful grace.
>
> —*Colossians 1:6 NLT*

The good news of Jesus is that our sins are forgiven and our relationship with God is restored through his saving work on the cross. This seed, when planted, grows and bears fruit for generations.

As a dad, you have a remarkable twofold calling. First, you are called to embrace the good news wherever you are, making the grace and truth of Jesus the central component of your life. Second, you are called to share this good news with anyone who comes across your path, perhaps most notably your children. Sow the seeds of the gospel of Jesus within their lives. Cultivate their faith. Provide the water, the light, the nutrients, and the environment for their faith to flourish. And watch with joy as the good news of Jesus spreads through them.

You know Jesus has impacted your life when he leads you to start impacting others. It has been said that your faith in God isn't actually yours. Rather, your faith in God is yours to give.

> God, let me never cover up my faith. Continue to change my life by your Spirit, and empower me to be bold in the way that I live out my commitment to you. Amen.

Why We Work So Hard

So we tell others about Christ, warning everyone and teaching everyone with all the wisdom God has given us. We want to present them to God, perfect in their relationship to Christ. That's why I work and struggle so hard, depending on Christ's mighty power that works within me.

—*Colossians 1:28–29 NLT*

If you were called to a meeting with God, and if it was your special responsibility to introduce your family to him, what would you say? How would you describe your family to God? What would be the important aspects you would want God to know as you presented them to him?

If you had your lifetime to prepare for this meeting, how would you spend your life? To what would you devote your time each day? What sorts of habits or characteristics would you hope would rub off you and onto them?

Paul tirelessly invested the qualities of his own life into others. His desire was to present people to God, perfect through Christ. He sought God's wisdom in the practice of his own faith so he would know how to teach and represent God to those he cared about. He worked so hard, not for his own gain but so others would discover and embrace the forgiveness and abundance that comes from knowing Jesus.

God, may the work of my heart and hands today be determined, strong, and courageous on behalf of my family. Amen.

CONTINUE TO LIVE

> And now, just as you accepted Christ Jesus as your Lord, you must continue to follow him.
>
> —*Colossians 2:6 NLT*

Just because at some point in your life you committed yourself to Jesus, doesn't mean that your faith is to remain static. To be a disciple means to be a learner. In other words, a disciple of Jesus is a learner of Jesus.

Therefore, continue to follow Jesus. In fact, follow him with more attentive steps than yesterday. Learn his thoughts, learn his actions, and learn his will. Seek out his decisions for you, search out his advice, and call out for his wisdom. Run to his healing, walk where he miraculously stands, and get down into the messes in which he so willingly places himself. Embrace him as tightly today as you did at any point in your past.

If Jesus is to be your Lord, let him be your Lord in every practical way today.

God, give me the resolve to continue to trust myself to your guidance, your steps, and your presence in my life. I want to follow you again today, as I did yesterday and as I will tomorrow. Amen.

DON'T GET CAUGHT

Don't let anyone capture you with empty philosophies and high-sounding nonsense that come from human thinking and from the spiritual powers of this world, rather than from Christ.

—*Colossians 2:8 NLT*

In Genesis 3, satan captured Adam and Eve in the Garden of Eden. He hunted them, he lured them, and then he snared them. They bought his shrewd, high-sounding nonsense. In Matthew 4, satan tried his alluring arguments again, this time to trip up Jesus in the desert. Each statement and question lobbed by satan was a like a high-arching softball grenade. If Jesus had taken the bait, the consequences would have been explosive. But he stayed the course. He didn't let the evil one capture him with falsehoods. In fact, he freely dispatched satan's empty philosophies by being even shrewder than the snake.

How did he resist while Adam and Eve had fallen? What was Jesus' weapon? It was the uncompromising ballistic missile of truth.

Staying alert and on course isn't just for your sake. The arguments you buy and the conclusions you accept impact the generations that follow you. Your kids will likely mimic your thoughts. Your grandchildren will likely reflect their grandfather's beliefs. If you get lost, it's likely that they will as well.

God, as for me and my family, we will serve you. Help me, then, to stay true, for the sake of those around me. Amen.

NEW NATURE

Put on your new nature, and be renewed as you learn to know your Creator and become like him.

—*Colossians 3:10 NLT*

In Genesis 1, God merely spoke, and the stars were born. He said, "Let there be …" and there was. In the beginning, Christ was the Word (mentioned in John 1) who declared to the darkness that there should be light.

Jesus has spoken into your life today. He declares you free from sin. He proclaims the year of the Lord's favor, release for those who are captured, and sight for those who have lost their vision. He speaks a new vocation for your days. He calls you to him, and he calls you to change the world. His words beckon you to draw near, and empower you to move mountains. He asks you to speak with his voice, his authority, his commands, and his creativity.

Be refreshed today. Put on the new nature given to you by Jesus, the creator of the world.

God, by your Word, create in me a clean heart, and renew a right spirit within me. Let me be refreshed in my soul today. Draw me close to you, and help me to share this newness of life with those around me. Amen.

CONTENT

I know what it is to be in need, and I know what it is to have plenty. I have learned the secret of being content in any and every situation, whether well fed or hungry, whether living in plenty or in want.

—Philippians 4:12

We often think of contentment as the satisfaction of all our needs. If that were true, it would only be possible to be content when everything is perfect. God gives us the power and the peace to be okay even when everything around us is not.

Our decision-making and leadership is better when we learn to be content no matter the outcome. God frequently reminds us that true peace and contentment comes from our relationship with him and not the circumstances of our life.

God, please give me your perspective on my life. Help me to be content even when there are things I wish I could change. Keep me from acting in fear, or worrying about things that are not how I wish they would be. Help me to trust that, no matter what, you are enough. Amen.

WITNESSES

Therefore, since we have so great a cloud of witnesses surrounding us, let us also lay aside every encumbrance and the sin which so easily entangles us, and let us run with endurance the race that is set before us.

—*Hebrews 12:1 NASB*

We often perform better when someone is watching. We fight harder, strive further, and endure longer when we know others are paying attention. When we forget we're being watched, it becomes easier to succumb to our struggle. We might rest our defenses and end up tangled in things we wouldn't want others to see.

The everyday people in our lives surround us like a cloud. They are paying attention even when we might think they're not. Through them, God cheers for us to wrestle free from the things that would hinder our relationship with them and with him. Our hearts will fight for others more fiercely than we fight for ourselves.

Lord, I desire to be a good example for my family. Please keep in my mind the truth that they are learning from my actions. Help me to trust that they are cheering for me, and that my successes are their successes. I believe they are worth any struggle, so please use them to inspire me to keep fighting. Amen.

GOD-BREATHED

All Scripture is God-breathed and is useful for teaching, rebuking, correcting and training in righteousness, so that the servant of God may be thoroughly equipped for every good work.

—*2 Timothy 3:16–17*

There's a mysterious weight to the words of Scripture. It's easy to live with a more-or-less understanding of God's ideal life gleaned from the general idea of a verse. When we forgo the specific words of the Bible, we pull its punches a little bit.

Even though our kids might respond with glazed eyes, it is worth quoting relevant verses at relevant times. When we do, the life God has breathed into those words will help it come alive in the heart of the listener. The entire Bible is available to give just the right wisdom in just the right way.

God, I want to know your Word so I can apply it when opportunities arise. Help me to recall the verses I have read whenever they can be of use in my life or the lives of those around me. Encourage me to cling to your specific promises and not just my own paraphrases. Please sharpen my spiritual mind. Amen.

OBEDIENCE

"Go and gather together all the Jews of Susa and fast for me. Do not eat or drink for three days, night or day. My maids and I will do the same. And then, though it is against the law, I will go in to see the king. If I must die, I must die."

—*Esther 4:16 NLT*

God rarely asks us to produce a specific result. What he most frequently asks of us is simply obedience. We don't always know what the result might be, or even what God's will is in a certain moment. What we can be sure of is that he desires our devotion and commitment no matter the consequences.

Esther was unsure what would come of her action, but she was certain it was what she needed to do. The result would possibly be death, but her only concern was obedience. We can miss opportunities to serve God when we focus on the outcome. God's desire is to grow us through an experience and to have us trust him with whatever happens. Life with God is not about results; it is about obedience.

God, thank you for inviting me to be a part of what you are doing in the world. I confess I often worry about what might happen, instead of trusting you to work through every situation. Remind me that it pleases you when I obey, and that you want to take care of the rest. Amen.

DOING GOOD

As for you, brothers, do not grow weary in doing good.

—*2 Thessalonians 3:13 ESV*

It is worth it to keep doing what is right and good. It may be thankless and difficult, but it is always worth it. You might feel like it doesn't matter or that nobody notices how hard you work to live how God says to live. Perhaps you feel cheated because, despite your efforts, things just aren't working.

Keep going. Don't grow weary now. It's possible you won't see the results of your devotion, but nothing you give to God is fruitless. Lower your shoulder and keep pressing on. Every decision you make to do what is good gives God one more tool in his toolbox, and he is working to build something beautiful for his kids. Keep going. It is worth it.

God, strengthen me to keep living how you ask me to live. Give me the endurance to make the decisions that please you, even when I'm worn. I pray you will restore my energy and help me to keep moving forward toward the life you want me to have. Thank you for being with me and for helping me live a life of doing good. Amen.

ADDING WORDS

"Every word of God is flawless; he is a shield to those who take refuge in him. Do not add to his words, or he will rebuke you and prove you a liar."

—*Proverbs 30:5–6*

When we believe the Bible is on our side, we must take great care in how we convey its truth. It is good to understand what the Bible says about any situation, and following what God says helps us keep our integrity.

However, we must be careful to not exaggerate what Scripture says just because we think we're right. Let Scripture speak for itself. It's not our job to make the listener agree. We can simply share what the Bible says and trust that God will water and grow his truth for his purposes. God delights in our righteousness, but he also yearns for the righteousness of others.

Lord, help me to speak only your truth when helping others to see your light. Please protect me from injecting my own opinions into the work you're trying to do. I want to gladly share your Word with others, and I trust that it speaks for itself. Thank you for helping me be an amplifier for your truth instead of my own. Amen.

POINTING

"You search the Scriptures because you think they give you eternal life. But the Scriptures point to me! Yet you refuse to come to me to receive this life."
—*John 5:39–40 NLT*

Approaching Jesus can be intimidating. We're often afraid of what he might say, or ask, or already know. This fear will drive us to keep doing the "safer" spiritual discipline of just reading the Bible. Secretly, we hope that rushed prayers and memorized verses won't disrupt our lives too much.

But Jesus wants to disrupt our lives. He wants to shake up our routine and replace the parts that are lacking with the vibrant life we crave in the depths of our soul. Scripture is good precisely because it begs us to intimately connect with our Savior. Don't shy away from the spiritual tug of Scripture, frightening as it may be. If you let it lead you to Jesus, you will find what are you are looking for in every verse.

God, I believe that you want to bring satisfying life to every part of who I am. I confess that I sometimes hesitate to come to you for fear of what you might say. Please remind me that you are not interested in shame or judgment and that your core desire is for me to experience the life you created me to live. Amen.

INFINITELY MORE

Now all glory to God, who is able, through his mighty power at work within us, to accomplish infinitely more than we might ask or think.

—*Ephesians 3:20 NLT*

God delights in surprising us. Like a father building an incredible treehouse for his child or a husband unveiling a dream vacation to his wife, God takes joy in doing things for us that exceed our expectations. He wants us to stare at him in wonder and realize that he is so much more impressive than we give him credit for.

Often, our dreams aren't big enough. We'd settle for a response to prayer that helps us just get by. Our heavenly Father wants so much more than that! We convince ourselves we aren't worth his time, but he says, "I want your life to be abundant, and I'm going to do that *through* you." The power of God is most beautifully demonstrated in his ability to exceed our expectations by working through us.

God, you are so much better than I can imagine. I know that even my grandest request seems small compared to what you want to accomplish through me. Help me to remember that you are at work in my life to create something better than I could ever create on my own. Amen.

BIGGER

I pray that out of his glorious riches he may strengthen you with power through his Spirit in your inner being, so that Christ may dwell in your hearts through faith. And I pray that you, being rooted and established in love, may have power, together with all the Lord's holy people, to grasp how wide and long and high and deep is the love of Christ.

—Ephesians 3:16–18

God is so big that only he can show us how big he is. Our understanding of God begins with that first aha moment where his power becomes reality to us. That first taste creates a hunger for more, and we strive to learn all we can about God. As our understanding of God grows, so does his stature and power in our mind.

But eventually we realize that God exceeds our ability to understand. For some, this stunts their growth, as they refuse to chase the Holy Spirit into the "unknown." For believers, however, the "unknown" is an invitation to experience God in a way we can't explain. God's power, working within us, pushes out the boundaries we've created around our creator. God is actively working to help you experience even deeper satisfaction in your relationship with him.

God, thank you that I can never understand in this life just how truly wonderful you are. Thank you that every day is a chance to be amazed by your character. I pray that you will let my heart and soul continue where my mind wants to stop, and that I would feel the deep connection you desire with me. Amen.

MERCY
THROUGH MENTORSHIP

Fathers, don't exasperate your children by coming down
hard on them. Take them by the hand and lead them in
the way of the Master.

—*Ephesians 6:4 MSG*

For most people, the first understanding of God is directly
connected to how they experienced their earthly father.
Fathers are models of the Lord whether we intend to be or
not. A child with a strict father will usually first assume God is
judgmental. A child with an absent father will often first perceive God as uncaring. Fathers shape the lens through which
children first see their Savior.

Through Jesus, God set his example of mercy through
mentorship. It's easy to dole out reactionary punishment when
we are upset, but the Holy Spirit works to direct that angry
energy into opportunities for growth and learning. When we
do that, we paint a more accurate picture of God for our children to follow.

God, I want my kids to know you. Please help me to conduct myself in a way that makes you look good. I pray
that I will choose opportunities for growth over angry
punishment. Help me to see the best way—your way—to
respond to my frustrations as a father. Amen.

NOTHING WITHOUT

"I am the vine, you are the branches. The one who abides in me while I abide in him produces much fruit, because apart from me you can do nothing."

—*John 15:5 ISV*

Many times we treat God like a turbo boost for life. For the most part we do our own thing, work hard to achieve our goals, and muscle through each day. But sometimes, when things are really hard, we finally relent and pray that God would help us over some particularly difficult hurdle in life.

If the above verse were written with regard to how many of us live, it would say "apart from me you can do *most things*."

Of course, Jesus knew what he was saying. His point was clear: we shouldn't save our reliance on him like some sort of power-up. We are designed for constant connection to Christ. We function best—and really only function at all—when we choose to connect with God at all times, not just in tough times.

God, thank you for being my source of strength every day. I pray that I will reflexively turn to you in every situation instead of leaning on you only when I feel I've exhausted all other options. Thank you for caring about even the things that seem small or insignificant. I know life is more enjoyable when you're in all of it. Amen.

WEARY

Even youths shall faint and be weary, and young men shall fall exhausted; but they who wait for the Lord shall renew their strength; they shall mount up with wings like eagles; they shall run and not be weary; they shall walk and not faint.

—*Isaiah 40:30–31 ESV*

Whenever you feel worn out, it should serve as a reminder to connect with God. When we try to do things with our own power, we often find ourselves drained before the task is accomplished. But when we trust that God is at work and we are simply assisting him, we find a deep supply of energy to keep doing his will.

The next time you're exhausted, pause and talk to God. He may encourage you to keep going, he may insist you stop worrying and rest, or he may convict you to shed the added weight of a sin in your life. No matter how he responds, he promises to help you keep going in a way you might have thought impossible before.

Lord, thank you for giving me strength and energy when I feel I'm running out. Help me to continue experiencing your goodness even when I'm weary. I pray that I will realize the difference it makes to trust in you each day and that I will experience the vitality of living for you. Amen.

COMFORT

Yea, though I walk through the valley of the shadow of death, I will fear no evil; for thou art with me; thy rod and thy staff, they comfort me.

—*Psalm 23:4 ASV*

President Theodore Roosevelt famously said, "Speak softly and carry a big stick." Sometimes we focus too much on the gentle and comforting shepherd image of God, forgetting that one of the primary jobs of a shepherd is defender, which he is prepared to do.

It is in the darkest and most terrifying places that we are keenly aware of any source of safety. As our fight-or-flight reaction kicks in, we pay attention to anything that offers protection. Perhaps this is the reason that God sometimes leads us through dark periods of life, so we are reminded of the safety found in him.

Your heavenly Father has every intention of protecting you with his might, and that fact should bring you deep peace when you're scared.

God, thank you for protecting me. I can take great comfort in knowing you are with me and you are powerful. Thank you for leading me through things that are intimidating, and for promising to help me fight when the time comes. Amen.

WORSHIP THE SPLENDOR

Honor the LORD for the glory of his name. Worship the LORD in the splendor of his holiness. The voice of the LORD echoes above the sea. The God of glory thunders. The LORD thunders over the mighty sea. The voice of the LORD is powerful; the voice of the LORD is majestic.

—*Psalm 29:2–4 NLT*

Worshiping God is the only natural response to his power. When we find ourselves in seasons where worship is difficult, we can think it's because we don't feel close to him. Intimacy is often the result of worship, and worship is the result of focusing on God's power and goodness.

God's might is the source of the good things we experience in him. In times of difficulty we rely on his strength to protect us. In times of joy we celebrate his power working within us. In all situations we benefit from placing our focus on the splendor of God. In doing so, we pave the way for a deeper sense of intimacy with and connection to our Creator.

God, you are powerful and mighty. Help me to focus on your characteristics so that I can see my own life with a better perspective. I want to worship you no matter my circumstances. Your power is the most helpful thing for me each day. Amen.

IMITATE

So I encourage you to imitate me.
—*1 Corinthians 4:16 GW*

You're a Christian not just because someone told you about Jesus, but because they also demonstrated what it means to live a Christ-centered life. The person who showed you is also following the example set for them by another, who is in turn copying yet another. For every Christian, there is an unbroken line of imitators that can be traced back to Jesus himself.

Your job, then, is to live in such a way that the chain continues. Is an invitation to live like you also an invitation to live like Jesus? Your imitation becomes an invitation, to those around you, into a satisfying life.

Lord, help me to live how you taught us to live. I want my life to be an example of what it means to follow you. I pray you will give me the strength to be an example to my family of what it means to have a life devoted to you. Amen.

FULLNESS

I want you to know all about Christ's love, although it is too wonderful to be measured. Then your lives will be filled with all that God is.

—*Ephesians 3:19 CEV*

Christ's love brings fullness of life. It was his love for humanity that pushed him to sacrifice so much on our behalf. It is through that same love that we are invited into a rich and satisfying life. It is Christ's love that is the missing puzzle piece for all those who have yet to follow him.

The promise of Christ's love is that we have been made complete. Our own lives are transformed, and we are able to live with more power and purpose than we ever could alone. Through that power we can help others experience the same amazing love and invite them into the full life God intends for us.

God, please continue pouring into me. Help me to experience your love in a way that fills my life. Amen.

YOUNG EXAMPLES

> Let no one despise you for your youth, but set the believers an example in speech, in conduct, in love, in faith, in purity.
>
> —*1 Timothy 4:12 ESV*

It's our job to teach our children, and nearly every day we find ourselves explaining or modeling something we wish for them to learn. Perhaps we feel like a spigot of knowledge, constantly pouring out what we know into the young vessels. There is deep satisfaction in seeing what we've taught take hold in the lives of our kids.

We can easily view it as a one-way street, but while God is using us to teach our children, he is also revealing himself to us through them. Some traits of the Lord are best demonstrated through youthful innocence and purity. If we pay close attention, we'll see the nature of God in our children.

When you do, celebrate it and encourage your son or daughter. Let them know that God is using them right now, in their youth, to teach others about himself.

God, please give me eyes to see what my children can teach me about you. Help me to experience what they know about you, that I have yet to learn. And Lord, please remind me to thank them each time they remind me of who you are. Amen.

CALLED UP

"You should also look for able men among all the people, men who fear God, are trustworthy, and hate dishonest gain; set such men over them as officers over thousands, hundreds, fifties, and tens."

—*Exodus 18:21 NRSV*

When God is at work, he recruits men with hearts pointed toward him. He is less concerned about skill and experience, and more concerned with motivation and love. Men who are intentionally living for Jesus are the most likely to be called into faithful action.

It is in day-to-day life that people demonstrate their readiness for leadership. A man who waits for his marching orders to begin conditioning will find himself woefully underprepared. Instead, the most useful followers of Jesus are those who put his teachings into practice each day. It is never fruitless to follow Jesus with daily devotion.

God, I want to be the kind of man you can call on when you are at work around me. I also want to be the kind of man that others would seek out in their times of need. Please use my everyday experiences to strengthen and grow me into someone who can serve you well. Amen.

SAFETY IN NUMBERS

Where there is no guidance, a people falls, but in an abundance of counselors there is safety.

—*Proverbs 11:14 ESV*

There is truth to the old saying, "It takes a village to raise a child." Fathers can easily fall into the trap of believing that they alone must provide protection and instruction for their children. But living this way robs kids of experiencing the richness of many voices.

We are called to be both discerning and generous with the guidance of our children. We should surround ourselves with godly men and women. Then we set an example for Christian community and provide a buffet of positive influence for our children. We should collect friends who are a blessing to both us and our children.

God, thank you for the other positive voices that speak into the life of my children. I pray you will bless anyone who has a place of influence in the lives of my family. Through your Spirit, please use them to back up the things you are teaching through me as a father. Amen.

WARNING AND PATIENCE

> And we urge you, brothers and sisters, warn those who are idle and disruptive, encourage the disheartened, help the weak, be patient with everyone.
>
> —*1 Thessalonians 5:14*

Correction and patience must go hand in hand. Correction without patience is anger. Patience without correction is avoidance. Being a godly leader requires both in equal balance.

The Bible urges us to follow God's example when encouraging right living in others. We are to point out God's expectations and highlight clearly when they're not met. This provides a chance to do the right thing. But the entire process falls apart if not done with encouragement, strength, and patience. Those are the three main ingredients of godly direction.

> God, when times arise that I need to encourage others to live how you say to live, please help me correct them the way you say to correct. Give me the strength and patience to truly encourage change in their lives, and continue to change me in the process as well. Amen.

TELL THEM

Parents will tell their children what you have done. They will retell your mighty acts.

—*Psalm 145:4 NCV*

We know an experience has profoundly changed us when we begin telling others about it. There is great power in stories, and the most powerful stories are those of God changing us. Throughout your life, God has worked to bring transformation, blessing, and wisdom. You're an expert in how God has worked in your life.

No doubt each of your children has a favorite story. We connect to stories in an incredible way, and the fastest route to a person's heart is through story. You're an expert in your story, and sharing the ways God has worked in your life is not only your responsibility but also one of the most effective ways to explain how God works within us. It helps the more famous stories of the Bible feel more alive when you know the same God is at work right now with someone you love. Tell your children what the Lord has done—and is doing—in your life.

God, please help me to be authentic in talking with my children about how you are at work. I want them to know you by hearing about the work you are doing in me. Remind me that my story is powerful and that you have given me experiences precisely so I can share them with others. Amen.

EVERYTHING YOU DO

In the same way, encourage the young men to live wisely.
And you yourself must be an example to them by doing
good works of every kind. Let everything you do reflect
the integrity and seriousness of your teaching.

—*Titus 2:6–7 NLT*

The only way to demonstrate that we really mean what we
say is to live it. Our actions are our primary way of teaching;
our own lives are the ultimate visual aid for any life lesson we
try to convey. If we want our children to listen to our advice,
we must live it clearly for them to see.

But if we want our children to listen to our advice, we must
also speak it. The best way to instruct is the one-two punch
of teaching and modeling. We must live correctly and then
explain why we have chosen to live that way. Your children
will learn from your life, no matter what it teaches.

God, please help me to be consistent in what I teach my
child. Give me the strength and wisdom for my life to
serve as a wonderful lesson for what it means to be a man
of God. Amen.

Rest

> It is useless for you to work so hard from early morning
> until late at night, anxiously working for food to eat; for
> God gives rest to his loved ones.
>
> —*Psalm 127:2 NLT*

Failure to rest is usually the result of failure to trust God. There are many valid things we could do with any hour of the day, and danger comes when we forget that rest is one of them. We were created to rest; in fact, the first full day that Creator and man spent together was a day of rest.

We know God disapproves of laziness, but we often forget that it is also sinful to never rest. No amount of work will ever supply the deep sleep and rest that God offers. He beckons us to rest so we can remember our dependence on him. When we do, we are more likely to depend on him on the busy days as well. Take time today to rest.

Lord, I know I need rest. Give me the courage to make time for rest by delaying or declining the things I need to do. Please provide peace that everything will be okay if I take time and obey your command to rest. I pray it will help me to trust even more that you are with me. Amen.

KNOW YOUR FLOCK

> Be sure you know the condition of your flocks, give careful attention to your herds.
>
> —*Proverbs 27:23*

It's not enough to simply watch for trouble with our children. We are called to keep our finger on the pulse of their heart and soul. We can easily lose that pulse in the normal rhythm of our everyday relationships, but as fathers we must give special care to our flock—the people in our care.

The beauty is that when trouble comes, we're more prepared for it. In fact, we're likely to catch it earlier if we already know the condition of our family's spiritual life. We're called to diligently keep watch over the ups and downs in our kids' lives.

> God, please give me the ability to sense how my family is doing spiritually. Help me remain consistent in my attention to their lives, and please highlight the things you want me to see. Amen.

AUGUST

STRONGER TOGETHER

Two are better than one, because they have a good return for their labor: If either of them falls down, one can help the other up. But pity anyone who falls and has no one to help them up.

—*Ecclesiastes 4:9–10*

Strength is so often defined as a man who needs no help. Our culture celebrates the stoic man who is able to face his battles singlehandedly. We see the lone wolf celebrated as the ultimate in masculine strength. Ironically, such a man is likely the weakest and most vulnerable type of man you'll find.

Only weak people believe that receiving help is a sign of weakness. In the same way that we delight in offering strength to others, there are others who are eager to offer their strength to us. We need only be courageous enough seek help, and to keep seeking until we find it. When we do, we will find our strength multiplied by those we join with.

Lord, please keep me from believing the lie that I have to do things on my own. Help me to trust others to carry the weights of my life with me, just as I work to help others with their burdens. I pray that you will fill my life with people who help make me stronger. Amen.

IT'S WHAT'S INSIDE

But the LORD said to Samuel, "Do not look on his appearance or on the height of his stature, because I have rejected him. For the LORD sees not as man sees: man looks on the outward appearance, but the LORD looks on the heart."

—*1 Samuel 16:7 ESV*

God often chooses the unexpected man to accomplish his goals. This is because God's method of choosing tends to be much different, and much deeper, than how we tally the score. The only person we're likely to assess accurately is ourselves, and even then we often exchange God's criteria for one less fitting.

God is able to look at our hearts, and he often uncovers positive traits even we have overlooked. He draws out of us a deeper strength than we thought we possessed. He produces from us more than we thought ourselves capable of. God is actively working to draw the very best out of the core of who he made you to be.

God, help me to see myself and others the way you see us. Please grow in my heart the qualities you desire, and keep me from focusing on traits that don't matter. Thank you for working to grow me. Amen.

COMPLETELY NEW

> Whoever is a believer in Christ is a new creation. The old
> way of living has disappeared. A new way of living has
> come into existence.
>
> —*2 Corinthians 5:17 GW*

The promise of the Christian life is not a better life or an
improved life. The promise of following Jesus is a completely
new life! The transforming power of God is so strong that it
actively erases our old desires and ways of thinking. It is when
we forget this that we start to beat ourselves up. We carry the
weight of our mistakes around, which slows our growth.

You are a new creation, having been made new simply by
choosing to follow Jesus. You don't need to worry about your
past any longer. Just keep living in the direction of Jesus.

> God, thank you for making me new. I'm grateful that you
> did more than just polish me up or make me presentable;
> you completely re-created my way of living. Please help
> me to remember the powerful work you've done in me.
> Amen.

STRONGHOLD

The Lord is good, a stronghold in a day of trouble; he protects those who take refuge in him.

—*Nahum 1:7 NRSV*

In order for God to protect us, we must run to him. God is good, and he promises to offer us safety in times of trouble. But the deal is we must go to him. We need to actively seek his help when trouble comes our way.

He does this so that we keep in mind the true source of strength. In the act of retreating to God, we make great advances against our enemy. In turning to the stronghold of God, we deal an incredible strike against everything meant to harm us. How can it harm us if it is what brings us closer to our Savior?

God, you are the true strength in my life. In times of weakness or danger, please call to me. I pray that I will hear your voice warning me to draw near to you. Thank you for using potentially harmful things as a way to bring me closer to you. Amen.

WORKING IN YOU

For God is working in you, giving you the desire and the power to do what pleases him.

—*Philippians 2:13 ESV*

God does not give us a list of demands and leave us to sort it out. He uses his power to help strengthen us. He is both the motivation and the destination for our spiritual lives.

We can make the mistake of thinking we must please him in order to experience closeness with him when, in fact, the inverse is what happens. When we draw close to him, he begins to produce in us the desire to do what pleases him.

Lord, I confess I sometimes avoid you because I'm afraid I'm not living how you want me to live. I pray you will help me realize that you are the source of the daily strength I need to live for you. Help me to come to you so you can grow healthy desires in me. Amen.

PEACE AND STRENGTH

> The Lord gives his people strength. The Lord blesses them with peace.
>
> —*Psalm 29:11 NLT*

Both strength and peace are things we often think of as being from within. *Inner strength* and *inner peace* are common phrases. While it's true that we perhaps *experience* those things internally, the source of them is both external and eternal. God gives us strength and blesses us with peace.

When we go through challenging times, we can be tempted to "dig deep" inside ourselves to find the strength to carry on. The truth is we should "reach out" to the source of that strength. If we feel we have nothing left, it's a sign that we are looking in the wrong place for peace or perseverance. The wonderful news is there is an endless supply, and God wants to bless us with both strength and peace.

God, thank you for giving me strength to face difficult challenges. And thank you for going even further, and for offering peace even in incredibly hard times. You are the source of all I need, and I am grateful. Amen.

Wisdom

With God are wisdom and might; he has counsel and understanding.

—Job 12:13 ESV

It's no accident that God is the supplier of everything we need in life, be it strength, peace, or wisdom. When the Creator set up the universe, he did it in a way that we would be naturally drawn to him at every turn.

God and wisdom are one and the same. As the Creator, God is innately correct, wise, and right. Because of this, when we are closely aligned with our heavenly Father, we are more likely to know which decisions we need to make. The act of decision-making becomes an act of worship as we rely on our relationship with God to lead the way.

God, I am glad your wisdom and understanding are so great. And I am thankful that you choose to use your power to help me live how you created me to live. Please guide me, and help me to end up where you desire me to be. Amen.

GROWING GOOD

Let us not become weary in doing good, for at the proper time we will reap a harvest if we do not give up.

—Galatians 6:9

Every time we make the decision to do good, we start a countdown until the inevitable moment when we ask, "Is it worth it?" If we're honest, there are plenty of days when it feels like doing good isn't everything it's cracked up to be. People don't notice, life is still hard, and sometimes it seems like more trouble than it's worth.

Don't give up. Each time you do good a seed is planted, and a life centered around Jesus causes those seeds to grow and grow. We usually don't know the result of every good deed, but we can trust that God does and that he is helping them grow to their fullest potential. The more seeds of good you plant in your life, the more likely it is for your life to become vibrant and full.

God, sometimes I grow tired of working to do what is right; it often feels like an unfair fight. Please help me to trust that you are working through me each time I choose to do what is right. Please bless me with a chance to see some of the fruit of following your way. Amen.

SPEAKING LIFE

"Don't be afraid," he said, "for you are very precious to God. Peace! Be encouraged! Be strong!" As he spoke these words to me, I suddenly felt stronger and said to him, "Please speak to me, my lord, for you have strengthened me."

—*Daniel 10:19 NLT*

God's words bring life. Whether they come through Scripture, through family or friends, or from some unexpected place, they have the power to invigorate us at our very core. When we actively search for what God is speaking to us, we will find a vitality we might otherwise miss.

We can also speak those words to others to bring them life. We may be hesitant to intrude with Scripture when speaking to our family or friends, but we should be courageous enough to speak life to them as well. God has gifted us with the wonderful power of his words, and he encourages us to share them freely.

God, thank you for speaking life into me. Your words have the power to heal, direct, and strengthen. Please help me to share timely wisdom from you in the lives of my children. Amen.

CHOSEN

But you are the ones chosen by God, chosen for the high calling of priestly work, chosen to be a holy people, God's instruments to do his work and speak out for him, to tell others of the night-and-day difference he made for you— from nothing to something, from rejected to accepted.

—*1 Peter 2:9–10 MSG*

God intentionally picked you. He didn't settle for you, and he didn't begrudgingly accept you; he chose you on purpose and for a purpose. You have been called into a role of great significance: you're an ambassador for Jesus Christ himself.

You're invited to tell anyone who will listen of the great change God has brought in you. You're encouraged to explain that such transformation is available to them as well. You have an endless supply of spiritual VIP passes to hand out. Let others know how important they are to God.

Father, thank you for choosing me. Thank you for making me different. Thank you for accepting me instead of rejecting me. Please give me opportunities to tell others about the life you invite them to live. Amen.

HOPE

Hope deferred makes the heart sick, but a dream fulfilled
is a tree of life.

—Proverbs 13:12 NLT

Don't put off hope. It's far too easy for our worries to shush
the dreaming voice that asks, "What if?" We then delay in pursuing our deepest desires under the guise of safety or prudence.
God invites us into adventure, and we reply with, "Someday."
Replacing hope with waiting leads to an unhealthy life.

True peace comes from seizing the invitation to live a
God-centered life. It almost always requires risk, but the
reward is the rich and satisfying life we were created to live.
Our children will not be shaped by "someday," but they will be
forever transformed by a father who dares to ask, "What if?"

God, I want to chase the dreams you've instilled in me.
Please help me to fulfill the purpose you have for me,
and to experience you by not waiting for what I hope will
someday happen. Thank you for desiring a life of fullness
for me. Amen.

LIVING OUT DEPENDENCE IN CHRIST

> But God chose what is foolish in the world to shame the wise; God chose what is weak in the world to shame the strong.
>
> —*1 Corinthians 1:27 ESV*

As a father, you'll need to showcase not strength but life-dependent weakness to the creator of the universe—God. Your children don't need a superman father who can fix all the unsolvable problems of the world; they need a committed, God-structured dad who lives his life on his knees in total submission to the Lord. They need to see the air you breathe (John 3:5–6), the bread you eat (6:48), the God who leads your life (15:5), and the obedience that comes by faith (8:31; 14:21, 23). Be intentional about living dependently and relying on the strength of God. These ideas are not contrasting in the Lord, but complementary to faithful parenting.

Heavenly Father, I come to you through the blood of the cross. Teach me to live my life in total dependence. May your Spirit align me with your Word, and may my heart's affection be stirred to your truth. Teach me to acknowledge my weaknesses so I can lean on your strength. Teach me to model dependence in you to the children you've blessed me with. Thank you that you're my strength, my rock, and my shield. Carry me today for your name sake's. Amen.

MODELING THE FATHER

> Husbands, love your wives, as Christ loved the church
> and gave himself up for her.
> —*Ephesians 5:25 ESV*

Masculinity, in our current society, has a vast array of meanings and implications. The necessity to biblically define and model it, regardless if you have sons or daughters, will shape and mold how your children grow up as godly men and women. Your sons will need a clear model of what it means to operate in servant headship (Ephesians 5:23), while your daughters will need a strong figure to emulate (v. 25) as they filter through the plethora of potential husbands throughout their adolescent life. In a day and age when the lines of sexual identity have blurred, the church must stand in the organic areas of life and practice biblical truths in order to faithfully press forward God's creative design. May you serve your family today with a trajectory of eternity in mind (Colossians 3:2).

Lord Jesus, I thank you for your cross. May your Spirit grant me the eyes and the heart to model, display, and imitate your grand design for fatherhood. Help me to paint a picture that will assist my children in seeing the beauty of your divine construction. May my service to my family be a resounding gong for your fame and a sweet aroma of your grace. Shape the minds and hearts of my children for your great name! Amen.

TEACH WITH TRAJECTORY

Set your minds on things that are above, not on things that are on earth.

—*Colossians 3:2 ESV*

With the instantaneous lures of our modern day, children (and adults) need to see the value of viewing life through the lens of trajectory. Model and train your children to see that the choices made today impact the pathways for tomorrow—and that life is not merely what our eyes can see, but what the Lord has promised (Psalm 119:154).

And yet, don't just look toward the future, but set their minds on eternity. The love, compassion, sacrifice, and service forged in these days for the sake of the gospel will have a ripple effect for eternity (Matthew 25:29–30). Let us teach our children that the people of God operate within the confines of life for the eternal glory of God.

Father God, I praise you for the salvation you grant to me through the Lord Jesus Christ. It is by his work that my eternal destiny has been forever changed. Help me to live my life with eternity in view. Remind me that my choices should be seasoned with a trajectory toward your eternal kingdom. Teach me to walk and guide my children in such a way as to set their gaze upon the Lord Jesus Christ. Amen.

CHARACTER

> I therefore, a prisoner for the Lord, urge you to walk in a manner worthy of the calling to which you have been called.
>
> —*Ephesians 4:1 ESV*

Walking with integrity and character is the hallmark of the Christian faith. Not that we can merit salvation. But the fruit of our salvation produces in us a coherence to the commandments of God (1 John 5:3). Our *call* to salvation, is not to an isolation away from God's decree, but rather to exemplify His character, quality, and virtue. The father's decree, then, is to lead his children not toward individualism, but rather to be a unique image bearer that reflects the grandeur, wonder, and glory of God (Romans 8:29; Ephesians 4:23–24; Colossians 3:10). Model character in your daily living and teach Christian virtue through the life, death, burial, and resurrection of Jesus Christ.

Father God, may your Spirit empower me through the blood of Christ to walk in a manner that is worthy of your call for called me. May the virtue and character that I reflect—first to my family and second to the world—be honoring to your name. Grant me the grace to confess when I fail and the compassion to extend when my children do likewise. May the life of my family be saturated by your grace and solidified by your goodness. Amen.

IDENTITY

> So Jesus said to them, "Truly, truly, I say to you, the Son can do nothing of his own accord, but only what he sees the Father doing. For whatever the Father does, that the Son does likewise."
>
> —*John 5:19 ESV*

Jesus, eternally generated by the Father, found his identity in him. Sons and daughters will grasp their value and worth by the display of love, grace, and affection that is afforded to them by their earthly fathers. As we look to Christ, "the founder and perfecter of our faith" (Hebrews 12:2), let the river of life flow from him onto your children with constant currency. This will form and establish a foundation for a Christ-centered identity that is firmly grounded in biblical truth. Identity, then, is grounded in the Creator, not creation (Romans 1:23). Usher your children to the foot of the cross that they may find their creative purpose in the one who grants purpose.

Lord Jesus, I thank you that your sacrificial love granted me access to be called a child of God. It is through my union with you that I am adopted into your family. Help me to find my value and worth in you. Help me to be a vessel through which my children will experience the beauty and majesty of your great love. May they truly find themselves when they root themselves into your life-giving love. Grant it to us for your name's sake. Amen.

A STOREHOUSE OF WEALTH

> I have stored up your word in my heart, that I might not sin against you.
>
> —*Psalm 119:11 ESV*

In an age of information, may the fountain of your lips be filled with the Word of God. May the truth of his Word flow from your mouth into the hearts of your children. How gracious would God be to allow your daily usage of words to be filled with his life-giving truths. And how equally amazing would he be to have your children be recipients of such treasures. Be intentional about having the Scriptures be the centralizing principle in the life of your family, and model a seriousness in handling the text. Saturate the minds of your children, remembering that Jesus said, "Apart from me you can do nothing" (John 15:5 ESV). Abide! Be a storehouse of beauty that oozes out truth that shapes the mind, heart, ears, and eyes of your children.

Lord Jesus, incline my heart to your ways and etch in my mouth your words. Draw my affections that they would be thrilled at the beauty of your truth. Stir in me a great adoration for the Scriptures that overflows into the hearts and minds of my children. Give them ready ears and fertile hearts to embrace the seeds of life. And guard our hearts from the evil one who seeks to kill and destroy. May your Spirit be ever present in pointing our eyes to you. I lift up these prayers for the glory of your name and the joy of your people. Amen.

GRATEFUL HEARTS PRODUCE A FIRM FOUNDATION

> Behold, children are a heritage from the LORD, the fruit of the womb a reward.
>
> —*Psalm 127:3 ESV*

Many men treat their cars with extra care and precise precision. The reason is because they understand the value and worth of the vehicle that they pour their time into. The Scriptures tell us that children are a blessing from the Lord. They embody the miracle of life that only God can provide while resembling his beauty, majesty, and grandeur in being made in his image. Take a moment to realize the value that God granted to you to steward and raise in accordance to His ways. Realize that God has granted you a partnership in bringing forth life, and that life has value, dignity, and worth. Shower your children with the love that flows from the Father through Christ Jesus.

Father God, I praise you for your unending love and mercy. It is by your grace that I'm granted the privilege to be called a child of God. My value and worth is intrinsically rooted in who I am in you. Lord Jesus, teach me to see through your eyes, and help me to cherish my children in a way that would bring you glory. May the love that is exemplified between me and my children be a picture of the gospel to the world. Thank you, Lord Jesus. Amen.

RESPECT

Hear, my son, your father's instruction, and forsake not your mother's teaching.

—*Proverbs 1:8 ESV*

Respect for authority is a trait learned by observing a father who lives it well. The value of community and the profit of parents is understood by the tutelage and guidance of a fatherly figure. Instill in your own demeanor a posture of respect that will permeate into your family. This will be a fountain of wisdom that your children will have at their disposal as they enter adolescence and beyond.

Lord Jesus, teach me humility that I may not overstep my bounds with you. Help me view others as you want me to see them. Amen.

REALITY OF SIN, SUPREMACY OF CHRIST

> Since therefore the children share in flesh and blood, he himself likewise partook of the same things, that through death he might destroy the one who has the power of death that is, the devil.
>
> —*Hebrews 2:14 ESV*

Children have an innate ability to sense the inaccuracy of ordinary life. Not only can they detect the inconsistencies of their parents, but they also often find in themselves the disparity that is rooted in their fallenness. As fathers, it is essential that we bring to the forefront the colossal shortcomings that surface, in order to magnify the supremacy of the cross.

The charge for fathers is not to sweep these blunders under the rug, but to teach our children that the cross of Christ cleanses us from all discrepancies. Though the sinfulness of our hearts can be heinous and, at times, unbearable, the magnitude of the cross conveys the message that the love of Christ stretches as far as the east is from the west (Psalm 103:12). Point your family toward the cross of Christ, and make your home at his feet.

Lord Jesus, forgive me for the times when I move away from the cross and assume that I have developed beyond its impact. Teach me to rest at the foot of your cross where salvation, restoration, and reconciliation is found. Teach me to model and teach my family to be saturated by the gospel. Grant us the grace to ground ourselves in your goodness, and to always be stirred by the glorious cross. Amen.

LOVE THE CHURCH

> By this we know that we love the children of God, when
> we love God and obey His commandments.
>
> —*1 John 5:2 ESV*

Model a great affinity toward the community of saints. This is sustained not by the self-generated will, but by a proper perspective of the biblical scope inflamed by the Holy Spirit. Being infused into the local assembly of saints will grant you the capacity to see life in God's larger scale. Service to the beloveds will create a disposition that will align you with God's redemptive work in using the church to bring forth restoration through Jesus Christ. We all long to be a part of something that is greater than ourselves. It is through "the church [that] the manifold wisdom of God might now be made known to the rulers and authorities in the heavenly places" (Ephesians 3:10).

> Lord Jesus, grant me an affection for your people that I may faithfully serve her for your name. Teach me to pour out myself for the good of your people and the joy of my heart. Amen.

TRANSPARENCY

If we confess our sins, he is faithful and just to forgive us
our sins and to cleanse us from all unrighteousness.

—*1 John 1:9 ESV*

Strength, from a biblical perspective, is not an innate or
self-generated sustenance; rather, it is grounded in a deep
dependency on the Lord (Psalm 18:2). Confession of sin
acknowledges the inability of the self and gravitates toward
the one true God that sustains, restores, and redeems.

As a father to your children and a husband to your wife, it
is imperative to demonstrate the humility of confession, first
to the Lord and second to your family, which will embody
a transparency that evokes the fruit of the Spirit (Galatians
5:22–23). Not only does it demonstrate the supremacy of
Christ in your life, but it also models a clear picture of gospel
living.

Lord Jesus, help me to not lean on my own righteousness.
Teach me a humility that will make much of you. Amen.

FOLLOW IN HIS FOOTSTEPS

> Whoever says he abides in Him ought to walk in the same way in which He walked.
>
> —*1 John 2:6 ESV*

As a young athlete, you may have watched the greatest basketball player in the world, Michael Jordan. After an intense and gripping game you may have even found yourself at the local court, shooting fadeaways and attempting acrobatic lay-ups with your tongue hanging out.

Likewise, we are not to become our own man per se; we are to mimic and imitate the God-man himself. He has come to show us what true humanity looks like, and by his Spirit we are to emulate him. As you walk through today, ask the Spirit to align your heart with his ways for his glory.

> Lord Jesus, grant me the favor to walk in your ways. Incline my heart and stir my affections to your truth. Amen.

LOVE YOUR CHILDREN, LOVE YOUR WIFE

Let marriage be held in honor among all, and let the marriage bed be undefiled, for God will judge the sexually immoral and adulterous.

—*Hebrews 13:4 ESV*

One of the greatest gifts that can be given to your children does not necessarily involve them directly, but it has profound implications for them in terms of security, assurance, and fortitude. Assurance is not necessarily a physical protection (though that is extremely important); it is a cultivation of atmosphere that brings forth life, vitality, and clout.

The strongest influence and shelter that a family can sustain is the well-being of a marriage that is grounded in biblical servitude and Christ-centered grace. Be intentional about loving your spouse and, in turn, your children. Your family will be the better for it!

Lord Jesus, teach me to love my wife like Christ loved the church. Humble me that my pride might not hinder my wife's growth. Guard my children and keep them by your hand. Amen.

HOLINESS

> Strive for peace with everyone, and for the holiness without which no one will see the Lord.
> —*Hebrews 12:14 ESV*

Autonomous identity is what society etches into the minds and hearts of its people. Uniqueness is pursued in order to standout, be distinct, and find ourselves in a class of our own. Yet what the biblical data conveys is a wholeness that is contingent upon linking oneself to the creator God, which brings forth a sanctity that sets us apart. Holiness, meaning to be set apart, is obtained through a divine union with him though the work and person of Jesus Christ. Our distinction from the world is our disposition, through the rebirth of Christ, to live counterculturally—and to embody the new nature that is grounded in the Spirit. Pursue holiness through the access of the Spirit for the glory and fame of his name.

Lord Jesus, thank you for your sacrificial love, which granted me salvation. Thank you for imputing in me a righteousness from the Lord. Transform my heart so that it will be sensitive to your truth. Amen.

GROW IN MATURITY

> So flee youthful passions and pursue righteousness, faith, love, and peace, along with those who call on the Lord from a pure heart.
>
> —*2 Timothy 2:22 ESV*

Biblical manhood is not saturated with shallow definitions of bench press markings, sexual mischievousness, or financial achievement. A godly man is defined by his Christlike attitude that is expressed in consistent sacrificial servitude for the good of the family and the joy of their hearts. Maturing men seek to grow in pouring themselves out for the development of their loved ones while continuously being poured into through the mercies of the gospel. Righteousness, genuine faith, selfless love, and gentle peace are characteristics that describe the mark of a godly man.

Lord Jesus, help me to grow into the man you have called me to be. Align my heart with your purposes. Grant me a steadfastness in your truth. Amen.

SUBMIT TO MENTORSHIP

Follow the pattern of the sound words that you have heard from me, in faith and love that are in Christ Jesus.

—*2 Timothy 1:13 ESV*

You can only lead as far as you are being led! The task of headship for husbands and fathers is not for the faint of heart. To properly take hold of the biblical mandate to shine forth the character of Christ—first to your family and second to the world—must be undergirded by the guidance of a biblically saturated individual who engages the blind spots of life. It is no small feat or fancy cliché that the biblical imagery consists of "iron sharpens iron, and one man sharpens another" (Proverbs 27:17 ESV).

Find solid men to surround yourself with. Growth occurs by being with people who will challenge you. Scripture says, "Whoever walks with the wise becomes wise, but the companion of fools will suffer harm" (Proverbs 13:20 ESV).

Lord Jesus, bring into my life a mentor who will point me toward you. Help me to trust and open myself to his critique. Bring forth growth and development that will honor your name. Amen.

Training for a Marathon

Rather train yourself for godliness.

—1 Timothy 4:7 ESV

"Rome wasn't built in a day."

"Olympic athletes don't shatter world records on their first day."

"Ball games are won in the off season."

"Preparation allows you to play fast."

All these sayings are marks, within athletic or warlike scenarios, that paint a picture of process. Though we are sold on the motto "quicker is better," the spiritual development of the heart takes time to marinate. The character of a man takes time to ripen. Don't take shortcuts in your sanctity, and don't despise the process. Buckle yourself in for the long haul, and embrace the fact that you are a work in progress.

Lord Jesus, grant me the patience to endure my own personal development. Give me zeal to pursue your goodness. Help me to keep my eyes on you, that I might not measure myself against anything else. Amen.

SEARCH THE INTENTIONS OF YOUR HEART

> The aim of our charge is love that issues from a pure heart and a good conscience and a sincere faith.
>
> —*1 Timothy 1:5 ESV*

Be sensitive to the motives of your heart, and keep watch on the intentions of your deeds. Saturate yourselves with the person of Christ, that his love might manifest itself in sacrificial deeds that will be "a fragrant offering and sacrifice to God" (Ephesians 5:2 ESV). Center your aim on the gospel, using the cross of Christ as the model to measure all your expressions of love.

> Lord Jesus, search the depths of my heart and reveal the severity of my sin. Pull me toward the cross that I may look at your goodness. May the sweetness of your love be the standard of my actions. Amen.

THANKFULNESS

But we ought always to give thanks to God for you, brothers beloved by the Lord, because God chose you as the first fruits to be saved, through sanctification by the Spirit and belief in the truth.

—*2 Thessalonians 2:13 ESV*

Gratitude postures the heart to not terminate one's thoughts, ambitions, and goals, but to see the gifts that have been given, ultimately, by God. In turn, we'll live in a manner that brings him praise. There is a tendency to be inwardly focused and, as a result, meditate upon all the things that we *don't* have. Thankfulness, on the contrary, centers its attention on the Blesser who has given to us beyond all comprehension. Eternal life. Bountiful meals. Amazing shelter. A beautiful family. Be thankful that in his providence you are blessed beyond comparison.

Lord Jesus, stir in me a heart of gratitude. Help me to be aware of your blessings in my life. Assist me in not forsaking your goodness, but seeing your faithfulness throughout my life. Amen.

HOLINESS THROUGH THE TRUE GOD

For God has not called us for impurity, but in holiness.
—*1 Thessalonians 4:7 ESV*

In an age of relativism, saturate your mind with a robust biblical view of the triune God of the universe. Do not settle for small glimpses of him, but be filled in awe with the mighty pictures that Scripture paints of our Creator. Meditate on the distinction between the creation and the Creator (Genesis 1:1). Marvel at the notions that he is everlasting and we are merely a mist within the wind (James 4:14). Ground yourself with the idea that the confines of time are not able to restrain him. Only then can we have a proper respect for holiness and begin to pursue it through the work of the cross.

Lord Jesus, grant me the desire to capture a clear understanding of you. May my thoughts of you be full of substance and richness. Amen.

SEPTEMBER

Marinate in the Word

Let the Word of Christ dwell in you richly, teaching and admonishing one another in all wisdom, singing psalms and hymns and spiritual songs, with thankfulness in your hearts to God.

—*Colossians 3:16 ESV*

We serve and lead out of the wealth (or lack thereof) that is stored up in our hearts. The value of life that permeates from our lives is intrinsically linked to the life that is within us. This life is not inherently ours; it's the breath of God that is blown into us through his Word. Therefore, saturate yourself with his breath and continue to root yourself in the life source of God through the living Word. Only then can you begin to serve in such a way as to have the eternal impact that God has designed for you. This was his intended purpose for you as an image bearer of God.

Lord Jesus, grant me a hunger and thirst for your Word that my heart would be a fountain that stores your truth. May the words that flow from my mouth be filled with life. Amen.

Uniting Love

And above all these put on love, which binds everything
together in perfect harmony.

—*Colossians 3:14 ESV*

As fathers, we tend to lean toward one of two extremes with
our children: overdisciplining or underdisciplining. Some
of us have a naturally tendency to overdiscipline because we
want to produce in our children a proper perspective and
an instinctive regard for the important things in life. Therefore, we seek to maintain order and discipline often at the
expense of being harsh (Ephesians 6:2). Others underdisci-
pline because we fall prey to laziness or don't want to deal with
our child's attitude. The biblical perspective gives hope in a
steadfastness that produces a sacrificial love grounded in biblical commandments. Embody a Christlikeness that expresses
itself in grace and truth (John 1:14).

Lord Jesus, may your Spirit bring forth unity that
expresses itself in love. May the impulse of my heart be
to personify your compassion, mercy, and grace. Amen.

ANXIETY STEALS

Do not be anxious about anything, but in everything by prayer and supplication with thanksgiving let your request be made known to God.

—*Philippians 4:6 ESV*

Today, the pressures of getting *there* (wherever *there* is) is the undergirding drive and influence that stimulates a posture of anxiety that steals the beauty of the *now*. What will best serve your spouse, children, and your own heart is the ability to strive toward God's purpose while simultaneously embracing your current season of life. Don't look ahead at the price of neglecting what the Lord has blessed you with now.

Whether you are in a season of diapers, car seats, and formula, or of teenage hormones, attitude, and drama, "make the best use of the time" (Ephesians 5:16 ESV) and disciple your family with a zeal for the Lord. Give thanks to the Lord for blessing you in your current season of life, and don't waste these learning opportunities by looking ahead to a season of life that you haven't even reached yet.

Lord Jesus, forgive me for not trusting you. Posture my heart in a fashion of hope that grounds itself in who you are. Grant me a proper view of you. Amen.

CHRIST-CENTERED AIM

> I press on toward the goal for the prize of the upward call
> of God in Christ Jesus.
>
> —*Philippians 3:14 ESV*

In the daily grind of life, it's imperative to see and understand the undergirding principles that drive the things we seek to do and accomplish. It's not enough to merely mule through the motions; we need to continuously evaluate the motives and intentions of our heart in order to clearly see the motivating factors that fuel our life. Without such evaluation, we will begin to place a weight upon our family, spouse, or career that they are not meant to carry. We will ask our loved ones to fulfill in us what only Christ Jesus was meant to fill. Therefore, we must fight valiantly to preach the gospel into our heart and keep center the person and work of Jesus Christ. Without such admonition, we are bound to crush the very people we love.

Lord Jesus, search the depths of my heart and incline my mind to your ways. May I meditate upon your precepts and find joy in your commands. Amen.

DISRUPTIVE PERVERSION

But sexual immorality and all impurity or covetousness must not even be named among you, as is proper among saints.

—*Ephesians 5:3 ESV*

The institution of marriage is meant to display the beauty and mystery of God's redeeming work in reconciling the church to himself (Ephesians 5:32). The nucleus of the family is a shadow of God's eternal inheritance fulfilled in the person of Christ (Ephesians 1:14). All these images are to be compounded in the kingdom of God.

Therefore, the perversion of sex is the expression of a deeply rooted bent toward the thwarting of God's divine design. Sexual perversion is not merely an outward aberration. It is, fundamentally, a treasonous act. Sexual immorality is the attempt of the evil one to destroy, thwart, and diminish God's redemptive picture (Romans 1:24–25). The health and vitality of your family points far beyond your own personal achievements, navigating and finding its fulfillment in the majesty of the triune God. Pour into your family for the sake of his name.

Lord Jesus, help me to see the world through your eyes—that the actions of my heart would point to your creative purpose and design, and that I would joyfully see the beauty of your design and express them for your fame. Amen.

LOVE IS A PERSON

God is love.

—1 John 4:8 ESV

Love is not merely an affection, a concept, or a devotion; rather, it finds its grounding in the person and work of Jesus Christ. Our society communicates the essence of love as an emotive principle that is gauged by the individual, but the biblical account forges a different reality. Love is unified with truth in the person of Jesus. Christ entered the tapestry of creation "full of grace and truth" (John 1:14 ESV). He is the standard to which we are to grasp and understand the power of love.

Immerse yourself in the person of Christ, and find yourself exemplifying the love that governs the universe. Suffuse yourself in the truth of the Scriptures, and find yourself permeating the divine love of the triune God. For the Lord himself said, "If anyone loves me, he will keep my Word, and my Father will love him, and we will come to him and make our home with him" (John 14:23 ESV).

Lord Jesus, forgive me for chasing concepts and principles. Holy Spirit, help me to chase after Christ, that I would grow in my love and affections toward him. Amen.

THE RIGHTEOUSNESS OF CHRIST

Filled with the fruit of righteousness that comes through Jesus Christ, to the glory and praise of God.

—Philippians 1:11 ESV

A caricature of the Christian faith is rooted in a moralistic approach to the law. Though the Lord's commandments are important to the faith, they are not the entry point to which union with Christ is obtained. The grounds on which the saints will stand before an infinitely holy God are cemented not in a meritorious righteousness that is harbored innately, but through a righteousness that is found in Christ.

When we come to grips with the fact that our right standing with God is dependent upon Christ's fulfillment of the law, we will begin to walk in humility, not only toward the creator God (though that is amazingly wonderful) but also toward those we encounter daily. Your righteousness is not your own.

Lord Jesus, help me to yearn for your righteousness, that the outflow of my heart would be the righteousness that brings you glory. Amen.

MANNER OF LIFE

Only let your manner of life be worthy of the gospel of Christ.

—Philippians 1:27 ESV

One's belief system governs the external expression of life. Verbal commitments are shallow, even meaningless, without a proper response in conduct, commitment, and propriety. In actuality, the common thread that is produced in one's exterior engagement communicates a definitive posture of the heart. The undergirding question, then, is, "What is informing one's belief system?" In order to properly establish a "manner of life [that is] worthy of the gospel of Christ" (Philippians 1:27 ESV), one must abide in his Word (John 15:4). "Manner of life" is not merely conduct from moment to moment, but a philosophy of living that is grounded in the gospel.

Lord Jesus, teach me to hunger for your Word, that the meditations of my heart would be saturated with your truth. Amen.

SUFFERING

For it has been granted to you that for the sake of Christ you should not only believe in him but also suffer for his sake.

—*Philippians 1:29 ESV*

The tendency of this age is to question the Lord's goodness in the midst of suffering. Yet, from a biblical standpoint, suffering is the means by which the Lord conforms us into the image of the Son (Romans 8:29). When "bad" things happen in our lives, may we not ask, "Why me?" but rather, "What are you teaching me?" If in Christ there is no condemnation (v. 1), then the suffering we face is not necessarily God's judgment. We can be assured that "for those who love God all things work together for good, for those who are called according to his purpose" (v. 28 ESV).

Lord Jesus, forgive me for pursuing my comfort over your glory. Teach me to walk in obedience, even if it means I must endure suffering. Help me to suffer well for your name. Amen.

THE POSTURE OF YOUR HEART

Do all things without grumbling or disputing.

—*Philippians 2:14 ESV*

As a believer of Jesus Christ, posture your heart in a manner that seeks to bring praise and honor to the Lord. As his child, put on his character and walk in his meekness. It should be your aim that in "whatever you do, work heartily, as for the Lord and not for men" (Colossians 3:23 ESV). Therefore, the intention of your heart is as important as the conduct of your behavior. Submit them both to his name.

Lord Jesus, incline my heart to your ways, that I may walk in contentment and serve in joy. May the posture of my heart be to see you glorified. Amen.

MORE OF HIM

That I may know him and the power of his resurrection, and may share his sufferings, becoming like him in his death.

—Philippians 3:10 ESV

Mimicking Jesus may not necessarily produce, from a worldly standpoint, the success that we are looking for. Yet reorienting our expectations and redefining advancement is necessary in seeing that the biblical definition of success is more about conformity to the image of Christ (Romans 8:29) and less about worldly recognition.

When we view the world through the gospel lens, we will find that trends do not dictate a faithful service to the Lord, but rather one's commitment to the biblical mandate of his disciples. In these scenarios, the Sunday school answer will never fail—Jesus!

Lord Jesus, teach me to see that you are my end goal. Sharpen my eyes to see that you are not a means to another end, but rather you are the end to my means. Amen.

COSTLY LOVE

> But God shows his love for us in that while we were still sinners, Christ died for us.
>
> —*Romans 5:8 ESV*

Love, service, and discipleship without cost do not resemble the biblical formation of gospel-saturated love. As the world continues to fight for convenience, may the saints of God embrace the sacrificial love that is personified through Jesus Christ.

The giving of yourself is posturing your heart in accordance with the Lord in order to convey the message of the gospel through deeds in service to others. In this way, you will mimic the creator God, who "so loved the world, that he gave his only Son, that whoever believes in him should not perish but have eternal life" (John 3:16 ESV).

Lord Jesus, forgive me when I serve you out of convenience. Remind me of how your call to discipleship is a call to death. Holy Spirit, help me see that Jesus is more valuable than my comfort. Amen.

ENDLESS SUPPLY

He who did not spare his own Son but gave him up for us all, how will he not also with him graciously give us all things?

—*Romans 8:32 ESV*

Discouragement, loneliness, and despair can find their way into our lives. The one thing we can rest assured in during those seasons of life is that our Lord is continuously faithful to his people. The creator God did not hesitate in giving his own Son on behalf of sinners in order to reconcile us back to himself.

How much more will he give to us in our time of need? He is an endless well of resources that brings forth life, vitality, and security. When the world strips us of our pride, hope, and assurance, he is the blanket that brings restoration to the soul. We have a heavenly Father who is good to his children.

Lord Jesus, forgive me when I doubt the sufficiency of your love. Your cross has displayed your love, and the resurrection has proclaimed your faithfulness. Teach me to trust that you hold me in your hand. Amen.

OUR DEBT OF LOVE

Owe no one anything, except to love each other, for the one who loves another has fulfilled the law.
—*Romans 13:8 ESV*

God demonstrated "his love for us in that while we were still sinners, Christ died for us" (Romans 5:8 ESV). This fact of divine love is a picture and a model to mimic, and it is to be payed forward, not for the merit of salvation but for the expression of gratitude. Service of love is in honor of the name that bought our salvation. Therefore, the Lord himself commissioned that we "let [our] light shine before others, so that they may see [our] good works and give glory to your Father who is in heaven" (Matthew 5:16).

Lord Jesus, I am in awe of your gift of salvation. Help me display your kindness. May the demonstration of your love draw people to the work of the Son by the power of the Spirit. Amen.

THE FUEL OF LOVE

We love because he first loved us.

—1 John 4:19 ESV

The extension of love in the Christian life finds its origin and fuel in the work and person of Jesus Christ. We love the poor because "he was rich, yet for [our] sake he became poor, so that [we] by his poverty might become rich" (2 Corinthians 8:9 ESV). We adopt because we "have received the Spirit of adoption as sons, by whom we cry, 'Abba! Father!'" (Romans 8:15 ESV). Our response in forgiveness is rooted in the fact that the call of Christ compels us to be "kind to one another, tenderhearted, forgiving one another, as God in Christ forgave you" (Ephesians 4:32 ESV). Christ is the fuel of love that empowers the soul!

Lord Jesus, grant me the power through your Spirit to extend the love with which you have loved me through the cross and resurrection. May your love shine forth from me to others today for your name's sake. Amen.

OUR PROVIDER

Abraham said, "God will provide for himself the lamb for a burnt offering, my son." So they went both of them together. … So Abraham called the name of that place, "The LORD will provide"; as it is said to this day, "On the mount of the Lord it shall be provided."

—*Genesis 22:8, 14 ESV*

Abraham's actions seem like those of of a mentally unstable father. God asked Abraham to do the unthinkable: to take his son and offer him up in sacrifice on Mt. Moriah. But something much deeper was going on in God's plan.

You see, God was also foreshadowing a greater event. Abraham put the wood for the sacrifice (v. 6) on his son and hiked up to the place on the third day (v. 4). The place? Moriah, which is only named one other time in the Bible (in 2 Chronicles 3:1), and it would be the place where King Solomon would build the temple one thousand years later. Moriah was also near the place of Calvary, where God would sacrifice his only Son, Jesus, two thousand years later. Same place, wood to be sacrificed on, and something about the third day. Sound familiar? The pain of a father's heart was felt by almighty God, who would offer up his own Son for our sin.

Our biggest tests are the opportunities for God's biggest provisions. His provision at that time was an unexpected lamb to sacrifice. His provision for us today begins with the Lamb of God, who died for us.

Father God, give me faith to know that in the times of my biggest tests as a father, you will always be there and provide me with everything I need. Amen.

PEACE

Laban said, "This heap is a witness between you and me today." Therefore he named it Galeed, and Mizpah, for he said, "The LORD watch between you and me, when we are out of one another's sight."

—Genesis 31:48–49 ESV

Laban and Jacob had a history. Jacob had asked to marry Laban's daughter, Rachel, but he was deceived by Laban and given her sister first, before he could marry the daughter he wanted. That was the start of a home filled with tension and jealousy. But God's blessing was on Jacob. Soon Jacob had twelve children. In his business he prospered in every way, and Laban became jealous. Distrust, resentment, and anger were starting to grow and infect their relationship.

Finally, they gathered stones—not to throw at each other, but to build a memorial. They couldn't even agree on its name. Jacob called this memorial Mizpah, or watchtower. Here they agreed to disagree, and to submit to God together. The fear of displeasing God became bigger than their disagreements with one another. They drew a line saying that their anger would go no further, and that they'd let the Lord watch between them. Finally, they celebrated with a feast and departed in peace.

Sometimes conflicts are unavoidable. We may each have our list of reasons for the conflict. But like Jacob and Laban, we need a "Mizpah moment" where we agree to disagree and don't allow the conflict to get any worse.

God, may I not sin against you in my disagreements. Help me learn where to draw the line and when to leave the problem in your hands. Amen.

THE GOD WHO ANSWERS

> God said to Jacob, "Arise, go up to Bethel and dwell there.
> Make an altar there to the God who appeared to you ..."
> So Jacob said to his household and to all who were with
> him, "... let us arise and go up to Bethel, so that I may
> make there an altar to the God who answers me in the
> day of my distress and has been with me wherever I have
> gone."
>
> —*Genesis 35:1–3 ESV*

A terrible thing had happened to Jacob's family. Jacob had just moved his family back to Canaan when the son of a local ruler took Jacob's daughter and raped her (Genesis 34:2). The local ruler, Hamor, tried to fix things by arranging for his son to marry Dinah, the woman he had defiled. But Jacob's sons responded with vengeance, murdering the men of the town and then plundering the village (Genesis 34:25–29). Jacob's family was in chaos, and he felt a target on his own life for the violence of his sons.

When life seems out of control, what's a father to do? God called Jacob back to Bethel. Bethel was thirty miles south, but more importantly, it was the very place where Jacob had met God thirty years earlier when he pledged that the Lord would be his God (Genesis 28:19). When we have drifted away from God, he calls us back to himself.

Father, thank you that you will never give up on me. Refresh me and give me a new encounter with yourself. You are the God who answers in the day of my distress. Amen.

COUNTING OUR BLESSINGS

"The blessings of your father are mighty beyond the blessings of my parents, up to the bounties of the everlasting hills. May they be on the head of Joseph, and on the brow of him who was set apart from his brothers."
—*Genesis 49:26 ESV*

Jacob had lived a long life filled with a few high points but also much conflict. He lost the love of his life as she birthed their final son, Benjamin. He lost his son, Joseph, through a scheme of his other jealous sons who sold Joseph into slavery and deceived their father that he had been killed. When Jacob was later reunited with Joseph in Egypt, he reflected on his life before Pharaoh, calling his 130 years "few and unpleasant" and not living up to his fathers before him (Genesis 47:9). But seventeen years later, he assessed his life differently, saying that God had indeed blessed him, even more than his own parents.

What changed? Jacob began to count the rich mercies of God in his life. It's easy to encounter adversity and think our lives are without meaning. We can focus on people who disappoint us, work that is difficult, or a life that seems unfulfilled. Or we can focus on the many ways God has blessed us.

God, today I choose to be thankful. Today I will put aside my complaints and take time to remember your goodness in my life. Thank you for your faithfulness, your protection, and the many ways you demonstrate that you love me. Amen.

GUIDANCE

> And he said, "My presence will go with you, and I will give you rest." And he said to him, "If your presence will not go with me, do not bring us up from here."
>
> —*Exodus 33:14–15 ESV*

Few would envy Moses and the task God called him to complete. Imagine leading millions of people for forty years through an uninhabited wilderness. Logistically, it took a miracle to provide food, water, and medical treatment for such a sizable and nomadic people. On top of this, the people were often filled with complaints and plots of rebellion. A three-day family road trip can be difficult enough. Imagine a forty-year trip!

Moses was wise enough to know what really mattered in life: to have God's presence in his life. God's presence includes his direction, protection, and blessing upon us and our families. Jesus told his disciples to abide in him, which meant to live in obedience and faithful relationship with him. God wants to be present with us. When God is present in our lives, there is rest and peace.

God, I thank you for the promise today that your presence will go with me and give me rest. May I faithfully follow you and enjoy your goodness in my life today. Amen.

COMPASSION, MERCY, AND GRACE

> Then the LORD passed in front of him and proclaimed: Yahweh—Yahweh is a compassionate and gracious God, slow to anger and rich in faithful love and truth, maintaining faithful love to a thousand generations, forgiving wrongdoing, rebellion, and sin. But He will not leave the guilty unpunished, bringing the consequences of the fathers' wrongdoing on the children and grandchildren to the third and fourth generation.
>
> —*Exodus 34:6–7 HCSB*

Moses had a special relationship with God. God spared his life at birth, called him, told him what to say, and did many miracles through him. But what Moses really wanted was to be shown the glory of the Lord (Genesis 34:18), to see God. This was impossible, because the glory of the Lord is too great for us to see (v. 20). So God arranged an encounter where Moses would be hidden in the cleft of a rock as God's glory passed by. As the Lord passed, the first words he used to describe himself were that he is compassionate, merciful, and gracious. Have you found this to be true in your own life?

Have you known the compassion and grace of God in your own family? While God has a righteous standard—and the consequences of sin can be felt for three or four generations—the grace of God can be felt for a thousand generations.

Thank you, Father, for your compassion and mercy on me and my family. May my children, grandchildren, and even my future generations know how good you are. Amen.

STRONG AND BRAVE

"Joshua, be strong and brave! You must lead these people so they can take the land that I promised their fathers I would give them. Be strong and brave. Be sure to obey all the teachings my servant Moses gave you. If you follow them exactly, you will be successful in everything you do."

—*Joshua 1:6–7 NCV*

Moses was dead, and Joshua was now being asked to do something that Moses was not asked to do. Yes, it took boldness and persistence for Moses to lead over six hundred thousand men (Numbers 2:23) plus the women, children, and uncounted Levites out of Egypt and travel through the Sinai Peninsula for forty years. Now the time had come to take the land that God originally promised to Abraham centuries earlier. Joshua would be entering a land filled with enemies and peril—no easy task. He was called to be strong, and that strength was based on two things: God's promise to be with him, and his own obedience in following God's commands (Joshua 1:5–6).

God is calling men to be strong today. Leadership is never easy. Like Joshua, our success depends on the same two things: God's promise to be with us, and our obedience to the God who calls us.

Thank you, Father, for the people you have brought into my life. You've called me today to be a godly influence. Remind me of your promises to be with me and never leave me. Strengthen me to obey you in all that you have commanded. Amen.

SUCCESS

"This Book of the Law shall not depart from your mouth, but you shall meditate in it day and night, that you may observe to do according to all that is written in it. For then you will make your way prosperous, and then you will have good success."

—*Joshua 1:8 NKJV*

Joshua followed a successful leader, Moses. He had served as Moses' assistant (v. 1), a role that had both military and religious responsibilities. But more important than being Moses' right-hand man, Joshua was commissioned by God as leader of Israel, and the Lord promised to be with him (v. 5).

When God calls, he empowers us. When God calls, he promises success. Here God gives a clear roadmap to our success in life. What was true for Joshua as he led the armies of Israel is true for us today. Success comes from meditating on God's powerful written Word day and night. Meditating means reflecting on the Bible so it becomes part of our thoughts and values. Success is directly linked to the place of God's Word in both our thoughts and our actions each day.

God, you know how I'm easily distracted with many things throughout the day. Give me a desire to spend time in your Word. Give me a desire to search the Bible, because in it I find the secret to success. Amen.

VICTORY

"One of you routs a thousand, because the LORD your God fights for you, just as he promised. So be very careful to love the LORD your God."

—*Joshua 23:10–11*

Joshua was now old and at the end of his life. He had fought many battles, and God gave Israel rest from their enemies. So Joshua called Israel together and recalled all their tremendous military success. He reminded them how the Lord had been fighting for them all along the way. Joshua also knew that life can get sloppy after a big win, that people can coast and forget to put God first. Now more than ever, they needed to be very careful to love the Lord God.

God is still fighting for us today. We face enemies of sin, including pride, lust, and greed. We have outside attacks on our health, our finances, and our business. We have family and loved ones who are being pressed by forces opposed to following God. But when God is fighting for us, amazing things happen. With God, we have the strength to rout a thousand enemies.

God, thank you for fighting for me and my family. May my eyes be on you today, to love you and obey everything you have asked me to do. And most of all, may I remember that the battle is yours and you never fail. Amen.

THE SIGHT OF VISION

So he answered, "Do not fear, for those who are with us are more than those who are with them." And Elisha prayed, and said, "LORD, I pray, open his eyes that he may see." Then the Lord opened the eyes of the young man, and he saw. And behold, the mountain was full of horses and chariots of fire all around Elisha.

—*2 Kings 6:16–17 NKJV*

Helen Keller was born without sight. She once said, "What is worse than being born without sight? Being born without vision!" Seeing and vision are not the same things. The prophet Elisha had vision but his servant did not. His servant could see only the Syrian king's army that surrounded Elisha at Dothan, ready to attack. It looked like Elisha and his servants were about to be destroyed. So Elisha prayed that his servant would "see" what God was doing. In God's hands they were completely safe.

We need vision to see what God is doing. Sometimes we are disappointed and discouraged. People let us down. Things don't turn out as we hoped. Resources appear slim. From our vantage point, there is little hope to cling to. But when God is at work, there is no reason to fear. Those with us are more than those who are with them.

God, give me your vision to see things your way. Open my eyes that I may see. Open my heart that I may love. Open my hands that I may help. Open my mind to understand the victories you have planned. Amen.

PRAISE

I will bless the LORD at all times; his praise shall continually be in my mouth. ... Oh, magnify the LORD with me, and let us exalt his name together!

—*Psalm 34:1–3 ESV*

For David, praise wasn't just a compliment to God. Instead, David's praise was an overflow of joy from a life made rich by God. As David wrote of God, his boasting was both continual and contagious (v. 3). He couldn't keep it to himself, wanting those around him to join him in praise.

Each of us is different in how we express our praise. Praise may be loud or quiet. Sometimes it is spontaneous and erupts unhindered, and other times it is a slow, steady crescendo of being in awe of God's presence. Praise may be expressed as a simple "thank you, God" that wells up within.

C. S. Lewis wrote that we praise what we enjoy and that our praise doesn't just express our joy but completes our enjoyment of God. John Ortberg contrasts true praise against selfish pleasure and hedonism. With selfish pleasure, we demand more and more to please us, but then the law of diminishing returns kicks in and what made us happy yesterday no longer does today. Our capacity for joy declines. But with praise of God, the more we magnify the Lord, the more our praise expands. Our capacity for joy increases.

God, hear the praise of my heart today. May my delight in you resonate within me throughout my day. Remind me that my deep joy is only found in knowing you. Amen.

DELIVERANCE

I sought the LORD, and he answered me and delivered me
from all my fears. Those who look to him are radiant, and
their faces shall never be ashamed. This poor man cried,
and the LORD heard him and saved him out of all his troubles. The angel of the LORD encamps around those who
fear him, and delivers them.

—*Psalm 34:4–7 ESV*

David sought the Lord. King Saul wanted to kill David,
so David ran to an enemy king, Abimelech, for protection
(1 Samuel 21). To survive, David acted like a madman and
Abimelech left him alone. Often in danger, David found deliverance in God. God delivered him from dreaded fears (v. 4)
and many troubles (v. 6). God gave David answers, made him
fearless, took away his shame, heard him, and saved him.
David's deliverance began with him seeking the Lord.

Too often men spend their lives seeking things and the
perfect circumstances. We start with "If I only had more …" or
"Someday life will be just right when things are …" We grew up
anticipating the next stage when life would be perfect: "when
I can drive," "when I get a job," "when I get a car," "when I get
married," "when I have children," "when I can retire," and on
it goes. But there is never enough stuff, never the perfect life.

However, when we seek the Lord, look for his direction,
listen to his voice, and rejoice in his answers, he offers a profound sense of joy.

Father God, may I be known as a man who seeks you. I
need you and your deliverance today. Amen.

Experience

> O taste and see that the LORD is good; how blessed is the man who takes refuge in Him! O fear the LORD, you His saints; for to those who fear Him there is no want.
>
> —*Psalm 34:8–9 NASB*

It takes time and practice to hear God; this is not for those of us in a hurry. Sometimes we encounter God the most when we are most desperate for him to come through and rescue us from trouble. I wish it wasn't that way, but God doesn't seem to mind, for he is always patient and full of lovingkindness. As we know God in the highs and lows of our everyday life, we discover just how good he is. For the writer of this psalm, the terror and dread of verse 4 that caused fear is replaced by the proper fear and reverence before God. The proper fear of God removes us from the fears of our daily life.

David wrote that the blessed person is the one who takes refuge in God (v. 8). Refuge is not found in the security of our investments, the authority of our job title, or even the devotion of our family and friends. Refuge is found in God. There is both joy and comfort when we step out and try God for ourselves. When we get a taste of the joy and goodness of God, both inner temptations and outer enemies lose their power against us. Those who taste, who drink deeply of God's presence and provision, will find their joy in him.

God, I'm ready to try something new. I'm ready to embark on a new adventure to see you work in my life. I want to experience more of you. In you there is no fear and no shortage. You are good. Amen.

PREPARING FOR BLESSING

Know that the LORD, he is God! It is he who made us, and
we are his; we are his people, and the sheep of his pasture.
—*Psalm 100:3 ESV*

How does a man become blessed by God? We want God's
blessing on our marriage, on our families, on our career, and
on every aspect of our lives. This verse holds a key for unlock-
ing the blessing of God.

To be blessed by God, we must grasp three core realities.
First, *know who God is*. Many misdirect their attention on
knowing themselves, but there is greater value in knowing who
God is. A. W. Tozer wrote that the most important thing about
any man is what he thinks about God. When we know God, we
find God alone is in charge; God is in sovereign control.

Second, *know who made us*. Back in 1859, Charles Dar-
win's *Origin of the Species* misled people to think there is no
creator, but that we are just an evolved accident. How different
to realize that God formed you and designed you in the image
of himself with a purpose to live out.

Third, *know who leads us*. Just like sheep, we are led by
a Good Shepherd who knows us, guides us, provides for us,
and protects us. This shepherd will one day lead us home to
heaven.

God, you know the times when I've struggled with doubt,
when I've wondered who I really am or even what I'm here
for. I thank you that I have a shepherd—a good one—who
has blessings planned for me as I follow your lead. Amen.

SATISFACTION / MARRIAGE

> Let your fountain be blessed, and rejoice in the wife of your youth, a lovely deer, a graceful doe. Let her breasts fill you at all times with delight; be intoxicated always in her love.
>
> —*Proverbs 5:18–19 ESV*

Marriage is a life-changing gift from God. A young couple promising their vows in a wedding ceremony is a beautiful thing. Both husband and wife are filled with hope, joy, and love. But over time it's easy to take the gift of marriage for granted.

These verses describe the personal love between a husband and wife. Sexual delight in marriage is one of life's great blessings given by God. As husbands, we are reminded of the great gift our wife is to us, and to be captivated—even intoxicated—by her love.

Proverbs 5 begins by describing the danger of being unfaithful. But when we get a taste of the good gifts of our generous Father, temptation outside marriage loses its power against us. Christian philosopher Dallas Willard has suggested that if we fail to attain a deeply satisfying life, sin becomes more attractive. But when we taste of God's goodness, temptation's power is reduced.

> Father, you are love and you designed me to love. I don't ever want to settle for the cheap substitutes the world tempts me with. Thank you for my wife. May I find my delight in her alone, and be satisfied by loving her. Amen.

OCTOBER

FEAR

"I, I am he who comforts you; who are you that you are afraid of man who dies, of the son of man who is made like grass, and have forgotten the LORD, YOUR MAKER, who stretched out the heavens and laid the foundations of the earth, and you fear continually all the day because of the wrath of the oppressor ..."

—*Isaiah 51:12–13 ESV*

Fear is a powerful force, and it can paralyze us from accomplishing the dreams God has for us. God allowed northern Israel to be defeated in 722 BC by the Assyrians for their unfaithfulness. In the south, Judah also stood in danger, as the king of Assyria threatened them also. But King Hezekiah of Judah took Isaiah's advice to pray to God, and Jerusalem was miraculously saved. God wanted his people to learn the lesson: the only way to conquer fear of man is to have a bigger fear—a healthy fear in God alone.

People who fear God need to fear nothing else. This fear of God includes a holy awe of who God is, a fear of disobeying him, and a fresh awareness of his power and plans for our lives. But when we fear people (v. 12), it demonstrates that we've forgotten God and his power (v. 13). John Calvin described fear as giving more power to the mortal man attacking you than to the power of God defending you.

Holy God, today I choose with your help to not fear others. Since you commanded me to not fear, I know you will also provide the power and resources I need to trust you. Today my heart is steadfast, trusting in you alone. Amen.

THE LORD'S PRAYER

"Give us this day our daily bread, and forgive us our debts, as we also have forgiven our debtors. And lead us not into temptation, but deliver us from evil."

—*Matthew 6:11–13 ESV*

Jesus taught his followers to pray for what is already on his Father's heart. When we pray this, we are agreeing with God, who wants his name kept holy, his kingdom to be established, and his will to be done on earth just like it is done in heaven. Prayer is an attitude of the heart that humbles itself before God and cries out, "I need you!"

Jesus tells us to pray for ourselves in three areas, which is what God wants for us. First, we ask our Father to give us what we need, because he is a generous giver and delights in giving his children good gifts. As we inventory all we have, we recognize that everything has come from him. Second, we ask our Father to forgive us, because he knows there are thoughts we've had, words we've said, unkind things we've done, and love we've withheld. He is a gracious forgiver. He wants us to confess them and be restored with him. Third, we ask our Father to deliver us from temptation because he knows what we face each day. He is a mighty deliverer who will always rescue us when we ask.

You are a good Father! Thank you for your thoughts about me and that you know what I need. Thank you for inviting me to come before you and pray with confidence for these things. As I come to you, you transform me and allow me to trust you more. Amen.

FAMILY WORSHIP

> Early the next morning they arose and worshiped before the LORD and then went back to their home at Ramah.
>
> —*1 Samuel 1:19*

Worship as a family is important to the Father. Early in the morning, at the beginning of the week, it should become one of the very first acts that the family does together. It will set the spiritual tone for the rest of the week.

Here are a few suggestions for fathers to pull this off weekly:

- Ensure that everyone gets plenty of rest the night before.
- Set out clothes for kids the night before.
- Wake up on time.
- Have breakfast together as a family.
- If your pastor has shared what will be discussed, read that text during breakfast.
- Leave home in time to arrive ten minutes early.
- Walk in as a family.

When we make worship a personal priority by being prepared, we will grow to anticipate the activity of God. When we live in this humble expectation, our kids will look forward to worship.

Lord, I confess, I have not taken worshiping you as seriously as I ought. Help me view worship in community with the same importance as you do, and to ensure that our family sees it as the priority for the week. Amen.

Visionary Prayer

I pray that the eyes of your heart may be enlightened in order that you may know the hope to which he has called you, the riches of his glorious inheritance in his holy people, and his incomparably great power for us who believe.

—*Ephesians 1:18–19*

Steve Jobs, the late cofounder of Apple, once said, "If you are working on something exciting that you really care about, you don't have to be pushed. The vision pulls you."*

Paul prayed that we'd have a God-shaped vision. He wanted us to see with our heart the hope, riches, and power God has for each one who believes. "Hope" expects God to fulfill what he promised. It doesn't live in limits, but instead lives in the realm of what God can do. "Riches" describes the believer's inheritance in Christ. All that Christ has is ours, and as we find promises in God's Word, we claim them in Christ.

But what good would it be to have wealth but be too weak to use it? So this God-shaped vision also includes "power"— the same power that rose Jesus from the dead. That power allows you to live with authority. Battles you face may try to intimidate, but greater is Jesus in you than anything in the world.

God, I need your vision to live with the hope, riches, and power you have for me. Pull me through today with this God-shaped vision. Amen.

---

* Steve Jobs, as cited by John C. Maxwell, *Put Your Dream to the Test: 10 Questions That Will Help You See It and Seize It* (Nashville: Thomas Nelson, 2009), 71.

RECREATED

> So then you are no longer strangers and aliens, but you are fellow citizens with the saints and members of the household of God, built on the foundation of the apostles and prophets, Christ Jesus himself being the cornerstone.
>
> —*Ephesians 2:19–20 ESV*

In Christ, everything has changed. Once Israel was God's only chosen nation, but now the people in Christ are. He has re-created us as fellow citizens. Once we were strangers to the things of God, but now we are members of God's family, adopted as full members of God's household. In the Old Testament days, non-Jews couldn't go into the temple area, but now we are being re-created as a holy temple to the Lord where his Spirit lives (v. 21).

What does this all mean? First, we look at ourselves differently. Habits, memories, fears, and past things need no longer control us, because we have been brought near to God. Second, we look at others differently. Judgment no longer comes pouring out of our mouths. We've been forgiven and are grateful. The blueprint has been written, and the Master Builder is following his plan in re-creating us according to new specs. The cornerstone marked the start of the foundation the builder would use so the building was square and true. In this new plan, Jesus Christ is the cornerstone, and all that is built will be true and according to God's plan.

Father, thank you for what you are creating in me. Thank you that I am no longer an outsider, but an insider in your family. Amen.

WALKING IN LOVE

Therefore be imitators of God, as beloved children. And walk in love, as Christ loved us and gave himself up for us, a fragrant offering and sacrifice to God.

—*Ephesians 5:1–2 ESV*

What an audacious statement. How could someone possibly imitate God? And how could one possibly ask us to be imitators of God? Doesn't the whole idea sound ridiculous?

The secret to this whole idea is found in the phrase "as beloved children." This is more than a kind expression. The original wording points to both the character and reason for that imitation. We are to be like God because we are his children. Can you think of some way you are like your dad? Maybe you have your dad's voice, his smile, his walk, his sense of humor, or his keen wit. He didn't have to teach you; as his son, you naturally resemble him in some way.

There are ways we'll never be like God, but we are to imitate him in one way: how we love. Jesus was both our example and the cause of this new ability. Because of what Jesus did, we have a new ability to love others around us. There's little room for complaining how hard it is to love another person because it is the love of Jesus—not our own—that we're giving.

Father, thank you for designing me to love like Jesus loves. It's now in my spiritual DNA. May your love leak out of me today, especially to those who have been hard for me to love. Thank you for making me your child. Maybe someday people will look at me and be drawn to you. Amen.

POWER

Be filled with the Spirit, addressing one another in psalms and hymns and spiritual songs, singing and making melody to the Lord with your heart, giving thanks always and for everything to God the Father in the name of our Lord Jesus Christ, submitting to one another out of reverence for Christ.

—*Ephesians 5:18–21 ESV*

When we became Christians, the Holy Spirit was given to us (1 Corinthians 12:13). Paul wrote to Christians who had the Spirit, but said they needed to be filled with that Spirit. He wasn't saying they needed more of the Spirit, but that the Spirit needed more of them. As we yield our will, our plans, and our self to God, the Holy Spirit can take control and lead us.

How do we know if we aren't filled? We may see conflict in our relationships, our prayer life may seem stale, we may be living a double life of tension between our old self and new life in Christ, or people around us may not be seeing the evidence of the Spirit in us (love, joy, peace, patience, kindness, goodness, faithfulness, gentleness, and self-control; Galatians 5:22–23). If any of this is true, we need to ask God to fill us with the Holy Spirit. Jesus reminded us that our heavenly Father will give the Holy Spirit to those who ask him (Luke 11:13).

Father God, I don't want just an experience; I desire you. Fill me with your Holy Spirit today. I don't want to live in my own strength alone; I need you. I want to love you with all my heart, soul, mind, and strength, and I want the Spirit of Christ to fill me completely. Amen.

God's Armor and Strength

Finally, be strong in the Lord and in the strength of his might. Put on the whole armor of God, that you may be able to stand against the schemes of the devil.

—*Ephesians 6:10–11 ESV*

At some point, we discover that life is more like a battleground than a playground. We encounter tests and tough times, and may even feel like we're under attack. As Paul wrote the words above, he was in prison in Rome and felt discouraged and isolated. He knew men needed to gain strength from the Lord.

Battle-time living forces us to be alert, strategic, and focused. We understand there are false ideas in our cultures that attack our values. We look within and know our old nature can rise up and resist the things of God. The Bible also reveals that there is a devil with schemes against men who follow God.

But God does not leave us defenseless in this battle. God gives us armor to wear: weapons of truth, righteousness, peace, faith, salvation, and God's Word (vv. 13–18). Martin Luther wrote "A Mighty Fortress is our God," including the words, "although this world with devils filled should threaten to undo us—we will not fear for God has willed his truth to triumph through us."

God has plans for your success. In Christ, you have a champion: the Lord, mighty in battle.

Lord, mighty in battle, show your strength in my life today. Protect those I love. Show me how to stand in your strength. Thank you that the enemies around me are no match for you, my Savior. Amen.

LIVING BY FAITH

And without faith it is impossible to please him, for whoever would draw near to God must believe that he exists
and that he rewards those who seek him.

—Hebrews 11:6 ESV

What is faith, and why is living by faith so difficult? Here we
see that the requirements of true faith are contrary to life in
our world. Faith is not blind. Faith is based on real evidence
that most people reject without testing—evidence that Jesus
resurrected from the dead and that there is a real God who
exists, created everything, and has demonstrated love to us.

Faith taps into God's story, which is more real than the
story of our natural world. God's story starts, "In the beginning, God" and ends with Jesus saying, "I am coming quickly,"
and is written in four acts. The first act is God's creation where
everything was good. The second act was the fall to sin and the
sentence of hard work, sorrow, and death. The third act began
immediately after the fall in the garden as God unfolded his
plan to redeem the people he created from their sin. The final
act, pictured in Revelation, includes God re-creating a new
heaven and earth and restoring all. To believe in God is to live
in his story, where he rewards those who seek him. Living by
faith is the only way we can please God.

God, thank you for your story. Life can wear me down,
and sometimes it seems like I'm stuck in the second act—
hard work, sorrow, and death. Remind me that your story
is at work. By your help, I will live by faith in you and your
story today. Amen.

OCTOBER 10

FAITH IN GOD'S PLAN

By faith Isaac blessed Jacob and Esau, even regarding things to come.

—*Hebrews 11:20 NASB*

Abraham's son Isaac had to live by faith throughout his life. The birth of Isaac's twin sons, Jacob and Esau, was no ordinary birth. In Genesis 25:23, the Lord said to their expectant mother, Rebekah, that two nations were in her womb and the older would serve the younger. Isaac loved Rebekah, but each favored a different one of the twins.

The verse above portrays the closing event of Isaac's life. As Isaac prepared to give the inheritance to the older, preferred Esau, Rebekah and Jacob intervened and gained the inheritance by deceit. When Isaac discovered that the "wrong son" gained the inheritance, he did not try to undo his action. By faith he stepped into God's plan of blessing even when it went against his own. Isaac realized there was a bigger story at work, and he determined to live by God's plan and not his own.

Each of us is called to live by faith. What does that look like in your life? Is there something God has asked you to do, even if it goes against your own plans and desires? Isaac lived "regarding things to come." And that life of faith made all the difference.

Father, help me to live by faith in you this week. I realize there are times when I only want to do what I want to do, and I can make my decisions based only on what I see and what benefits me. Thank you for calling me to live in your bigger story. Amen.

MENTORING

> Never forget your leaders, who first spoke to you the Word
> of God. Remember how they lived, and imitate their faith.
> —*Hebrews 13:7 PHILLIPS*

As men, we're never alone. We grow by observing the examples of others, and each of us needs someone to lead us. Hebrews 11 gives a long list of courageous heroes who have stood strong in the faith, and each generation has more faith-filled leaders for us to learn from. We observe how they live and how they show faith that is rock solid. We watch how they make decisions, how they love as husbands and fathers, how they pray, how they handle finances, and how they face conflict. We watch so we can follow and be stronger ourselves.

To stand strong, we also need someone to walk alongside us. We need a brother to pray with and share with as we grow together in faith. We're also part of the passing of the baton of faith to the next generation. That means we need to invest our lives and our faith in a younger man.

Father God, I thank you for the godly men in my life. May I remember their lives and imitate their faith. I pray that others see the same faith in me to follow. Amen.

WISDOM FROM ABOVE

But if any of you lacks wisdom, let him ask of God, who gives to all generously and without reproach, and it will be given to him.

—*James 1:5 NASB*

When Solomon began his reign as king in Israel, he prayed to God for one thing: wisdom (1 Kings 3). God was pleased that he didn't ask for long life, riches, or vengeance on his enemies. Solomon asked for the most important thing. So God rewarded him, giving him a discerning heart like no other. God then blessed Solomon with riches and honor in addition to the wisdom.

Each of us faces trials and challenges where our own human understanding is not enough. We don't see the answer. We don't have the resources. Maybe something unexpected has happened. Maybe our best plans didn't work out. Maybe there is a conflict with someone, and we don't see the way out. We need God's wisdom. The good news is that God tells us to ask for wisdom, and that he will give it if we ask. And God is not stingy but generous in giving us wisdom.

Father, thank you for your wisdom. You know the challenges I am facing right now. I need you to get me through this. I thank you that you are a generous Father, and I trust you now. Amen.

Steadfast

Let what you heard from the beginning abide in you. If what you heard from the beginning abides in you, then you too will abide in the Son and in the Father.

—*1 John 2:24 ESV*

If you have ever replaced a light fixture, you know you have to connect the black wires and white wires to each other. The hot wire supplies the power, and a neutral wire carries that current back. But the third wire is very important. Electricity is always looking for the shortest path back to the earth, so if there is a problem, the third wire—the grounding wire—provides a direct path back to the ground, preventing you from becoming that shortest path and suffering serious shock.

Some people live life without the ground wire attached. When the unexpected happens, we need to be grounded. John wrote that we need to abide in Christ. What was so clear to us when we were younger can become unclear and confusing. Remembering what we have learned and experienced in Jesus allows us to remain grounded and unshakeable when life gets stormy.

Father God, make me unshakeable. I remember a time when things seemed more clear. May Jesus be my anchor point, my grounding wire today. Amen.

FAMILY

See what kind of love the Father has given to us, that we should be called children of God; and so we are. The reason why the world does not know us is that it did not know him.

—*1 John 3:1 ESV*

Here is an amazing truth: In Christ we are part of God's family. Everyone is God's creation, but the Bible is clear that those who have received the Son are the ones who are called children of God (John 1:12). The first word, "see" or "behold," is a sharp command to pay attention because something marvelous is about to be said. The title is real, so John adds here "and so we are."

We are God's family. God hasn't just forgiven us; he has also given us himself. Martyn Lloyd-Jones said, "The Son of God became the Son of Man that we, the sons of men, might become the children of God."* And as children, we stand in a unique and certain position. We have a legal position defining our status as part of God's family. We are heirs, we have access to come boldly into our Father God's presence in prayer, and we can know His love every day.

Father God, I am amazed that you have made me your child. You have placed me in your family. You have forgiven me, and your thoughts of me are wonderful. I will live in the joy and honor of the family name today. Amen.

---

* Martyn Lloyd-Jones, *Life in Christ*, vol. 3, in *Children of God: Studies in 1 John* (Wheaton, IL: Crossway Books, 1993), 19.

FUTURE

Beloved, we are God's children now, and what we will be has not yet appeared; but we know that when he appears we shall be like him, because we shall see him as he is.

—1 John 3:2 ESV

There's a future event God's children look forward to: the return of Jesus. In 1 John 2:28 and 3:2, John uses two words to describe this: Jesus' "coming" and his "appearance." In the Roman Empire, when a ruler visited, there was great celebration and rejoicing. Here, we read of Jesus' appearance that we will see. Jesus said he will return when the Father decides, and when all peoples have heard (Matthew 24:14).

When Jesus returns, we will be changed. In Christ, we already have been changed to have a new nature, to be aware when we sin, and to have a desire to live for God. But when Jesus returns, the change will be complete because we are destined for glory. We will be like him because we will see him as he is, face-to-face.

Lord Jesus, I rejoice that you are coming again. I don't understand everything about that great event, but I take comfort that I am your child and you have a great future planned for me. Amen.

SHOWING GOD'S LOVE

> Little children, let us not love in word or talk but in deed and in truth.
> —*1 John 3:18 ESV*

Love, for a child of God, is not just a duty but a way of knowing who you are. The preacher Martyn Lloyd-Jones observed that in the New Testament, we are never called to do anything without first being reminded of who we are. And because of Christ, we love. We don't make ourselves Christians by showing love; we show that we are Christians by our love.

There may be some people who you don't like very much. Maybe they are negative, mean, pushy, lazy, thoughtless, insulting, or irritating. But this is different. Loving isn't based on our personality differences or whether or not we like the other person. Because God is love (1 John 4:8) and we are God's children, we love. And love is not an idea or a soft, sentimental feeling. Love must express itself. Who will you show God's love to today?

Father, you are love. You made me to love. May I live out your design in me today. Amen.

OVERCOMERS

Little children, you are from God and have overcome them, for he who is in you is greater than he who is in the world.

—*1 John 4:4 ESV*

At the end of the first century, John wrote to Christians who had much to fear. Christians lived a fragile existence that found few comforts in daily life, and they were persecuted by Jewish Zealots and then the Roman government, which often made Christians scapegoats for national problems. As well, false teachers twisted truths about Jesus and the Christian life. John wanted the Christians to know who they were (from God) and the power they had.

Overcoming is natural in the life of the believer. We overcome when we don't give up in our faith, when we refuse to live in fear, and when we continue to obey when others around us don't. We overcome when remember that the Jesus in us is greater than any force in the world. Victory is certain when we remain in Christ.

Lord Jesus, thank you that because of you I am an overcomer. You know my situation today. I claim this truth that you are greater than any force I face. In you my victory is certain. Amen.

SACRAMENTAL PEOPLE

Beloved, if God so loved us, we also ought to love one another.

—1 John 4:11 ESV

Love is one of those subjects that is easy to talk about but difficult to put into practice. It was said that twentieth-century theologian Karl Barth was asked what the greatest theological truth was, and he replied, "Jesus loves me this I know, for the Bible tells me so." On a cold, winter's day, your dog delights in curling up in front of the fire and soaking in the warmth. God's love is like that. It does no good to think about the concept of love; we have to soak it in and let its warmth penetrate us, so we can love others.

A sacrament is a means of grace, a channel of God's grace to us. Greg Ogden uses the term "sacramental people." We are to be God's sacraments to others, the channel by which they feel the warmth of his love. Once Jesus was asked what is the greatest commandment, and he responded to love God and our neighbor as ourselves. When he was asked about the neighbor, Jesus dialed up the discussion and gave the story of the Samaritan who showed love to the man attacked by thieves. Love gets down to the nitty-gritty details of reaching out to people's needs. And when we do that, we are a sacrament, a channel of God's love to others.

Father, I thank you that you are love and you designed me to love others. Show me who you want me to love today. May others see how loving you are based on my actions. Amen.

FEARLESS

There is no fear in love, but perfect love casts out fear. For fear has to do with punishment, and whoever fears has not been perfected in love.

—*1 John 4:18 ESV*

Did John say "perfect"? Can you ever imagine telling your spouse or close friend, "Yes, I'm perfect in the way I love"? John isn't writing that we are now perfect, but that we are being completed and developed as we reach for our intended goal as God designed us to be.

We've been designed to love. Before we knew Christ, we were designed to respond to someone in the same way they treated us. If someone pushed us, we'd push back a little harder. But the new design is quite an upgrade. The Christ in us does not respond like that; in fact, we show love to those who don't love us first.

This new love makes us fearless. We are fearless as we face death, and we are fearless as we face everyday life. The key to living without fear is to have a greater power that drives out fear. That greater power is the love of God. Consider the dad who would run into a burning house to rescue his child trapped in there. The love for that child is greater than the fear of that fire.

God's love makes us fearless.

Father, I thank you for your love. Remind me who I am. I don't need to live in fear because the God of the universe loves me. I no longer fear your judgment since you love me. Make me fearless today. Amen.

CONFIDENCE

And this is the confidence that we have toward him, that
if we ask anything according to his will he hears us.

—1 John 5:14 ESV

Men are expected to be confident. If we don't believe in ourselves, then who will? But, what does that confidence look like?
Fake it until you make it? Speak louder than the other guy?

There's a quiet confidence shown by the man of God. Blus-
ter and acting confident will only go so far. The apostle John
spoke of a different kind of confidence. This is confidence not
based on our performance, but in the one who sent his Son,
called us his children, and promised us eternal life. He has
called us to come into his presence boldly and to pray with
confidence.

When we pray confidently, we enter the the throne room
of heaven, the universe's largest arena. As men, we bring ourselves, and especially those who depend on us. Our families,
our friends, and our coworkers need us to be confident in
prayer. And when we pray—because we are his children—we
know that God hears us.

God, thank you for inviting me to come into your presence every day. Help me to pray bold prayers filled with
faith because people in my life need me. Thank you for
your promise that if I pray, you'll listen. Amen.

DREAMING AGAIN

When the LORD restored the fortunes of Zion, we were like those who dreamed.

—Psalm 126:1

Life has a way of stealing, crushing, and shrinking our dreams. There was a time when our dreams motivated us, stirred our hearts, and fueled passion in our souls. We were small, but our dreams were huge. The writer of Psalm 126 reminds us that it is never too late to dream again. After a generation of captivity in Babylon, God set his people free. They were free to return home, and they were free to dream again. Not just set free, but set free to dream.

A new season is a great opportunity to dream again, to rediscover old dreams and to ask God to give us new ones. When you consider God's faithfulness, his trustworthy character, and his call to adventure, asking him to give us new dreams seems a small thing for his big heart. Be courageous and invite God to give you a renewed ability to dream again.

God, you showed your faithfulness to your people, restoring them and giving them a new dream. In this new season in my life, I invite you do this incredible work in my heart. Let me dream again. Release your great big dreams into my life today. Amen.

LAUGHING AGAIN

Our mouths were filled with laughter, our tongues with songs of joy. Then it was said among the nations, "The LORD has done great things for them." The LORD has done great things for us, and we are filled with joy.

—Psalm 126:2–3

When was the last time you laughed at the ridiculous, scandalous, and radical love of God expressed in Jesus Christ? Consider for a few moments the impact of your experience. Laughter and joy are a witness to the work of God in our lives. The psalmist makes this point with incredible, exaggerating language. The very nations will declare the goodness of God when they see your expressed joy.

Dads, imagine the impact we could make on our kids if we began to discover the power of laughter and joy. If nations can be impacted by the joyful return of God's people to Jerusalem, surely our emotional energy can impact our home. Maybe if we can tap into joy and begin to laugh again—if we can open our mouths and express ourselves in worship—just maybe our sons and daughters might declare, "The Lord has done great things for them."

God, remind me today of your incredible saving work in my life. Let the power of your love overflow and overwhelm me. Fill my heart with joy and my mouth with praise, and help me to display my joy to my world. Amen.

FINDING HOPE AGAIN

Those who sow with tears will reap with songs of joy.
Those who go out weeping, carrying seed to sow, will
return with songs of joy, carrying sheaves with them.

—*Psalm 126:5–6*

God takes his time to accomplish his work. It's frustrating but true. As busy dads, we sometimes wish he would pick up the pace. Then we remember how carefully, intentionally, and graciously he is doing his transforming work in our lives, and we remember that his timing is perfect. He really understands his children.

The writer of Psalm 126 understood two things. He understood farming, and so he understood that timing is everything. Preparing, planting, caring, watching, and reaping—everything has a season. But the writer also understood that with God's deep transforming work, a spiritual miracle is needed. If a farmer sows tears, then it would stand to reason that he would reap tears. As we work in partnership with God's perfect timing, our reward is lasting change. We might sow in tears, but at harvest time the fruit of those tears will be revealed in powerful joy.

God, I wait on you to do your powerful transforming work in my heart. I long to grow again. I hope for a new season, one where lasting change takes place in my life. Give me patience to trust your timing, and give me commitment to your processes. Amen.

LETTING GOD'S LIGHT SHINE IN

The people who walked in darkness have seen a great light. For those who lived in a land of deep shadows— light! Sunbursts of light!

—*Isaiah 9:2 MSG*

Common sense is overrated. It's not bad; it's just overrated. God calls people to trust him deeply and radically, and even to follow him at the expense of common sense. Faith is our ability to trust God right now, today, in this moment. Hope is our ability to trust God for the future. That's hard.

Isaiah's message was one of incredible hope. Just a few chapters before the words above were unleashed, the prophet was explaining to God's people that they had chosen darkness as their path. Their rebellious hearts and their consistent disobedience had led them down a path of darkness. The prophet might say it this way: "I think you are lost."

That sounds a lot like our wives when we get lost on a road trip. It's hard to admit it, but those amazing ladies sitting beside us are usually right. But there is hope. In the car we call it Google Maps, and in our faith journey we call him Jesus. He comes to illuminate our lostness and to gently lead us back into his perfect plan. Common sense says, "Figure it out yourself." But Jesus says, "I am the light of the world" (John 8:12; 9:5).

God, let your light shine in my heart today. Illuminate my ways. Help me to trust you radically and fix my eyes on you for the future. Amen.

WANDERING SOUL

All of us, like sheep, have strayed away. We have left God's paths to follow our own. Yet the LORD laid on him the sins of us all.

—*Isaiah 53:6 NLT*

Something is broken inside of us, and as dads we know it. We watch our kids grow, and we struggle to keep them in line with the values and vision of our family. Truthfully though, we know something is broken from looking inside ourselves. We are prone to wander. We see it in our children, but more importantly we feel it in our own journey with Christ.

The prophet Isaiah described this predicament by using an image from the world of shepherding. He was speaking to the elders of God's people, known as the shepherds of the flock. He reminds them that they were no different from the people they had been called to shepherd.

What an amazing encouragement! If godly men who are called and empowered as leaders struggle to walk on God's path, I think we can stop beating ourselves up. Instead we can lean into truth. Here is one incredible theological truth: Jesus did not wander from the path. He was committed to his journey to the cross and to his substitutionary death. Now, no matter how many times we find ourselves wandering from God's path, we can, through Christ's power, find our way back to the flock and to a restored soul.

Thank you, Lord, for being my shepherd, for giving me all I need. Guide me along your paths day by day. Amen.

Following for Others

Be imitators of me, as I am of Christ.

—*1 Corinthians 11:1 ESV*

Have you ever been working out at home and had a strange sense that someone was watching you? Then you turn around to find your son there. And he isn't just watching you; he is copying you. What a moment! Your son wants to be just like you.

When Paul spoke the above words to his church family in Corinth, he was inviting them to intentionally watch and copy his life in Christ. He was learning to follow Jesus and was living openly for all to see so that they could follow.

Dads, live your faith out loud for your kids to see, to copy, to follow, and to become.

God, help me follow you in such a way that those who are following me see you and see Jesus. Amen.

IN MY PLACE

God made him who had no sin to be sin for us, so that in him we might become the righteousness of God.

—2 Corinthians 5:21

As young dads, we have to learn the art of the diaper change. If we don't, the mess in our child's diaper will undoubtedly end up on us. And while our child will be clean and shiny from the baby wipes, we will now be the messy one.

The apostle Paul uses a similar illustration to help his church understand the amazing work of Christ on our behalf. Jesus entered our messy lives and took all that mess onto himself. This transaction left us clean, pure, perfect, and holy. Christ makes us completely righteous before God, while he, on the cross, hangs in the darkness of our sin and shame.

Our mess becomes his mess. His perfect nature becomes our perfect nature.

What an amazing work.

God, thank you for Jesus, my Savior and my substitute. Thank you that he enters my messy story and takes all that is mine and makes it his and gives me all that is his. I'm in awe. Thank you for this incredible work. Amen.

GENEROUS WITH IDENTITY

> Even before he made the world, God loved us and chose
> us in Christ to be holy and without fault in his eyes. God
> decided in advance to adopt us into his own family by
> bringing us to himself through Jesus Christ. This is what
> he wanted to do, and it gave him great pleasure.
>
> —*Ephesians 1:4–5 NLT*

There is something about being a dad and being generous.
Did your dad bring you a gift when he got back from a road
trip? Do you bring your own children a gift after a trip away
from home? It is such an enjoyable thing!

In Ephesians 1:5, the apostle Paul expresses God's father
heart by explaining that he gave his children something that
"gave him great pleasure." As we receive gifts from our heavenly Father, he experiences pleasure in our receiving them.
Verse 4 explains that on this occasion, God's gift to us is the
gift of belonging. We are in his family. We are his children.

Generosity seems to work in two ways. We get to give
gifts to our children while we ourselves receive the pleasure of
being generous. Perhaps the most incredible gift we can give
our children is the gift of family.

> God, thank you for your generous heart. Help me to give
> my children the gift of belonging today. May I speak iden-
> tity over my little ones today—who they are to me and
> who they are to you. Amen.

I NEED MORE

He is so rich in kindness and grace that he purchased our freedom with the blood of his Son and forgave our sins.

—*Ephesians 1:7 NLT*

I think every dad wishes he had more to give. More money, more time, more talent, more heart, and more energy. We're all giving all we have, but the issue is capacity. There are limits to our output. What if there was another source to tap into? A limitless reservoir that could provide all we need for our calling as dads.

Ephesians 1:7 gives us a beautiful picture of God's capacity. He is so rich. He is rich in kindness and rich in grace. He has so much kindness and so much grace that he was able to purchase our forgiveness and redemption from the slave market of sin.

This verse also gives us an idea of the depths of resources available to us in our parenting. We might have a limit to our kindness and a very real limit to our grace, but our heavenly Father has an abundance and he is clearly willing to share it with us.

God, when I run out of capacity, when my ability to show kindness and grace to my family is extended to the limit, help me tap into your great big heart and abundant resources. Amen.

SAFE AND SECURE

And when you believed in Christ, he identified you as his own by giving you the Holy Spirit, whom he promised long ago. The Spirit is God's guarantee that he will give us the inheritance he promised and that he has purchased us to be his own people.

—*Ephesians 1:13–14 NLT*

Often in our journey as dads, we get a little lost. Those crazy moments when we're dropping the kids at basketball practice and we drive to the soccer fields. Oops! We also get lost in ourselves. We lose our sense of identity. We are so busy driving around, working, parenting, and husbanding. Along the way, we forget that we have a greater identity. Before we are a dad, a husband, or an employee—before we belong to the system, the rat race, or the coaching team—we belong to God.

We might feel lost, but we are not lost. He has placed inside of us a gift of security. His Holy Spirit has found his way into our heart and has taken up permanent residence. His job is to transform us, to equip us and unleash us, and to also just to remind us. The apostle Paul tells us that the Spirit is God's guarantee that he will give us the inheritance he promised. In simple terms, the Spirit is the down payment that secures us into the contract. We might lose our way and our sense of who we are along the way, but we cannot lose our place among the purchased people of God. We belong to him.

God, let your Spirit speak to my spirit today. Remind me of your place in my heart. Awaken my soul to your Holy Spirit and call me back to Jesus again. Amen.

IDENTITY AND CALLING

This letter is from Paul, chosen by the will of God to be an apostle of Christ Jesus. I have been sent out to tell others about the life he has promised through faith in Christ Jesus.
—2 Timothy 1:1 NLT

As dads, one of our greatest challenges is staying focused. There's always so much background noise! And we can find ourselves running from crisis to crisis or from activity to activity. Who are we, what has God called us for, and what is our role as a dad? If we can keep our eyes on the vision, then all the little things make more sense.

When the apostle Paul introduced himself in 2 Timothy, he wasn't speaking to the church but to himself. He was locked in a prison, awaiting his execution, missing his friends, and hurting from the pain of his ministry journey. Yet his words sound like a rallying call. He was rallying himself for one final push toward the finish line, no matter what was happening in the background. So he reminded himself of his identity and mission in Christ.

Who are you, and what are you called to be and do?

God, speak to me today. Speak to my identity, speak to my calling. Remind me of the big picture, and help me focus my heart on it. Amen.

NOVEMBER

BE REAL

I remember your genuine faith, for you share the faith that first filled your grandmother Lois and your mother, Eunice. And I know that same faith continues strong in you.

—2 Timothy 1:5 NLT

The little word *genuine* that the apostle Paul uses here is a term that means real, or without hypocrisy. Really, it means that there's an alignment between who you say you are and who you are. It's a challenge toward authenticity, toward being straight and unwavering. Amazing, awesome, and epic seem like little hills against the mountain of genuine faith. Genuine faith lived out in the context of family gives our kids hope, something to admire, and something to follow. Timothy learned this from his mother and grandmother—with the noticeable absence of a dad!

Do you love a challenge, and do your kids need you to be a mountain climber? Start climbing today!

God, help me straighten out the crooked ways within me. Make me one person, inside and out, and allow my kids to catch a glimpse of a genuine faith, a real relationship between Jesus and me. Amen.

BE PASSIONATE

This being so, I want to remind you to stir into flame the
strength and boldness that is in you, that entered into you
when I laid my hands upon your head and blessed you.

—2 Timothy 1:6 TLB

The apostle Paul adopted some young men into his leadership team and treated them as his family. One of these was
Timothy, who struggled with the demands of leadership. In 2
Timothy 1:6, we get a behind-the-scenes glimpse of a father
motivating a son to be all he can be. Paul used the metaphor
of a fire, one that is lit but barely, like a summer campfire the
next morning. Some of the wood has a glow. With a little
work, it could be a raging fire again. Paul told Timothy that it
was time to restoke the fires of his heart.

This was really a moment of reflection for the young pastor. He was being asked, "Is there still a love for Jesus in your
heart, like there once was?" Paul was saying, "I've seen passionate faith in you. It's time to let the fire burn again."

Dads, take some time to remember when you were passionate for Christ. Remember when he had captured your affections
and the good news about Jesus was everything to you, and when
the fire raged as your heart was set on Jesus Christ. Let's ask God
to help us rediscover a passionate faith.

God, thank you for kindling my heart with power, love,
and self-control. Now I ask you to ignite the fire, let the
fresh wind of your Spirit catch the flame, and let my heart
rage for you once more. Amen.

BE BRAVE

For God gave us a spirit not of fear but of power and love and self-control.

—*2 Timothy 1:7 ESV*

We have so many fear-filled moments as dads. Fear for our kids as their world changes and we gaze into the craziness of their futures, fear with our kids as we consider the responsibility of raising them, and fear from our kids as we're afraid they will reject us or forget us, or even hate us. Parenting is a fear-filled space. Acknowledge the fear, but don't let it stop your moving forward. Instead, recognize that God lives inside you and that the tools he has equipped you with—power, love, and self-control—are greater than fear. When fear fills your heart and your knees tremble, it's time to go forward anyway, remembering that God is with you and in you.

God, fill me with courage, risk taking, and adventure, and let your power, love, and self-control overcome my fears. Greater is he that is in me than he that is in the world. Amen.

BE LOYAL

Join with me in suffering, like a good soldier of Christ Jesus. No one serving as a soldier gets entangled in civilian affairs, but rather tries to please his commanding officer.

—2 Timothy 2:3–4

When the apostle Paul challenged his young spiritual son Timothy to be a military man, he was not asking him to take up arms, join the army, and learn how to fight. He was challenging him to be loyal. In those years, many of the soldiers fighting on behalf of the Roman Empire were mercenaries. In fact, whole legions were financed and supported to go to war on behalf of one nation or another. History tells of entire armies switching sides because they got a better cash deal.

As dads, leaders, and believers, we have already pledged our allegiance to King Jesus. This Scripture is encouraging us to remain loyal. Don't get distracted by what seems like a better deal. There is no better deal. You're already on the winning team. Victory is ours through Christ Jesus. Death is defeated, sin is under our feet, and glory awaits for those who please the commanding officer.

Don't get distracted. Bow your knee. Receive your orders. Be obedient.

King Jesus, I humble myself before your leadership. As my commander in chief, I give you your rightful place as Lord and King. Help me to remain loyal to you and your call. Amen.

BE UNDIVIDED

And athletes cannot win the prize unless they follow the rules.

—*2 Timothy 2:5 NLT*

The Rio Olympics were marred by allegations of cheating and drug abuse by the Russian Athletics Federation. When Russian athletes competed, they were greeted by taunts and boos from the crowd. Cheating in sports is not a new thing. From the earliest documented history of the Olympic Games, we can track the problem of athletes not competing according to the rules. Records show details of athletes caught using bribery, match fixing, and even food poisoning to gain an edge over their opponents.

The entrance to the ancient stadium in Greece was lined with golden statues of Zeus and other gods. These statues were placed there not as a tribute to the gods but to remind athletes not to cheat. If caught cheating, the athlete would have to take a public flogging followed by paying the hefty bill for one of these statues to be erected in their honor as a cheat. At the bottom of the statue their name would be immortalized, known forever as one who didn't compete according to the rules.

In a culture where getting ahead is culturally acceptable, to be an athlete—a true athlete—you must be a man of integrity, living in a state of being whole and undivided. In other words, you are the same person off the track as you are on it.

God, help me be undivided. Make me a man of integrity. Show me how I can grow, and equip me for the race of faith. Amen.

GET YOUR HANDS DIRTY

Hardworking farmers should be the first to enjoy the fruit
of their labor.
—*2 Timothy 2:6 NLT*

The apostle Paul loved to communicate by painting pictures
with words. As a spiritual dad to a young man learning to
become a pastor, he liked to make his teaching memorable
and meaningful. A life of faith and leadership is like being a
soldier, an athlete, and a farmer. A soldier's life is marked by a
quest for glory. An athlete is chasing the dream of gold, fame,
and honor. The farmer's journey, however, is different. There
is no honor and no glory in the field. There is just mud, sweat,
and tears. But after lots of hard work, in the right time and in
the right season, there is a harvest and the farmer gets to enjoy
it first.

Being a dad is messy business. We find ourselves with dirty
hands from a life of shaping and forming our kids. We are
working in the muck and yuck of little broken lives. There are
seasons when it is all sweat and tears. The hardworking farmer
knows that the harvest is coming, and he is close enough to
the action to be able to appreciate it first.

Don't run away from the hard work of being a dad. Roll
your sleeves up and get mucked in!

God, give me a farmer's heart. Help me understand what
season I am in and to trust you that the harvest is coming.
Amen.

GET READY

You should know this, Timothy, that in the last days there will be very difficult times.

—2 Timothy 3:1 NLT

When the apostle Paul wrote about difficult times in the last days, he was talking about the very times we find ourselves living in now. The word *difficult* comes from a term that was used to describe a wild animal on a rampage or a ship at sea during a dangerous storm. In other words, there will be people and circumstances that come against you. Following Jesus well involves navigating through a complex maze of relationships and circumstances, none of which are guaranteed with comfort or safety. These were important words from Paul to his true son in the faith. It was important that he equipped Timothy for the real world.

The same is true of our calling as dads. It's an adventure of action-packed challenges, ups and downs, real relationships with conflict and healing, and real circumstances—some good some bad. It is not only our job as dads to navigate these experiences, but it is also our calling to equip our kids to do the same.

Paul was writing from a dungeon prison in Rome, awaiting his execution, alone and struggling and missing Timothy. This is a good word to us as dads. Let us use our life experiences to prepare and equip our children for theirs.

Heavenly Father, give me the wisdom to see opportunities when my journey can equip my kids for theirs. Give me courage to face the storms of life and to teach my family how to trust you in the midst of them. Amen.

Be Focused

For people will love only themselves and their money; they
will be proud and boastful, sneering at God, disobedient
to their parents, ungrateful to them, and thoroughly bad.

—*2 Timothy 3:2 TLB*

Our kids are no different than we are. It figures, given that
we were so heavily involved in the process that caused their
arrival into our world. We can easily get frustrated at their
behavior, their attitude, and their dysfunction, but the reality
is they're made of the same stuff that we are.

The apostle Paul is painting a picture of a generation coming along behind us with crumby relationships with their
parents, an unholy love of stuff, and a selfishness that goes
right to the core. Sometimes we gaze into the lives of the next
generation without realizing the role we play in shaping and
creating those who are coming along after us.

This is why we need a holy focus. Our lives, our values,
and our ethos—in other words, what matters to us—will be
reflected deeply in the little ones following at our heels. If we
have an ungodly love of stuff, guess what, our kids will too. If
we treat people with a lack of respect, good chance junior will
as well. It's time for us as dads to focus. Our lives matter, not
just here and now, but in the shaping of the lives to come after
us. Dads, the future starts here and now.

God, help me to know who I am and who I'm becoming,
and help me show my children what is truly important.
Give me a holy focus. Amen.

Keep Going

> But as for you, continue in what you have learned and
> have firmly believed, knowing from whom you learned it.
> —*2 Timothy 3:14 ESV*

When it comes to being a dad, you're smashing it out of the park! All the time you've invested in your children, all of the hard work and provision for their needs, and all the time spent on your knees praying, weeping, and interceding for your little ones. Be encouraged today. You're doing a great work.

Being a dad feels like a boxing match sometimes. But whatever you do, don't give up.

Young Timothy, a pastor and leader in a New Testament church, wanted to quit. His calling was a tough one. But these words of wisdom were given to him from his spiritual father: "You know who you are. You know what you are about, you know what I am about. Now take a deep breath and let's get back into the fight."

You know who you are. You have been called by God to raise these kids, and you know what you are about. So refocus on your values and remember what is important. Get back in the fight today.

> God, speak to my identity today and use that to call me back into the game. Help me keep going. I trust you. Lead me. Amen.

THE WORD

There's nothing like the written Word of God for showing
you the way to salvation through faith in Christ Jesus.
—*2 Timothy 3:16 MSG*

There aren't many dads who feel adequately equipped for
their calling. We are growing, we are learning, and we are
being transformed, but truthfully we still feel the weight of
parenting, and it is heavy! It's a serious business, operating in a
dynamic environment and shaping little lives, who, as it turns
out, also have their own ideas about how things should go.

In the middle of all the changes, the ongoing transforma-
tion, the chaos of relationships, and the growing pains of life,
Paul reminds young Timothy of two things that never change:
God's Word and his gift of salvation through Jesus Christ.
Whatever your journey is throwing at you, learn to hold on
tight to these two immovable objects.

Allow God's Word to be your daily guide. Let it shape you
and strengthen you for your calling to fatherhood. Hold fast
to the amazing gift of your salvation. You are no longer your
own, but your life is hidden with Christ. You are secure in
him. No matter what comes your way today, choose to listen
to his Word and cling to the one who is holding tight to you.

God, let your holy Word guide my day, equipping me to
be a great and godly dad, because of Christ Jesus. Amen.

THE MAIN THING

> Preach the word of God. Be prepared, whether the time is favorable or not. Patiently correct, rebuke, and encourage your people with good teaching.
>
> —*2 Timothy 4:2 NLT*

Every family is telling a story. As they live their lives, manage their resources, and leave their relational footprint in the community, they're all making a noise—leaving a mark. Your family is no different. What story are you are telling your world?

In the verse above, Paul was teaching Timothy about the importance of connecting our story to God's story, and letting the noise we make be the noise God is making. This young pastor was being encouraged to keep the main thing the main thing. He was being encouraged to be open and ready to be used by God. Finally, he was being reminded to take his learning and use it to build up those around him.

How can you connect God's Word to your story today? How can God use you to see his story extended into your world? How can you take his Word and use it to encourage your family, to build them up and connect them to God's story?

> God, make me a man of your Word. When I read it, let it read me. Make your Word the living Word for me, that I can learn your ways and help others discover them. Amen.

DON'T FOLLOW THE CROWD

> There will come a time when people will not tolerate sound teaching. They will collect teachers who say what they want to hear because they are self-centered. They will turn their back on the truth and turn to myths. But you must keep control of yourself in all circumstances.
>
> —*2 Timothy 4:3–4 CEB*

As dads, we love to see our kids stand out. We get so excited when they score a goal in soccer, get an assist in hockey, or master the back walkover in gymnastics. We love to see our kids shine bright and are thrilled when they step out of the ordinary into the extraordinary. In short, we love it when our kids go against the flow. Maybe this is something we can learn as dads.

The apostle Paul was forecasting a time in the future when his young son Timothy would be under serious pressure to conform to the overwhelming flow of his culture. The pressure to run with the pack would be so great, and the bright light of Timothy's calling would be extinguished.

Just like a good coach in the locker room, Paul looks his quarterback in the eye and inspires him to get out onto the field and get the win. Timothy is challenged to get his helmet on and get to work. It's his time to shine. What a great word to us dads. The pressure is on and the culture is squeezing, but we were made for so much more. You were made for so much more.

Father, thank you for making me unique, special, and specific in my calling. Help me to shine for you today. Amen.

LET'S GET THE JOB DONE

Keep the Message alive. Do a thorough job as God's servant.

—*2 Timothy 4:5 MSG*

Dads love to be practical. Whether it's teaching our kids to shovel snow or wash the car, we love to see our team mobilized, active, and participating in the practical realities of life in the family. As Jesus followers, we are called to do the same. When the apostle Paul wrote to his son Timothy encouraging him to keep the message alive, he was telling him it's time to get practical. He wasn't talking about preaching; we know that because just a couple of verses previously, he instructed the young pastor to "preach the word" (v. 2 NLT).

No, in this particular Scripture we're being challenged as believers to make sure our message has hands and feet. Just as Jesus came to serve and demonstrate the good news, we are being asked to do the same. What an amazing opportunity to teach our kids about the practical realities of life in the family! So today look for practical, tangible ways to express the message that we proclaim. Show your children that we're not just a people with a book; we are a people with a mission! Let's get the job done!

> God, you are awesome. Thank you that we don't all need to be preachers. Show me practical and helpful ways today that I can lovingly demonstrate the kingdom of God to my world. Amen.

Eyes on the Prize

> I have fought the good fight, I have finished the race, I have kept the faith. Now there is in store for me the crown of righteousness, which the Lord, the righteous Judge, will award to me on that day—and not only to me, but also to all who have longed for his appearing.
>
> —*2 Timothy 4:7–8*

There probably isn't a more manly verse in Scripture than 2 Timothy 4:7–8. The apostle Paul considers his life to have been a wrestling match. There are many days like that for dads too. Some days there is actual wrestling, when our little ones jump on us from behind the sofa and strong-arm us to the floor. Some days the wrestling is on a deep, spiritual, and transformational level. It is rough, gritty, and dirty. But we were made to be in the fight.

Our journey is also likened to a long-distance race. Perhaps you're a distance runner and so you know well how to strategize, organize your energy, and dig deep for that inner resolve to press on to the finish line. Listen up, dads, we are fitter and stronger than we realize. We were made for the fight, and we were designed for the race.

The key to being successful is keeping your eye on the prize and your ears attuned to the coach. The crown of righteousness awaits, and your coach, King Jesus, is cheering you on, shouting instructions and sharing his experience. Don't stop fighting and don't stop running. Your kids will thank you in eternity.

King Jesus, fill me with courage to fight the good fight, and energize my soul to run hard today. Help me fix my eyes on the prize. Amen.

BROTHERHOOD

> But the Lord stood at my side and gave me strength, so
> that through me the message might be fully proclaimed.
>
> —*2 Timothy 4:17*

In ancient warfare, there was nothing more important than the man who stood at your side. When the Roman troops prepared to defend themselves against the arrows flying through the air, they formed a tight wall and each soldier's shield covered the man to his right. You were completely dependent upon the man on your left side; he was your shield and defender.

Dads, it's time to get some good men around us. This fight of faith is too big, too dangerous, and too scary to go alone into battle. Yes, we want the Lord at our side, but part of how he designed discipleship is that we stand side by side with our brothers. They take care of us and we take care of them. We were not made to do this alone.

Who is standing at your side, covering you with his shield, fighting for you, encouraging you, and covering your back? If you know, then praise God for that man or those men. If you don't know who that is, it's time to ask God to bring these men into your life.

God, help me to reach out to other dads today. I want to stand side by side with other men who are fighting the good fight of faith. Connect me to men of courage, honor, and integrity. Amen.

Everything You Need

The Lord be with your spirit. Grace be with you all.
—*2 Timothy 4:22*

Here goes another crazy day in the life of dad. Driving, working, driving more, homework, family time, church, and sports. Let's be real for a moment. It's a lot. It's nonstop. It's hard. It's a wrestling match. It's a long-distance race. Being a dad really is a special calling.

The apostle Paul, as he signed off from a life of ministry, had one final word for his young son spiritual Timothy. This rookie pastor, overwhelmed by his calling, his weakness, and his limitations, must have been taking a deep breath as the aging apostle handed him the leadership of the gospel movement. In the last sentence of his final letter, Paul tells Timothy that everything he needs for all that's ahead is found in two things: God's presence and God's grace.

Dads, let's learn to lean in to these important things today. God is with us, and his grace is for us. Our resources are limited, but his are not. Our emotional capacity is small and our ability to fight temptation and sin is little, but his grace is great. It is strong. It is enough.

Your challenge today is to remind yourself of the abiding, unrelenting presence of Jesus and to accept his grace into your life.

God, help me to take a deep breath. Instead of being stressed and overwhelmed, may I realize that you are with me, you are in me, and your grace is over me. Amen.

THE AMAZING NEWS

"The time has come," he said. "The kingdom of God has come near. Repent and believe the good news!"

—*Mark 1:15*

God is near. Really near. He's just a decision away.

Did your children ever color on the walls, but when it came time for them to clean it off they just weren't strong enough to get the job done?

With tears in their eyes, they said, "Daddy, help."

Repentance is a beautiful gift. It's the simple, Spirit-led moment of realizing we don't have the capacity to wash the walls of our lives. Then, by God's amazing grace, we simply turn around, and when we do, we find that God is near. The King and his kingdom are at hand. Our Daddy help has arrived.

God, I can't believe you're so close. I'm sorry for always trying to do everything in my own strength. Forgive me, and let your kingdom power come into my life. Amen.

New Things

> As he walked along, he saw Levi son of Alphaeus sitting at the tax collector's booth. "Follow me," Jesus told him, and Levi got up and followed him.
>
> —*Mark 2:14*

Jesus called Levi to be a disciple, even though nobody liked, trusted, or communed with tax collectors, such as Levi. It's pretty amazing that someone so despised would be so welcomed into a religious community.

There's a deeper story here though. Levi is identified as the son of Alphaeus. In all likelihood, Levi was a tax collector because that was the family business. Levi was who he was because his father was who he was. Then Jesus entered his story, called this publican, and invited him into a different story. Levi accepted and was never again identified as the son of Alphaeus. This is incredibly freeing news, but it's also deeply challenging.

First, we dads don't need to be defined by who our fathers were or how they raised us. Second, we must face the reality of our lives and the impact they have on our children. We desperately need Jesus to call us into a new story and to equip us to raise our kids to find their place in his story too.

> Lord Jesus, thank you for your beautiful call to follow you. I want to live in your story today. Thank you that I am not defined by my past and that your call is a call into new things. Amen.

WELCOME TO THE FAMILY

"Whoever does God's will is my brother and sister and mother."

—*Mark 3:35*

Every family has issues, including Jesus'. Ponder that for a moment and maybe even quietly enjoy the deep encouragement that this simple thought from Scripture gives us. Jesus, the Son of God, had a dysfunctional family. Not everything was Instagram perfect.

Jesus had been busy in his ministry, training his disciples, teaching about his kingdom, and healing the sick. Crowds were following him, and everyone was getting excited. Well, everyone except for Jesus' own family. Their response was pretty shocking: "When his family heard about this, they went to take charge of him, for they said, 'He is out of his mind'" (Mark 3:21). After the dust had settled, Jesus explained to his followers that in his movement—his emerging kingdom community—family and belonging were being redefined. To be in Jesus' family, the priority must be to discover and do the will of God.

As dads, it's critical that we remember how family works in the kingdom. We need to ensure we're helping our children to first discover and second to do the will of God. Sometimes this might mean setting our plans, our leadership, and our understanding out of the way.

Lord, thank you for my family. They are a gift, and I want to honor that. Help me, as a dad, to passionately pursue your will, and give me the courage to help my kids to the same. Amen.

JESUS, MESSIAH

"Why are you so afraid? Do you still have no faith?"

—Mark 4:40

The people of Israel had a love-hate relationship with water. They had been delivered through the Red Sea during their Exodus, but their fear of the depths was still hanging over from Noah's flood. As they waited for their promised Messiah to arrive, a man named Isaiah foretold of his coming and his relationship to water: "When you pass through the waters, I will be with you; and when you pass through the rivers, they will not sweep over you" (Isaiah 43:2), and "Was my arm too short to deliver you? Do I lack the strength to rescue you? By a mere rebuke I dry up the sea" (50:2).

When Jesus was in the back of the boat after calming the storm and rebuking the disciples, he was really taking them back to Isaiah's promises about their deliverer. He was essentially saying, "Do you still not get it? I am the Promised One, and the Promised One can take care of a little storm on the sea." The disciples needed to connect the promises in the Word to the Promised One who was the Word.

Dads, let's take Jesus at his word. He is the one who his people waited for. He is the Messiah. The Promised One. We need not fear any storm. We may pass through the waters, and he will be with us.

Lord God, thank you for sending your Messiah, King Jesus. Take my fears from the storms in my life and make your redeeming presence real to me today. Amen.

STORYTELLING

Jesus did not let him, but said, "Go home to your own people and tell them how much the Lord has done for you, and how he has had mercy on you."

—Mark 5:19

As dads, one of our primary roles is being a storyteller. Our kids love to hear stories about their mom and dad—our childhood adventures, family legends, and tales of romance and tragedy. Storytelling has always been the primary vehicle of transferring faith from one generation to the next. But in our times it has become a lost art. Too often we parents are relying on someone else to help our kids connect their lives to the good news about Jesus. This is actually a movement away from the very plan God showed his people in Scripture. The psalmist explains, "We will tell the next generation the praiseworthy deeds of the Lord, about his power and his mighty wonders" (Psalm 78:4 NLT). It is our responsibility to tell stories of faith to our kids.

You don't have to be Bible school graduate or an ordained minister. You just need to discover your own story again. Jesus put it this way: "Go home to your own people and tell them how much the Lord has done for you" (Mark 5:19). Take some time today to tell your kids about some of the amazing things that God has done in your life.

Lord, you are amazing. Thank you for the many ways you have changed my life. Give me a renewed passion for telling stories to my kids—stories of hope, stories of provision, and stories of mission. Amen.

SENT

> Calling the Twelve to him, he began to send them out two by two and gave them authority over impure spirits.
>
> —*Mark 6:7*

What a momentous occasion for these rag-tag teenage Jesus followers. Most of them were blue-collar workers, semiskilled in religious studies, and marred by negative cultural legacy. They were from Galilee, second-class citizens at best. Completely and utterly unqualified for the task ahead of them. Inexperienced, uneducated, and immature.

The amazing thing about the generosity of God is that he doesn't just invite us to join him in his work; he also generously supplies all we need to live on a mission with him. For the disciples, he practically supplied teammates to journey with, to pray with, and to support and care for. He also spiritually provided the ability to get the job done. A certain set of tools are needed for kingdom building, and the King generously supplies them.

You have a massive calling on your life. Your kids remind you of it every day when they shout, "Dad!" Remember that you are inexperienced, you are a work in progress, and you are completely unqualified. The great news is that when the King calls, the King supplies. All you need today can be found in him. So ask God to show you his generosity today. You are called, and so you will be equipped.

> Lord, replace my doubt, my fear, and my feelings of inadequacy with a deep sense of call, a confidence in my being sent by you. I look to you to supply all the resources I need today to get the job done. Amen.

FEAR NOT

"Fear not, for I am with you; be not dismayed, for I am your God. I will strengthen you, yes, I will help you, I will uphold you with My righteous right hand."

—Isaiah 41:10 NKJV

What is the one thing that helps to calm your children when they wake up in the middle of the night from a nightmare? More than likely, they just want to be in your presence. There is something comforting and assuring about being next to someone you trust.

When you find yourself facing fear (fear of the future, fear of not being able to provide, fear of failure), remind yourself that you are not alone. God has promised that he is with you and that he will offer the strength you need. That he will uphold you and protect you. You can take shelter in his presence.

Just as your children run to you when they are fearful, run to God in your fear. Just as you wrap your arms around your children and remind them that you are with them, God will wrap his arms around you and remind you of his perfect, powerful, and unwavering presence.

God, help me to be willing to come to you with my fears. Thank you that you have promised to be a shelter for me. Help me to find comfort, encouragement, and strength through resting in your presence. Amen.

THANKSGIVING

And whatever you do or say, do it as a representative of the Lord Jesus, giving thanks through him to God the Father.

—*Colossians 3:17 NLT*

Sometimes the point of Christianity gets relegated to going to church, saying a prayer before a meal, and maybe reading the Bible from time to time. Those are all great and should be elements of one's faith, but according to the verse above, our whole selves are to reflect a picture of what Jesus is actually like. And everything we do and say should lead toward gratitude.

This seems like an impossible task, but there is actually a science to this. As humans practice being thankful in their mind and in their speech, it actually rewires pathways in their brain in a way that trains them to live their whole lives through a lens of gratitude. Consider a keeping a journal of thankfulness or practicing gratitude verbally with your kids one or two times per day and see if it changes anything within you. You are most likely *the* person in your kids' lives who can be the best picture of Jesus for them. Don't take that lightly. Happy Thanksgiving!

God, train my thoughts and speech to be grateful so I reflect the heart and character of Jesus. Amen.

GREED

Then he said to them, "Watch out! Be on your guard against all kinds of greed; life does not consist in an abundance of possessions."

—*Luke 12:15*

Have you ever been shopping on Black Friday? Perhaps you've waited in crowded aisles, hoping to fill your cart with all the newest and hottest items for your kids, your wife, or yourself. It's chaos! All to get more stuff at the lowest price.

We live in a "more is better" culture—a culture that tells us that if we can just possess the right things, we will be happy and content. If we can purchase the best gifts for our kids, we are good parents. But what if our culture is wrong?

The reality is that within the next twelve to twenty-four months, most of what was purchased this year on Black Friday will be broken, tossed out, or useless. How can we instead give gifts that will not lose their value over time? This Christmas, how can your family give gifts that help share the true meaning of Christmas with others? Not only will you be sharing the gift of the gospel with others, but you'll also be creating memories with your family. Memories that will last a lifetime.

God, protect me from the greed for stuff. Help me to know my identity as a follower of Christ. Help me this season to share the true meaning of Christmas. Amen.

RELATIONSHIP RESTORATION

Do not cast me from your presence or take your Holy Spirit from me. Restore to me the joy of your salvation and grant me a willing spirit, to sustain me.

—*Psalm 51:11–12*

Can you hear the child's cry in these verses? *Don't send me to my room, Dad. I know I was wrong, but I want to stay in your presence.* "Cleanse me from my sin," the psalmist says just a few verses previously (v. 2). He knew that the relationship had been broken.

The psalmist knew there was nothing worse than to be banished from the presence and fellowship of the Lord. But he also knew that the way to restore his relationship was to seek forgiveness, to plead for mercy from a loving God.

Today, rest assured that your loving heavenly Father wants you to be in relationship with him as you want to be in relationship with your children.

Father, thank you for Jesus and providing a restored relationship with you no matter what I have done. Restore to me the joy of your salvation. Let me more fully be in relationship with you. Show me where I am unclean and cleanse me. Amen.

FAITHFULLY COMMITTED

> Jesus Christ is the same yesterday, today, and forever.
>
> *—Hebrews 13:8 NLT*

Jesus has never left a project unfinished. He has never started a season and quit because he got bored with the sport. His garage is not filled with late-night impulse buys from a home shopping channel that he used once and never came back to. Jesus and his mission are the same yesterday, today, and forever.

Take heart that the Savior still has plans for you. You may not be the new model or the latest craze, but Jesus is still committed to his relationship with you, to fulfilling his plan for your life. He is committed to you!

> Jesus, thank you for sticking with me even through my dark days. You have never left me, and you never change your plan for my well-being. May I be faithful to your faithfulness. Amen.

Affirmation of Others

"My command is this: Love each other as I have loved you."

—*John 15:12*

It's easy to love others who already love us, and it's easy to love our kids when they are obeying. It's harder to love others when they are acting like jerks. Yet here the command we are given is to love others as we have been loved. As Jesus spoke to his disciples, they may have remembered being cheating tax collectors and dirty fishermen when Christ began to love them.

Love others as Christ has loved you. Love your coworker who cheated to get the promotion you deserved. Love your neighbor when you step in the present his dog left you. Love one another as Christ has loved you.

Jesus, help me to love the unlovable. Help me to obey you by loving as you loved—by loving those who may not seem like they deserve it. Thank you for loving me as I am. Amen.

WORSHIP

Guard your steps when you go to the house of God. Better to draw near in obedience than to offer the sacrifice as fools do, for they ignorantly do wrong. Do not be hasty to speak, and do not be impulsive to make a speech before God. God is in heaven and you are on earth, so let your words be few.

—*Ecclesiastes 5:1–2 HCSB*

We often speak before we think. The proverbial foot-in-mouth disease. Sometimes we catch it just a second or two after our words come out, and sometimes it's days later when we think back to the conversation and realize, *Oh, that's why they got mad.* The warning here is to keep your foot out of your mouth before God. Are we claiming to be holy as we walk into the house of the God for worship, while we spend our weeks living in unconfessed sin? Are we quick to tell others how they should live and love, while we ignore our own advice?

We serve a God in heaven who knows us completely. There is great freedom in knowing that. There is great comfort knowing that we can enter into worship because God knows us and loves us still. Let us be honest in our worship.

God, help me keep my words few and my worship true, and may my honesty spill forth before you. Amen.

ACCESS TO THE THRONE

Therefore, since we have a great high priest who has passed through the heavens—Jesus the Son of God—let us hold fast to the confession. For we do not have a high priest who is unable to sympathize with our weaknesses, but One who has been tested in every way as we are, yet without sin. Therefore, let us approach the throne of grace with boldness, so that we may receive mercy and find grace to help us at the proper time.

—*Hebrews 4:14–16 HCSB*

We all want special access. Administrative rights, all-access passes, VIP status, or the key to the executive suite. Through Christ Jesus we are given something even better than all these things. We are given access to the throne room of God. We get to walk in like we own the place and can approach the throne of grace with boldness. No fear that we don't belong. No fear that they will find out our credentials are not enough. The great thing is we are not relying on our credentials but on Christ's. He grants us access to the throne, where we receive mercy and grace right when we need it. All we need to do is enter in and ask. Come on in, access granted.

God, may I be bold in my requests. Thank you, Jesus, for giving me access to the throne room of God. May I stand before the throne in awe, but knowing that I belong there because of what you have done. Amen.

DECEMBER

PENETRATING TO THE HEART

> For the word of God is living and active, sharper than any two-edged sword, piercing to the division of soul and of spirit, of joints and of marrow, and discerning the thoughts and intentions of the heart.
>
> —*Hebrews 4:12 ESV*

One of the most difficult things we do as fathers is try to pass our faith on to our children. We often feel inadequate or unprepared, especially when children reach an age when they begin to ask questions and seek to understand God and his redemption story. Yet each of us has access to the most powerful tool for mentoring our children, the Word of God.

The Word of God penetrates to the heart of the matter. It speaks to intentions of the heart. The better we know it, the easier it becomes to use its insights to pass on wisdom to our children. A simple word of Scripture can bring to light our children's motives, helping us to better talk with them about the things of God.

God, thank you for your Word. Help me to better understand it and its place in mentoring my children. Allow your Word to wash over me and fill me, so I am full to share with my children. Amen.

INTEGRITY

"If we are thrown into the blazing furnace, the God whom we serve is able to save us. He will rescue us from your power, Your Majesty. But even if he doesn't, we want to make it clear to you, Your Majesty, that we will never serve your gods or worship the gold statue you have set up."

—*Daniel 3:17–18 NLT*

Faced with certain death, Shadrach, Meshach, and Abednego stood up to the only person who could have set them free. With a simple word, King Nebuchadnezzar could have shut the furnace off and sent them on their merry way. Yet the three, instead of waffling, doubled down on the God they served. With a certainty that came from walking hand in hand with God, they placed their hope in him alone.

How easy it is for us to compromise to make life easier. The integrity of these three men is amazing. A simple knee taken would have set them free. God would have known their true hearts, and yet they knew that, before God, their integrity would be more important than their lives. We too can have this type of resolve in the face of moral decline around us. Stand firm knowing that God is faithful no matter the circumstances.

God, thank you for the example of integrity of men who have gone before us. Help me to live with honor in every small circumstance as well as every dramatic event. Amen.

SUFFICIENCY OF GOD

The Lord God says, "I am Alpha and Omega, the one who is and was and is coming. I am God All-Powerful!"

—*Revelation 1:8 CEV*

When was the first time you wondered how your child would turn out? Was it when you first held your baby in your arms? Was it when you signed your adoption papers or when you first heard the news of the pregnancy?

Whenever it was, God already had an answer for it. He says to us in our worries and questions, "I am the one who is and who was and is coming." He has seen all time, he is all-powerful, and he knows the answer to your questions. While you stare into the future, wondering what will come, God holds it in his hands and says to you, "I am God All-Powerful!"

God, as my worries as a father surround me and feel like they are overwhelming me, may I rest in you. May I find comfort in you being Alpha, first, and Omega, last. Thank you for knowing and holding the future so I don't have to. Amen.

FORGIVENESS

Be kind and loving to each other, and forgive each other just as God forgave you in Christ.

—*Ephesians 4:32 NCV*

Often one of the first thoughts that comes when someone reads this is, *But you don't know what they did to me.* Or we think that we'll forgive when they ask for forgiveness.

Being kind and loving to one another is something we as men also deal with often. Sometimes we think our love language is sarcasm and snide remarks, as we cut people down with words instead of building them up. Here we are encouraged to forgive, love, and be kind, not as unbearable burdens but as ways to live that will let us be free from bitterness and unforgiveness. Christ forgave our sins on the cross long before we had a chance to seek forgiveness.

Christ, you forgave my sins on the cross, so let me forgive as you forgive. Let my life be filled with kindness and loving others. Help me to speak words of comfort and affirmation to those around me. Amen.

CALLED TO PREACH

> But the believers who had fled Jerusalem went every-where preaching the Good News about Jesus!
>
> *—Acts 8:4 TLB*

These first-century believers who fled weren't the leaders of the church. They weren't people we would consider preachers in today's society. They were Spirit-filled followers of Christ. Under threat of persecution and death, these followers shared the love of Christ with those around them.

We are called to preach also. This can start with us sharing the good news of Jesus with our family and then include spreading the news to others around us as we grow deeper in our relationship with Jesus. As we know Jesus more, we can preach his good news more!

> Jesus, help me to know you more. Help me to preach your good news to others around me. May I not be afraid to share your love to those in need. Amen.

DEVOTION TO JESUS

> When they saw the boldness of Peter and John and perceived that they were illiterate and uneducated men, they marveled. And they recognized that they had been with Jesus.
>
> —*Acts 4:13 MEV*

What a compliment! Okay, the words *illiterate* and *uneducated* are probably not words you want to be known by, but the leaders marveled at them. Peter and John had silenced those who accused them. They had boldly declared the truth of the gospel to the rulers of the law. The rulers were amazed, as uneducated men had spoken truth in a way that they could not argue with or contradict. Then came the most beautiful compliment that a Christ follower could ever receive: "They recognized that they had been with Jesus." What a statement! We also want people to see that we have been with Christ.

Jesus, give me the same boldness you gave Peter and John. Remind me to spend time in your presence. May your light shine through me to those who need to hear your truth. Amen.

OUR SHELTER AND STRENGTH

God is our shelter and strength, always ready to help in times of trouble. So we will not be afraid, even if the earth is shaken and mountains fall into the ocean depths; even if the seas roar and rage, and the hills are shaken by the violence.

—*Psalms 46:1–3 GNT*

All around us the world seems to be falling apart. Watching the news, we can feel overwhelmed by the number of heart-breaking things happening around the world. Even closer to home there is pain: families in distress, children rebelling, the death of loved ones, and the list could go on.

The psalmist wasn't writing this psalm in blissful igno-rance. He knew the world is full of sorrow, but he held strong to the promise that he had seen—that God is our shelter and strength, always ready to help. In our situation God is there. He wants to help and will help no matter what is happening in or to us. He is our shelter. As the storms rage around us and even on us, he is still there sheltering us.

God, I need your shelter and strength. The pressures of today seem to overwhelm my hope. Reveal your strength, and may my hope not fade even as the world roars around me. Amen.

Longing for God

> As a deer pants for flowing streams, so pants my soul for
> you, O God. My soul thirsts for God, for the living God.
>
> —*Psalms 42:1–2 ESV*

If we're thirsty, we're already partially dehydrated. It's our body's way of telling us we need hydration. We need fluid before our systems start to shut down. Growing up, we quickly realized the signs of thirst. Dry mouth, itchy throat, feeling the need for liquid. When we're thirsty, we drink something.

But what about the soul? Do we know the signs of soul thirst? Do we know the signs of longing for God? Sometimes soul thirst is revealed through a short temper, unkind words to those we love, or feeling far from God. What is the answer to a soul thirst? Time with God. Like a deer who runs full bore to the river to drink, in our times of soul thirst we need to run toward God and let his living waters restore our soul.

God, when my soul thirsts, may it thirst only for you. Help me to recognize the signs of soul thirst and run to your presence. May I long for you and your presence as the deer longs for flowing streams. Amen.

TIME WITH GOD

> Yet the news about him spread all the more, and enormous crowds collected to hear Jesus and to be healed of their diseases. But he slipped quietly away to deserted places for prayer.
>
> —*Luke 5:15–16 PHILLIPS*

Jesus knew he was the one the crowds wanted to see. He knew he was the one who brought healing and hope for the people pressing in around him. Yet in the midst of enormous crowds, faced with all the pressure of healing these people, Jesus retreated to quiet places to pray. He knew the priority of being in right relationship with the Father as he ministered.

As fathers, the best thing we can do is make sure we're right with God. Sometimes slipping quietly away means setting our alarms earlier than those around us, or staying up just a little bit later to spend time talking with the Father. The best thing an earthly father can do is spend time talking with his heavenly Father.

> God, help me to follow the example of Christ. Help me to slip away to be with you. Wake me up to be with you. Keep me up to be with you. May our conversations together be life-giving as I father those you have entrusted to my care. Amen.

ENCOURAGEMENT MATTERS

> So speak encouraging words to one another. Build up
> hope so you'll all be together in this, no one left out, no
> one left behind. I know you're already doing this; just
> keep on doing it.
>
> —*1 Thessalonians 5:11 MSG*

We have all received at one time or another. A kind word
or note brings light into our life. An encouraging word can
brighten our day. Encouraging words cause us all to do more
together. The Scripture here encourages us to be an encouragement. So many times it is easy to be critical, thinking that
will encourage people to do good. But an encouraging word
goes so much further! We can be an encouragement to others
simply by telling those close to us what they mean to us.

As a father, you are important. Take courage that you can
do this!

> God, I want to encourage those close to me. Help me to
> see others around me who might need an encouraging
> word today. Open my mouth to speak words of encour-
> agement to those who are in need. Amen.

SALVATION THROUGH CHRIST

Here is a trustworthy saying that deserves full acceptance: Christ Jesus came into the world to save sinners—of whom I am the worst.

—1 Timothy 1:15

This is not something most of us would include in a letter going to our church. But here Paul remembers who he is, thanks to Christ and where he would be without him. Christ came to save sinners. We all need Jesus. We all need to be saved from our sins. This is why Jesus came to earth. Paul, who gave his approval for murdering those who followed Christ, never forgot from what he was saved. He is no longer living in condemnation. He knew full well that his sin was covered at the cross and that is why he freely said, "Of all the sinners, I am the worst."

No matter our past, in Christ we are saved. We too have been saved from death to life and can live in freedom because Christ Jesus came into the world to save sinners—us!

Thank you, Jesus, for your salvation. Thank you for forgiving all my sins. Past, present, and future, my sins are forgiven. Thank you! Amen.

INTERCESSION

First of all, then, I urge that supplications, prayers, inter-cessions, and thanksgivings be made for everyone, for kings and all who are in high positions, so that we may lead a quiet and peaceable life in all godliness and dignity. This is right and is acceptable in the sight of God our Sav-ior, who desires everyone to be saved and to come to the knowledge of the truth.

—1 Timothy 2:1–4 NRSV

Our prayer list just got a bit longer. We may be used to praying for those close to us—for our family, friends, and coworkers—but Paul adds a few more people to the list: everyone. That list just became over seven billion names long. And what should we pray? Pray that all will be given the opportunity to be saved and come to a knowledge of the truth.

We have people around us who we know need the Savior's love, but there are also billions of people we don't know who need salvation. One of our roles as a Christ follower is to pray. By praying we enter into the work of God. We are invited to pray for others around the world, not just those close to us. We can ask God to intercede in their lives and reveal himself to them.

God, reveal yourself to those in need of you. I ask that you would intercede in their life in powerful ways. May your love be revealed to those both near and far who are in need of your love. Amen.

EQUIPPING

Fight the good fight of the faith; take hold of the eternal life to which you were called when you made the good confession in the presence of many witnesses.

—*1 Timothy 6:12 RSV*

It's not easy. Every day we're faced with opportunities to cheat or lie, to cut corners or to not be men of integrity. This struggle is not something new. Here Paul is equipping his protégé Timothy to fight the good fight of faith. The fight of faith is often internal. We might question our convictions, but we must cling to the salvation to which we were called. We may fight a battle each day to stand our ground in faith, but take heart—it's a battle worth fighting.

God, help me to fight the good fight of faith. Help me to cling to the hope of eternal life. As pressure pushes in all around me, may I fight for what is right and true. Thank you for strength to fight. Amen.

SAVED BY MERCY

> He saved us, not because of the righteous things we had done, but because of his mercy. He washed away our sins, giving us a new birth and new life through the Holy Spirit.
>
> —*Titus 3:5 NLT*

These verses are often hard for us to understand. We're saved not because of anything we have done, but only because of his mercy. As we believe this truth, our faith deepens. If we had done something that could have earned salvation, then it makes sense in our minds that we deserve salvation. We think we can rely on our good deeds or righteous acts to bring salvation, but in Christ's economy our deeds cannot bring salvation. So we must have faith in his promises.

It is this faith that saves us by his mercy. We are then given new birth and life through the Holy Spirit, to live according to the mercy given to us. Our righteous deeds flow out of and not into salvation. We do what is right because of God's mercy given to us and not to earn his favor.

God, increase my faith so I may continue to live in this understanding of how your mercy works. You love me and saved me by your mercy, not because of things I had done. Thank you. Amen.

RITES OF PASSAGE

"I pray that the LORD will bless and protect you, and that he will show you mercy and kindness. May the LORD be good to you and give you peace."

—Numbers 6:24–26 CEV

God instructed Moses to teach Aaron to use these words to bless the people of Israel. Since then, these words have been prayed over people at the end of worship services and repeated often as young people set off on another phase of their journey. They're not just words to be repeated but a prayer of blessing over the people of God.

In the same way, we can pray this blessing over our children. God not only hears this prayer but answers it. As we pray it over and with our children, we instill in them an understanding of where good comes from. As we ask God to be good to them, we can have conversations with our children about where good things come from. This can become a daily conversation as we talk not only to God but also about God.

God, please bless and protect my children from things that would bring them undo harm. Show them mercy and more kindness than they can even begin to fathom. God, be good, oh so good to them, and give them peace that is real, lasting, and eternal. Amen.

RITES OF PASSAGE

"This may be a sign among you. When your children ask in time to come, 'What do those stones mean to you?' then you shall tell them that the waters of the Jordan were cut off before the ark of the covenant of the Lord."

—*Joshua 4:6–7 ESV*

God knew how quickly we would forget. He knew how easy it would be to not share our faith story with our children. We so quickly forget the amazing things that God has done for us. We forget the financial provision and the healing he has done.

It's important to use reminders to help us pass on our faith to our children. Just as God instructed the people of Israel to build memorials, we to can build modern memorials to pass the stories of our faith down to the next generation.

God, remind me of the things you have done in my life. Help me to share these stories with my children. When I forget, please bring to mind all you have done. Amen.

BOLD FAITH

"Now give me this hill country the LORD promised me on that day, because you heard then that the Anakim are there, as well as large fortified cities. Perhaps the LORD will be with me and I will drive them out as the LORD promised."

—*Joshua 14:12 HCSB*

Caleb was eighty-five years old at this time. After wandering in the wilderness for forty years and fighting for five years to get to this land he had been promised forty-five years before, he didn't shy away from the battles that still were before him, instead holding to the promise in the Lord.

God is not always looking for the youngest, fastest, or most equipped to do his will. He is looking for people of faith who remember his promises and say, "I will take the hill before me, because God has promised that he would give it to me." Remember God's promises as you face the mountains of your life, and trust him to go with you.

God, may I have the faith of Caleb. Help me to remember your promises and trust only in them. May I see your promises and not the battles before me. Help me to be as bold today as Caleb was at eighty-five. Amen.

INTEGRITY

> Joseph's master was furious and had Joseph arrested and put in the prison where the king's prisoners were kept, and there he stayed.
>
> —*Genesis 39:19–20 GNT*

The world tells us do the right thing because if you do, good things will happen. God says do the right things because it's the right thing to do. Joseph has just stood up to sexual temptation. He has kept his purity, and instead of being rewarded, he was thrown into prison. "And there he stayed," verse 20 concludes. Joseph had done the right thing and yet here he sat in prison.

Even so, the right thing remains the right thing. As fathers, we want our children to see us doing the right thing even if it costs us. Doing the right thing is *always* the right thing.

God, I pray you would help me to always do the right thing. I want to do right—not to be rewarded for doing right, but because I want to be right in your eyes. Thank you for revealing to me the right thing to do today and each day. Amen.

FORGIVENESS

"Now, do not be upset and do not be angry with yourselves because you sold me here, for God sent me ahead
of you to preserve life!"

—*Genesis 45:5 NET*

Sold as a slave, falsely accused, and thrown in prison. This all
happened because Joseph's brothers had hated him. Yet here
we see Joseph not only forgiving his brothers for this mistreat-
ment but also asking them to forgive themselves. Imagine how
many times Joseph had opportunity to reflect on the wrongs
done to him because his brothers hated him. But he did not
become bitter. Instead, by the grace of God, he began to see
things through God's eyes. All this happened so he could later
save lives. Joseph granted forgiveness to his brothers because
he could see that God was in control and had a plan, even for
the pain that he endured.

The same is true for us. God has a plan for the wrongs that
have been done to us, and we need to forgive, knowing that
God can yet redeem the pain we have experienced.

Help me to forgive as Joseph forgave. I want to see things
in the light of eternity. Amen.

DISCIPLINES

"A good man brings good things out of the good stored up in his heart, and an evil man brings evil things out of the evil stored up in his heart. For the mouth speaks what the heart is full of."

—Luke 6:45

If we want good things to flow from our mouths and into the lives of our children, we need to spend the time it takes to fill our hearts with good things and empty them of evil. When we confess our sins to God, we empty our hearts to him. This is a good practice to go through daily with God. Ask him to reveal any evil in you, and confess it to him and ask him to replace the evil with his good. Our hearts must be consistently filled with Christ so we can speak good things to our family and children. Daily Scripture reading helps us to fill our hearts and minds with his Word and good things.

God, I confess to you the evil I have harbored in my heart, and I ask that you would fill my heart with you so I may speak right and good words to my loved ones. Amen.

FILLED TO OVERFLOWING

> May the God of hope fill you with all joy and peace in believing, so that you may overflow with hope by the power of the holy spirit.
>
> —*Romans 15:13 NTE*

Hope is contagious. When hope starts to show in someone, it can't be held back from spreading to others. Here the author of Romans prays that we may be filled will all joy and peace so that we may overflow with hope by the power of the Holy Spirit. We do not have a false sense of hope, joy, or peace; these things come from the God of hope. These things fill us to overflowing. And we don't store hope only for ourselves; it is to overflow to those around us by the power of the Holy Spirit. The hope in us brings hope to others and opens doors for us to share the gospel with those we know.

> Lord, fill me to overflowing with hope, joy, and peace. May those around me see the hope I have in you. Guide my heart in peace, bring joy even in sorrow, and give hope to overflowing for those around me. Amen.

GOD IS FAITHFUL

> And he guarantees right up to the end that you will be counted free from all sin and guilt on that day when he returns. God will surely do this for you, for he always does just what he says, and he is the one who invited you into this wonderful friendship with his Son, even Christ our Lord.
>
> —*1 Corinthians 1:9 TLB*

Some guarantees are better than others. There are lifetime guarantees that are only good for a few years, and there are some guarantees that aren't even worth the paper they are written on. The guarantee is only as good as the person or company backing it.

The guarantee given here is one that is worth more than any gold or silver could buy. We will be counted as free from all sin and guilt, because our guarantee is from God himself. And God always does what he says. This guarantee is one we didn't have to purchase; it was given to us through Christ and sealed with the Holy Spirit.

Thank you, God, for keeping your promises. Thank you for being faithful and true to what you say. Amen.

IDENTITY

> So then, you are no longer a slave but a child. And since you are his child, God will give you all that he has for his children.
>
> —*Galatians 4:7 GNT*

This is no small change of identity. From slave to son is a huge change. We are given the right status to walk hand in hand with our heavenly Father. We don't follow him around out of obligation but instead walk side by side with him as he calls us son. The relationship we are given with God through Christ is an amazing opportunity to sit knee to knee with God and converse, to hug and to see the smile that only a father can give a child. A smile that says, *That man there is my son, and I love and am proud of him.*

Thank you, God, for calling me son. Thank you that you smile upon me and call me your own. When I am discouraged, remind me that I am your child and have all that you have for me. Amen.

A MUCH BIGGER STORY

> But after he had considered this, an angel of the Lord appeared to him in a dream and said, "Joseph son of David, do not be afraid to take Mary home as your wife, because what is conceived in her is from the Holy Spirit."
>
> —*Matthew 1:20*

Even for a carpenter from Nazareth, this was a rough situation. His wife-to-be was pregnant and the baby wasn't his. In fact, his bride claimed that she was found pregnant through the Holy Spirit. He loved Mary, and he didn't want to shame or embarrass her. But his reputation and livelihood was on the line. Joseph was well within his rights to quietly end their relationship.

That's when the angel appeared to him. "Joseph," the angel said, "Don't be afraid to take Mary as your wife." In essence, the angel was reassuring him, "Yes, this is stressful, but there is a much bigger story going on. God is in this, Joseph. God wants you to step up, to love her, to stand with her through everything that is to come, and to accept the joy, salvation, and hope that will come through this child."

> God, help me see the bigger reality of Jesus in my life. Let me see the responsibility I have to love and serve those around me, for your sake. Amen.

THIS CHILD

"She will give birth to a son, and you are to give him the name Jesus, because he will save his people from their sins."

—Matthew 1:21

Imagine trying to raise a child whose birth was announced by angels. Imagine rocking him to sleep, burping him, cleaning him up, playing peek-a-boo, and making silly noises. Imagine his hand wrapped around your finger. Imagine the sound of his measured breathing and the quirky movement of his arms stretched out.

Imagine this child, with the whole world in his hands, entrusted to your calloused, hardworking ones. The responsibility for the one who would shoulder the sins of the world, placed upon the shoulders of this inexpectant father. Joseph was given the incredible privilege and great responsibility to take Jesus as his own.

"Jesus," Joseph said. "That's the name I give you. You will be called Jesus, meaning 'the Lord saves.'"

That's the message of Christmas. This baby, so meek and mild, so full of power, ready to be embraced in your arms.

God, I recommit myself fully to the salvation that comes through the birth of the Savior. Amen.

RESTORING OTHERS

Brothers and sisters, if someone is caught in a sin, you who live by the Spirit should restore that person gently. But watch yourselves, or you also may be tempted.

—*Galatians 6:1*

As fathers, sometimes we're tempted to put our children into the place we want them to be. We see them misbehaving and demand that they are obedient immediately. Sometimes we need to do this as they are younger or when they put themselves into situations where their disobedience will cause them harm. It is harder, however, to walk gently with them as we see them doing wrong. We want to force right choices on them. That may work for a time, but it doesn't help them deepen their faith and make the right choices when we're not around. We need to work gently to restore them, to mentor them in right choices, letting natural consequences take place, as we lovingly help them to understand right choices.

God, help me to be gentle in mentoring my children. Help me to know when to step in and when to step back. Give me patience with them. Amen.

POINTING OUT JESUS

Again the next day John was standing with two of his disciples, and he looked at Jesus as He walked, and said, "Behold, the Lamb of God!" The two disciples heard him speak, and they followed Jesus.

—John 1:35-37 NASB

John the Baptist really understood what it meant to point people to Christ. Here we see just a brief encounter between two of his followers and him. These two people had agreed to some extent to follow John, to listen to his teaching. They were standing there, perhaps learning from John, when John sees Jesus and says to his followers, "Behold, the Lamb of God!" Either John didn't know how to stay in business or he knew his role as the one to make the way for the Savior. Our role in parenting is similar to John's: we are to continue to point out Christ, and when our children become his disciples, we let them go and follow him.

God, help me to point out Jesus in the lives of my children. Help me to release them as they follow you. I want to know you well enough to know when and where you are moving so I can point to you and say to my children, "Behold the Lamb of God!"

FAITH

Simon Peter answered Him, "Lord, to whom shall we go? You have the words of eternal life."

—*John 6:68 MEV*

Simon Peter puts his foot in his mouth many times throughout Scripture. He wasn't one to truly think before he spoke. Here, however, he said something that can and should be repeated.

Jesus, after many who were following him left him, asked his closest followers if they too were going to leave. Peter spoke these words and made a confession that has been repeated throughout the ages: "You have the words of eternal life." He had seen it, and we can see it too; Christ's words bring life for eternity. For ages, people have continued to look elsewhere for these words, but they are only found in Jesus.

Jesus, thank you that your words and teachings are much different from any others we have heard. Your words bring eternal life to those who listen and believe. Thank you. Amen.

MISSIONS

"But you will receive power when the Holy Spirit has come upon you, and you will be my witnesses in Jerusalem and in all Judea and Samaria, and to the end of the earth."

—*Acts 1:8 ESV*

Just before Jesus was taken into heaven before their eyes, he told his followers how things would unfold. The Holy Spirt would come and then they would share his story with all people everywhere. The Creator and Sustainer of the universe has given us the task of sharing his story with the world. He chooses to involve us and to rely on us to continue to share his story everywhere, including in our own backyards. But the great thing is that we have the Holy Spirit to help us and give us the power to do it.

God, help me to be involved in sharing your story with those all around the world. Help me to lean in to the Holy Spirit and follow his leading to tell the story of Jesus. Amen.

UNITY

> Behold, how good and how pleasant it is for brethren to dwell together in unity!
>
> —*Psalm 133:1 ASV*

Often we forget to meet face-to-face with people. Our lives are so filled with texts, e-mails, Skype calls, and Facebook updates that it's easy to forget that we haven't see our friends in some time. In the verse above, the psalmist agrees that it's good to dwell together. *Dwell* is a good word here; it means to spend time together—significant amounts of time, not just the passing "Hey, how's it going?" time together. We need to dwell and converse with others in a way that brings true relationship. Belly laughter, deep connections, and honest pushback and accountability can all be included in the word *dwell*. It is good to dwell with others in unity.

Heavenly Father, help me to dwell in your presence with others. Help me to be present in the lives of others so we may be blessed by each other and by you. Amen.

GOD IS NEAR

The LORD is near to all who call on him, to all who call on him in truth.

—*Psalm 145:18*

God is never far off when we call to him. He may seem distant, but God is near. He wants to hear our call, and he wants to answer our call. He never lets our call go to voicemail or asks us to quickly text him because he doesn't have time for us. He is near to all who call. He is there. Sometimes our perception of him is skewed because of our sin. But he is near. He is always near to us.

God, help me to see how near you are to me. Help me to not feel that you are far off. I want to feel your presence and know that you are here when I call. You have promised you are near, and I want to know you are near. Amen.

"This is my command—be strong and courageous! Do not be afraid or discouraged. For the LORD your God is with you wherever you go."

—*Joshua 1:9 NLT*